LEWIS NAMIER AND ZIONISM

LEWIS NAMIER AND ZIONISM

NORMAN ROSE

CLARENDON PRESS · OXFORD

1980

Oxford University Press, Walton Street, Oxford OX2 6DP

London Glasgow New York Toronto
Delhi Bombay Calcutta Madras Karachi
Kuala Lumpur Singapore Hong Kong Tokyo
Nairobi Dar Es Salaam Cape Town
Melbourne Wellington

and associate companies in
Beirut Berlin Ibadan Mexico City

Published in the United States by
Oxford University Press, New York

British Library Cataloguing in Publication Data

Rose, Norman Anthony
    Lewis Namier and Zionism
    1. Namier, Sir Lewis
    2. Zionism – Great Britain
    I. Title
    956.94′001′0924   DS151.N3/80–40841
    ISBN 0–19–822621–7

Typeset by Macmillan Company of India Ltd.,
Printed in Great Britain
by Billing & Sons Ltd.,
London, Guildford and Worcester

Preface

In this volume I have attempted to keep strictly to Lady Namier's bidding, namely to write 'a political sketch' of her husband. This work makes no pretence to be anything other than an account of Namier's political activities. This proved to be a serious constraint. The temptation to wander beyond the narrow confines of my terms of reference and to embark upon a more comprehensive biography was very great indeed. But in fact there is no justification for such an exercise. Lady Namier herself has written what is probably the definitive personal biography of her husband, and it would serve no purpose to go over the same ground again. I have also made no real attempt to evaluate his professional achievements. His place as an historian has yet to be assessed; that task must be left to those more qualified than I. If I stray occasionally from my brief, it is merely in order to round off Namier's political personality. 'No man is an Island, entire of itself', wrote John Donne; every biographer, even the most limited in scope, ignores his words at his peril.

Acknowledgements

Lady Namier's untimely death in December 1977 prevented her from seeing the publication of this volume. I can only hope that it would have met with her approval. She first requested that I write a political sketch of her husband; and to ease my task she kindly placed at my disposal a considerable amount of private papers and notes (referred to throughout this work as Lady Namier's Notes) which she had collected over the years. I remain greatly in her debt, for without her encouragement and generosity this book would never have been completed.

Others also unselfishly gave of their time. I am most grateful to Miss Constance Babington Smith, Sir Isaiah Berlin, Professor John Brooke, Mr A. Fergusson, Mr Martin Gilbert, Mr J. Mirelman, Mr S. Rosenne, Professor J. Talmon, Mr A. J. P. Taylor, Professor M. Vereté, and Professor D. C. Watt, for their patience and understanding. I am also indebted to the archivists, librarians, and staff at the British Library of Political and Economic Science at the London School of Economics; the Library at Carleton University, Ottawa; the Central Zionist Archives, Jerusalem; the Kaplan Library of the Faculty of Social Sciences at the Hebrew University, Jerusalem; the National Library at the Hebrew University, Jerusalem; the Public Record Office, London; and the Weizmann Archives, Rehovoth, for their help and expertise. My thanks are also extended to Mr A. Nachmani and Mr T. Ben Moshe who pursued further enquiries on my behalf. The Research Fund of the Faculty of Social Sciences at the Hebrew University supported this project from its inception, a speculative act of largesse for which I remain deeply grateful.

I also wish to thank Miss Constance Babington Smith, Lady Namier's literary executor; Balliol College, Oxford, who hold the copyright for Namier's published works; and Mr A. Fergusson, Mrs Dugdale's literary executor, for allowing me to quote freely from the material placed in their charge. My thanks are extended to those authors and publishers (listed in the bibliography) for quotations I have used from works of which they hold the copyright. I should put down in advance my apologies for those cases which I have inadvertently overlooked.

I am also grateful to the officers of the Canada–Israel Academic Exchange Foundation and Carleton University, Ottawa, for inviting me to spend a year in Canada. The staff and students of the Department of History at Carleton received me most warmly and ensured that my stay there was a pleasant and fruitful one. Thanks to their kindness, I succeeded in surmounting the main obstacles in my researches and writing.

I must also record my deepest gratitude to the Reich family of London. For two consecutive summers they endured, with stoic patience, the foibles of my family, and in particular of myself, thereby enabling me to complete the writing of this book. Theirs has been an act of hospitality above and beyond the normal calls of friendship.

It remains finally for me to record my profoundest thanks and admiration to my wife and daughter for their confidence in my ability to complete this task, and their encouragement in my efforts to realize their conviction. Only those who have embarked upon a risky venture of this nature can fully appreciate the importance of being subject at all times to such consistent support.

The Hebrew University, Jerusalem   NORMAN ROSE

Contents

Abbreviations

CZA Central Zionist Archives
PD   Parliamentary Debates, Hansard, 5th Series
PRO Public Record Office
WA   Weizmann Archives

Introduction

From the start Namier knew himself for a misfit. During the greater part of his seventy-two years he was driven by a formidable urge to get down to the root of his malaise. Enquiries into it involved him in a never-ending round of self-analysis, constantly seeking out the causes of his inability to relate smoothly to the outside world. In the fashionable jargon of today he would be said to be suffering from, or perhaps enjoying, a crisis of identity.

The reasons for his condition are not difficult to deduce. Anyone familiar with Lady Namier's graceful and revealing biography[1] will recall the incredibly complicated circumstances of his upbringing. Presumed dead at birth, regarded by his family as a weak and sickly child, he spent the first years of his life in a state of limbo, following his parents from one country home to another. It was not just a question of periodically moving house, of not being allowed to strike deep roots, unsettling though this undoubtedly was. His enforced travels familiarized him in the most practical manner with the nuances and ambiguities of Polish nationalism and its oppressor states. He traversed partitioned Poland from his birthplace in Wola in Russian Poland, to Koszylowce, his parents' final acquisition, an estate in eastern Galicia then under Austrian rule. Fully aware of its strengths and weaknesses, he became a strong advocate of Polish nationalism, though a violent opponent of its expansionist offshoot. With the collapse of the Austro-Hungarian and Tsarist empires, no one was better qualified than he, in particular linguistically, to assess the conflicting claims between the emerging national entities in central and eastern Europe.

But it was the relationship with his parents which proved crucial to his inner tranquillity. Both were Polonized Jews who, while not entirely rejecting their Jewish heritage,[2] wholly identified themselves with their Polish environment. Together with many members of their class, they

---

[1] Julia Namier, *Lewis Namier: A Biography* (OUP, 1971).

[2] There was indeed little to be ashamed of. Namier's paternal grandfather, Jacob, was a property owner and minor banker in Warsaw who had been imprisoned by the Russians in 1863 for his sole incursion into revolutionary politics; Jacob's wife, Balbina, boasted direct descent from the Gaon of Vilna, the most renowned Jewish scholar of the eighteenth century. His maternal grandparents, though less distinguished socially, were well-to-do landowners in eastern Galicia.

believed that assimilation into their Polish background was feasible and indeed necessary if the Jews were to break once and for all the terrible cycle of persecution at the hands of their Gentile neighbours. They took the obvious step and converted to Roman Catholicism; and, though they never displayed any ostentatious enthusiasm for their new faith, they brought up their children according to its rites.

On his tenth birthday, Namier underwent what might well be termed a traumatic shock. In the course of some family quarrel he was informed by his father, Joseph, that no one in his family could be considered either a Christian or a Jew. In the strict religious sense, with its accompanying national connotations, he was 'nothing'. His mother, Ann, later put his dilemma in a nutshell: her family was to be acknowledged as of 'Jewish descent, with strong Christian sympathies and Polish enthusiasms'.[3] This was a heavy intellectual baggage to have to carry around, and Namier never fully reconciled himself to its burden. Inevitably, his first confrontations with anti-Semitism compounded his anguish, as his tormentors taunted him as 'a Jew more Polish than the Poles'.[4] His mother's academic synthesis had been shattered at his first real encounter with the outside world. It was perhaps these episodes, more than any purely intellectual reckoning, which finally convinced him that his parents' way, far from resolving the Jewish problem, only aggravated it. He rejected their theories as inherently false, shameful, degrading, and ultimately self-defeating. He could no more escape his Jewishness than he could shed his own skin; and what was true for him was true for all Jewry.

His rejection of assimilation was the cornerstone of his Jewish–Zionist philosophy. He never deviated from this path. If anything, his experience as a mature adult only confirmed what he had sensed as an immature youth:

Many of us are happy to acknowledge the eminently fair treatment which we and our work have received in this country. Still, in every one of us there is, deep down, the consciousness that we cannot afford to slip: a fall for us is harder and more irretrievable than for a non-Jew . . . we all undergo assimilation in some measure or other; but those who long to be joined to their neighbours closer than they are, are the most unhappy among the Jews. For the desire to be 'assimilated' is a confession of inferiority, an attempt to divest oneself of one's inheritance in order to share in that of others.[5]

---

[3] Julia Namier, 37–8.   [4] Ibid., 54, 60–1.
[5] From his essay 'The Jews', *Nineteenth Century and After* (Nov. 1941), republished in *Conflicts* (London, 1943). See p. 27.

But his new-found Jewishness had little to do with religion. Quite the contrary, he rejected outright the pretensions of organized religion. All his life he fostered an intense detestation towards those representatives of the established church, whether clerics or rabbis, who dared to venture beyond the narrow confines of their vocation into the real world of politics. Having discarded his parents ideas as obsolete, he adopted others. He flirted with socialism as a means of removing class and national barriers. He was no Marxist. Indeed, he held an extremely low opinion of Marx whose works, he believed, were 'blinded by hatred';[6] and he neglected few opportunities to castigate Marxist ideologues whenever he could get hold of them. The furthest he ever got to translating his socialist notions into practice was by attending Fabian summer schools in the pre-1914 era. This was a passing phase. He swiftly came to recognize nationalism as the dominant motif in modern history. It was a force so primeval, so powerful that it swept everything else before it. It could not be denied. The conclusion was inescapable, in particular for himself. If the Poles could seek salvation through national renaissance, so too could the Jews. He once wrote: 'Scattered groups without a centre must not be exposed to the impact of nations. National emancipation is the meaning and essence of Zionism.'[7] He was not yet a Zionist, and was not to announce his conversion until after the First World War, but his ideas, as yet raw and undigested, were taking shape.

By the age of eighteen Namier had in effect broken with his parents. Driven out of Lwow University by the anti-Semitic provocations of Roman Dmowski's[8] followers, he left home in the autumn of 1906 to attend Lausanne University where he attended the lectures of Vilfredo Pareto. From there he migrated to the London School of Economics. After a year at the School, he finally came to rest at Balliol College,

[6] See Sir I. Berlin, 'Lewis Namier: A Personal Impression', in *A Century of Conflict, 1850–1950; Essays for A. J. P. Taylor* (London, 1966), ed. M. Gilbert.

[7] 'The Jews'.

[8] Roman Dmowski (1864–1939): Polish statesman and lifelong rival of Pilsudski; played a leading role in Poland's resurrection after the First World War; Leader of National Democratic Party in 2nd and 3rd Dumas; President of Polish National Committee, 1917; first Polish delegate to Paris peace conference; favoured incorporating the historic eastern provinces into a unitary Polish state. Namier, who violently opposed his anti-Semitic and ultra-nationalist policies, wrote of him: 'He was a strong man and an extremely skillful politician, a "boss" rather than a leader, strong willed, brutal, shrewd, hard-working, and persistent, a good speaker, a brilliant talker, endowed with a fantastic imagination and slender regard for the truth. His mind was crude and pragmatic but clear and alert; he had flair and judgement. Unscrupulous in the choice of means, he did what the indolent but fundamentally honourable Polish nobleman would never have done. He was a child of the Warsaw riverside and reproduced its type in the arena of international politics.' (*Manchester Guardian*, 3 Jan. 1939.)

Oxford. It would be gratifying to interpret these moves as the result of some carefully designed plan: a conscious awakening to the possibilities a tolerant, democratic, civilized society like England offered in contrast to the persecution and bigotry he had abandoned in eastern Europe. Namier himself encouraged this illusion in later years. In fact, it appears as though his decision to go to London resulted from his father's refusal to support him at the Sorbonne; while Balliol, his ideal of everything that Britain and British scholarship should be, presented itself as the outcome of the initiative of one of his London School of Economics acquaintances.[9] This is not to decry his move or his motives, for despite these cold facts, convincingly human in themselves, there was more than an element of truth in his self-justification. Namier, like many East European intellectuals insisted on regarding England through rose-tinted spectacles. And, in the course of time, those virtues which he so admired as being typically English—pragmatism at their head—came to coincide with his own outlook on life. Despite many disappointments and setbacks, he never fundamentally altered this view; and his deepening experience of politics, both national and world, only reinforced his conviction.

Namier was painfully conscious of his own faults; of his inability to escape the consequences of his background and in particular of his impossible relationship with his parents. He made every attempt to discover for himself the sources of his malaise. He regarded graphology in the highest esteem, believing passionately that it revealed subterranean facets of one's character. It is also common knowledge that he held psychoanalysis in high regard, though, from personal experience, he rejected its alleged therapeutic value. After many years of analysis he concluded that 'It deepened one's understanding without curing anything.'[10] He was constantly being psychoanalysed, first in Vienna, in the early 1920s, later in England for the remainder of his life. What did it reveal for him?[11]

[9] See Julia Namier, 67, 70–1. It should be clear that personal recommendation was the first stage of entry to all Oxford Colleges, confirmed, in the case of Commoners, by an interview. As a result of his recommendation, Namier had a long and successful one with Mr A. L. Smith, Senior Tutor at Balliol, on which he was finally admitted to the College.

[10] Ved Mehte, *Fly and the Fly-Bottle: Encounters with British Intellectuals* (Pelican ed., London, 1965); 221.

[11] When I first met Lady Namier she was unable, owing to the state of her health, to conduct long and detailed conversations. She tired easily, and could do no more than recount in the most superficial manner her impressions of Namier's attitude to these questions. Almost twenty years earlier, however, in an interview with a young Indian writer, Ved Mehte, she recalled more fully Namier's conclusions. Mr Mehte included these recollections in a fascinating book (op. cit.), and I have drawn extensively from it for the following passage.

It brought to the surface of his mind many things—such as the fact that his Zionism was really a result of the conflict between his Polish mother and his Galician father, and that his wish to unite the land and state of Israel was really an attempt to paper over childhood memories of his bickering parents.[12] And his conservatism—he always insisted he was a radical Tory—he discovered was a result of his loneliness as a child and as a grown-up. Because he never learned how to *consort* with people, he wanted to find out the principles by which people consort with others. And that is why he spent most of his life studying the politics of Parliament, and so on—because that was where people best consorted with each other . . . Not for nothing did he use an epigraph from Aeschylus' *Prometheus Vinctus* for his *Structure of Politics* . . .: 'I took pains to determine the flight of crook-taloned birds, marking which were of the right by nature, and which of the left, and what were their ways of living, each after his kind, and the enmities and affections that were between them, and how they consorted together' . . . He spent his life studying group life—the very thing that he didn't, he couldn't have.[13]

Early in adult life he had noticed that, sooner or later, in examining a situation he would perceive two mutually exclusive solutions to whatever problem he was grappling with. This state of mental indecision often produced a condition of tension so difficult to contain that at times he wondered whether he was not on the brink of madness. When his emotions were involved, as was the case with questions not of a purely academic nature, the issue became infinitely more complex, and he drifted off into periods of 'unmanageable turmoil', a condition his psychoanalysts later defined as his 'ambivalence'.[14]

His 'ambivalence' was most pronounced in his relations with Jews; or to define it more precisely, in his attitude towards Jewish nationalism and his place in it.

Though he was a Jew, he didn't basically like Jews. Lewis believed in character, which he thought was as fixed in all men as a stone in a ring; he didn't like what had become of the Jewish character. He thought that historical circumstances had made of the Jew a *petit bourgeois* and a rootless creature; money had taken

---

[12] In fact, his father's family was Polish, his mother's Galician (see Julia Namier, 4–6). This point later found expression in his academic work, (see p. 39), where he defines 'the native land' as the 'life-giving Mother' and 'the state' the 'law-giving Father'. See also p. 1.

[13] Mehte, 220–1.

[14] Together with his friend C. G. Stone, a medieval historian and moral philosopher, Namier had defined his condition in geometric terms. They took the concept of a hyperboloid which looks on paper like the middle part of a vase with a deeply curved waist but without top or bottom. Its two symmetrical lines constantly approach but never reach each other. The imagery of two lines forever moving towards each other but never merging owing to an inherent quirk of nature graphically describes Namier's state of mental turmoil.

the place of ties and roots. But Lewis, instead of leaving the Jews there, became the most ardent Zionist of his time, maintaining that the only way the Jews could become normal was to have roots, and the only place they could put down their roots was their original home, Palestine. His Zionism consisted of trying to join the land and the state.[15]

Lady Namier tells the following story from the Second World War:

One day Namier came to tea at the flat I then shared with a young friend engaged in war work . . . On the ground floor was a flat recently occupied by a dashing East European youth redrafted into one of H.M.'s services to perform hazardous tasks abroad. A forlorn girl, whom he kept there, apparently used his frequent absences to recover from the merciless beatings he gave her between times. That morning having heard he was on his way to her, she hanged herself. As my friend was telling Namier about it, I noticed his knuckles whiten as he gripped the arms of his chair. With lips grown livid he choppily asked if she was a Jewess. We didn't know. Later, when we were alone, I said that to me the girl's origins seemed totally irrelevant. But Namier retorted with searing heat that he was bound to every Jew with his gut, or rather an umbilical cord which became inflamed with detestation when one of them was obnoxious but tautened agonizingly when one, or a group, fell into dire adversity.[16]

Namier best expressed his predicament himself:

Hearing my foreign accent, people often ask me about my 'nationality'. I answer that I am a naturalised British subject and a Jew. 'But what was the first language you spoke?'

'I am in the habit of answering this question by saying: 'Hebrew'.

'Oh! You speak Hebrew?'

'I am sorry I don't.'

Non-plussed by this apparent contradiction, they try a different approach. 'But where were you born?'

'In the Galuth.'

'Where is that?'

'Anywhere outside Eretz Israel, which is our name for Palestine.' If they press any further, I tell them that my paternal grandfather came from the Ukraine, my paternal grandmother from Vilna, and my maternal grandparents from East Galicia. Will they kindly settle to their own satisfaction whether the Ukrainians are a branch of the Russian nation or a separate nationality? Whether East Galicia should count as Ukrainian or as Polish? Whether Vilna should belong to Lithuania, Poland, or White Russia? And if to White Russia, will they decide whether the White Russians are a branch of the Russian nation or a separate nationality? And by the time they have settled all these problems,

---

[15] Mehte, 219.   [16] Lady Namier's Notes.

will they tell me what origin I should claim to satisfy them? Had I a perfect English accent, they would call me a Jew. As it is, why will they not be satisfied with my calling myself a Jew, pure and simple and unhyphenated, but wish to saddle me with a prefix?[17]

He felt nothing but contempt for those Jews who refused to adhere to the Zionist creed. He told Sir Isaiah Berlin that he could not talk to English Jews about Zionism. 'The Jews of England were victims of pathetic illusions—ostriches with their heads in some very inferior sands—foolish, ridiculous creatures not worth saving.'[18] But, with the notable exceptions of Weizmann[19] and 'Baffy' Dugdale,[20] he was unable to talk to English Zionists also. Contemptuously he dubbed them as the 'Order of Trembling Israelites'.[21]

Namier never resolved his inner emotional battles, whether they concerned his Catholic upbringing, his Jewish heritage, his sympathy for Polish nationalism, his love-affair with England, or his commitment to Zionism. Each of these facets of his malaise were related one to the other: none were separable. Having abandoned religion in his 'teens, he returned to it at the age of fifty-nine on the occasion of his second marriage; a proud Tory radical,[22] he was viewed with suspicion by those he sought to emulate; a passionate Zionist all his life, it remained for him, in the final analysis, an intellectual abstraction, for he never fulfilled the ultimate duty of every practising Zionist, though he was urged on many occasions to do so. All that can be said with any certainty is that he mellowed with advancing years.

---

[17] 'Judaica', *Zionist Review*, 7 Nov. 1941.   [18] Sir I. Berlin, 219.

[19] Chaim Weizmann (1874–1952): President of World Zionist Organization and Jewish Agency, 1921–31, 1935–46; director of Daniel Sieff, later Weizmann, Institute of Science, Rehovoth; First President of Israel.

[20] Blanche Elizabeth Campbell Balfour (1880–1947): niece and biographer of Lord Balfour; the leading Gentile Zionist of her day. 'Baffy', daughter of Lady Francis Campbell and Mr Eustace Balfour, was related to two of the most powerful and prolific political clans in Britain, the Campbells and the Balfour-Cecils. She first met Namier when working in the Department of Naval Intelligence at the Admiralty during the First World War. For her political activities, see *"Baffy". The Diaries of Blanche Dugdale 1936–47* (London, 1973), ed. Norman Rose.

[21] See Namier's essay 'Numbers and Exodus', *The New Judaea* (Feb.–Mar. 1942), reprinted in *Conflicts*.

[22] In 1942 he wrote of himself as 'Pro-Russian and anti-German, a Conservative by instinct, predilections, and doubts, but not from material interest or fear—in short, a Tory radical' [*Conflicts*, p. 94].

Chapter 1

Tentative Reawakenings

Namier's first active interest in Jewish affairs occurred some time after he arrived in England in 1907. It is difficult to pin-point the date more precisely. His papers are replete with references such as: 'I was a strong Jewish nationalist since about 1905', or 'I was a theoretical Zionist since 1906.' But nowhere are such descriptions substantiated, expanded, or explained. His reference to his being a Zionist, theoretical or otherwise, was surely inserted as an afterthought. No evidence has yet been brought to light which indicates that he underwent a Zionist conversion so early in life. He was certainly aware of his Jewishness however. And during his years as an Oxford undergraduate, 1908–11, he attempted to draw closer to his Jewish contemporaries. His efforts were not crowned with conspicuous success. He first thought of joining a Jewish group called the Adler Society: 'but when I got there I found them discussing if there should or should not be organs in the synagogue. As I had never been to a synagogue and did not intend to go to one, I felt that a Society which carefully engaged in such discussions was no fit place for me.'[1] Shaken but not entirely disillusioned, he made a further attempt and attended a Zionist meeting at the home of Norman Bentwich.[2] 'But no sooner was that over than they started talking about preparing some kind of mysterious Sabbath ritual—it was Friday evening. I fled and never returned.'[3] These encounters were an apt prelude to his future relations with Anglo-Jewry.

Namier's concern for Jewry, his 'gut reaction', did not awaken as a result of these sad experiences. At Oxford he had struck up a friendship

[1] Lady Namier's Notes.
[2] Norman Bentwich (1883–1971): prominent English Zionist and scholar; Attorney-General of Palestine administration, 1920–31; Professor of International Relations at the Hebrew University, 1932; Director of League of Nations Commission for Jewish Refugees from Germany, 1933–6. Namier wrote that he attended the meeting at the home of 'a most amiable undergraduate', namely Norman Bentwich. This was clearly impossible as Bentwich, five years Namier's senior, had read classics at Trinity College, Cambridge, and had already completed his undergraduate studies. In 1908 he was called to the bar. Perhaps Namier attended the meeting at Bentwich's home in London.
[3] Lady Namier's Notes.

with Sir Reginald Wingate's son, Ronald,[4] and he was frequently invited to stay at their home, Knockenhair, near Dunbar. While there in August 1911, reports came through of anti-Jewish demonstrations, including the looting of Jewish shops, in the industrial valleys centred on Tredegar, Ebbw Vale, and Rhymney in Monmouthshire. The disorders were a by-product of the intense labour unrest of that summer, the hottest on record, when there occurred widespread strikes of seamen, dockers, and miners, which culminated in a national railway strike from 16 to 19 August. The anti-Semitic character of the reports stimulated Namier's curiosity. As soon as the strike was over, he secured introductions from an acquaintance, Thomas Jones,[5] and a trade union leader named MacTavish, and made his way to South Wales to discover for himself what had actually occurred. In later life he recalled the incident:[6]

I published nothing. I well remember having been asked by local Jews to let the matter die down. People in South Wales were ashamed of the whole business and discussing it in public would have served no useful purpose. It was fact that at Tredegar only Jewish shops were attacked, and only one Jewish shop escaped; the owner, a poor man, had begged the people to leave him alone, which they did. As the riots spread beyond Tredegar, they lost their distinctly antisemitic character; I believe that at Ebbw Vale a number of Welsh shops suffered, and still further afield, at Bargoed, more Welsh shops were attacked than Jewish.

This seemed to suggest an organising hand at Tredegar. But if there was, it could not be traced—as a Welsh friend told me, if anything was hatched underground, no non miner would know. I was further told that among the Tredegar magistrates there were very few professional people, who mostly lived in Cardiff or Newport; and the local shopkeepers among them took no action promptly.

[4] Francis Reginald Wingate (1861–1953): Sirdar and Governor-General of Sudan, 1889–1916; High Commissioner of Egypt, 1917–19. Created Bt. 1920. His son, Ronald Evelyn Leslie Wingate (b. 1889) rose to high office in the India Civil Service. These Wingates were cousins of Orde Charles Wingate, and perhaps imbibed something of the family's fundamentalist, protestant, philo-Semitism.

[5] Thomas Jones (1870–1955): Professor of Economics, Belfast, 1909–10; Deputy Secretary to Cabinet, 1916–1930; member of Unemployment Assistance Board, 1934–40.

[6] This passage is based upon extracts from a letter by Namier to Mr A. Gray-Jones contained in correspondence between Gray-Jones and Lady Namier, 17 Dec 1963 (CZA A312/60). Namier's original letter, dated sometime in the latter half of 1959, has not survived. Nor has a contemporary report he wrote for Claude Montefiore, then a member of the Jewish Board of Deputies. Mr A. Gray-Jones, at the time of the riots, was the son of the Presbyterian Minister at Ebbw Vale.

I remember a small Jewish shopkeeper who had been active in W.E.A. and other educational work. Heartbroken at the treatment received, he comforted himself that even the looters had no bad feeling against him personally: having found in a jacket which they stole a notebook of his with business notes, they pushed it one night under his door.

This 'small pogrom', as Namier called it, has to be judged in relation to the economic distress and social tension which then prevailed throughout much of industrial Britain. Yet Namier hesitated to draw the most obvious conclusion from it: that even the most civilized and humane of societies was not immune from the pernicious influence of anti-Semitism. He derived one small pleasure from this miserable experience. One evening he was entertained at dinner by an ultra-orthodox rabbi. Unable to comprehend the elaborate ritual, he explained to his host his ignorance of Jewish religious customs. The rabbi replied: 'You have to come to see what has happened to us. You have a good Jewish heart. That's all that matters.'[7]

*   *   *

Namier graduated in the summer of 1911 with a first-class degree in Modern History. His attempt a year later to gain a Fellowship at All Souls ended in ignominious failure, although he was the most strongly favoured candidate. He was at a loss to explain his lack of success. Yet the reason was patently clear. One member of the examining board, A. F. Pollard,[8] recorded the incident in a letter to his father: 'the best man by far in sheer intellect was a Balliol man of Polish-Jewish origin [the author here added a marginal note, "Namier"] and I did my best for him, but the Warden and majority of Fellows shied at his race, and eventually we elected the two next best.'[9] At the time, Namier preferred to ignore the rumours then currently circulating in Oxford that anti-Semitic prejudice had dashed his chance of obtaining this prestigious Fellowship.[10] Obviously, as during the South Wales affair, he felt more

[7] Julia Namier, 101.

[8] Albert Frederick Pollard (1869–1948): historian; Fellow of All Souls, 1908–36; founder and chairman of Institute of Historical Research, 1920–9.

[9] Julia Namier, 101.

[10] It is, however, probably an over-simplification to subscribe his failure *solely* to anti-Semitism. Some Fellows, not unnaturally, found his personality unpleasing and wondered how he would behave in the Senior Common Room. One Fellow made the legitimate point that 'he was clever but not as clever as he thinks he is' (Julia Namier, 100; and a private communication). Namier, characteristically, preferred to attribute his lack of success to the unorthodox brilliance of his presentation. At a later date, he claimed that he was turned down because his extreme anti-Germanism found expression in his examination answers. (See his correspondence with Kingsley Martin, Aug. 1942, p. 137.

secure with his idealized version of what English society should be, choosing to ignore its uglier face. Like his despised English Jews, he too was burying his head in 'some very inferior sands'.

In May 1913, after being granted a certificate of naturalization, Namier sailed for the United States. His purpose was twofold: to attend to his father's business affairs, and to collect material for his forthcoming book on the imperial problem in British eighteenth-century history. He remained in America for one year. Apart from his academic and business interests, both of which progressed, he was brought face-to-face with the most dramatic phenomenon of contemporary Jewish life: the mass exodus from eastern Europe to the West. His comments reveal his ambivalent attitude towards Zionism:

I was much interested in Jewish affairs but not in touch with Jews. I studied in books and reviews problems of Jewish immigration and development in America. In fact I was not wildly excited about Zionism which in those days seemed to me an interesting but rather impracticable and unimportant side-show. The thing which really interested me was the mass migrations of Jews from Eastern Europe to Western Europe and to America.[11]

He was, in a sense, mesmerized by the sheer weight of the numbers involved. Namier took the view that 'statistics were the biographical data of the new mass personality of nations', and much of his written work reflects his growing interest in demographic changes.[12] Nowhere, he felt, was this truer than for his own people.

*   *   *

When war broke out in Europe in August 1914, Namier was already back in London. A month later he volunteered for the army and was drafted into the Royal Fusiliers. He did not stay there for very long. Namier had plenty of enthusiasm, but was not the ideal soldier. Temperamentally he was quite unsuited for army discipline, and this, coupled with his atrocious eyesight, effectively debarred him from active service. He also endured unexpected indignities, for his foreign-sounding middle-name, Bernstein, and heavy central European accent made him easy prey for those in search of secret German agents. His talents were going to waste. His Oxford friends conspired to get him transferred to a Whitehall office where his intimate knowledge of

[11] Lady Namier's Notes.
[12] For example, his essays, 'The Jewish Question', in *Facing East* (New York, 1966), and 'Numbers and Exodus' in *Conflicts*.

Central and East European affairs could be best exploited. But he also had other, more powerful and influential acquaintances. At the end of September Sir Reginald Wingate, in the course of a letter to a friend of his at the War Office, raised the question of Namier's future. His letter tells us something about Namier's idiosyncrasies, and much about how a fairly typical representative of the English upper class viewed this strange phenomenon:

Mr. L. B. Namier [is] an exceptionally clever Jew . . . My son Ronald knew him at Balliol and brought him up to see us for a few days in Scotland—I was much struck with his ability and linguistic powers, and, for a foreigner, his knowledge of history was astounding. He professed the greatest hatred of Germany and it seemed to me that he had at times almost Nihilistic tendencies, but of his exceptional ability there can be no doubt . . . it seems to me that in such a war of nations as is now going on an individual of the type of Namier might be very useful if his loyalty can be absolutely depended upon and guaranteed.[13]

It was, however, Lord Eustace Percy,[14] who had been greatly impressed by the profundity of a number of Namier's articles, who finally managed to swing the appointment. In February 1915 Namier joined the staff of the Foreign Office.

*   *   *

He had still made no commitment towards Zionism, except to pass it off as an 'unimportant side-show'. But Turkey's entry into the war in November on the side of the Central Powers completely revolutionized the situation. Asquith, the Prime Minister, in a famous speech at the Guildhall, rang the 'death-knell of Ottoman dominion, not only in Europe, but in Asia'. 'The Turkish Empire', he proclaimed, 'has committed suicide and dug its grave with its own hand.'[15] Traditional British policy towards Turkey had turned one hundred and eighty degrees. From playing the role of the protectors of the crumbling Turkish empire, the British now appeared as partners in its eventual partition. This point was not lost on Namier. Soon after Asquith's

[13] Sir Reginald Wingate to Lt.-Col. Oswald Arthur Fitzgerald (then military secretary to Lord Kitchener), 28 Sept. 1914, PRO 30/57/45. I am grateful to my colleague Prof. M. Vereté for bringing this letter to my attention.

[14] Lord Eustace Percy (1887–1958): 7th son of 7th Duke of Northumberland; diplomat and politician; served in Foreign Office, 1914–19; Conservative MP for Hastings, 1921–37; President of Board of Education 1924–9; Minister without Portfolio, 1935–6. Created Baron Percy of Newcastle, 1953.

[15] Report of the speech in *The Times*, 10 Nov. 1914.

speech he approached another Oxford friend, Lionel Curtis,[16] and spoke to him about the future of Palestine and 'the possibility of doing something for Zionism'.[17] Curtis had no authority, but he did have an extensive range of influential contacts. Namier believed that he broached the subject with Herbert Samuel,[18] but received a dusty reply that 'nothing could be done'.[19] This was a fleeting episode. Before long Namier was wholly absorbed in his new duties at Wellington House, the newly established propaganda and information bureau of the Foreign Office.

Namier was sent to scan the Central and East European press. From his discoveries he was required to furnish the Foreign Office with weekly summaries of internal developments within the Austro-Hungarian Empire. Much of the material he gathered he used for his own purposes, churning out a never-ending stream of articles for publication in journals ranging from scholarly quarterlies to the weekly and daily press.[20] All the time he was consolidating his reputation as an expert. Initially, his main concern was for the future of the Austro-Hungarian Empire. He detested its master races, the Germans and the Magyars, and upheld the right of its subject peoples to national self-determination. He could not envisage a peace which included the survival of the empire: 'Austro-Hungary must cease to exist on account

[16] Lionel George Curtis (1872–1955): barrister; administrator in S. Africa, 1900–7; founded Round Table, 1910; appointed Beit lecturer in colonial history at Oxford, 1912; Fellow of All Souls, 1921; founder Royal Institute of International Affairs; advocate of imperial federation and of a world state.

[17] Lady Namier's Notes.

[18] Herbert Louis Samuel (1870–1963): prominent Anglo-Jewish politician; Liberal MP, 1902–18, 1924–35; Chancellor of Duchy of Lancaster, 1909–10; Postmaster-General, 1910–14; President of Local Government Board, 1914–15; Home Secretary, 1916, 1931–2; High Commissioner for Palestine, 1920–5; Leader of Parliamentary Liberal Party, 1931–5. Kn. 1920. Created Viscount, 1937.

[19] Namier's account does not tally with what is known about Samuel's interest in Zionism. On 9 November, the same day as Asquith's speech, he had discussed Zionism and the future of Palestine with Grey, the Foreign Secretary, and Lloyd George, Chancellor of the Exchequer, and had come away encouraged by their reaction. (See Viscount Samuel, *Memoirs* (London, 1945), 139–42.) As a result of these early talks Samuel drafted a memorandum for the cabinet (March 1915) in which he proposed the restoration of the Jews in Palestine under the aegis of the British Empire. His paper is rightly regarded as an important milestone along the road which finally led to the Balfour Declaration. Why, therefore, Samuel should have told Curtis that 'nothing could be done' is not clear. Perhaps nothing less than a wildly enthusiastic endorsement on Samuel's part would have satisfied Namier's expectations, a response quite out of keeping with Samuel's character.

[20] Some of these essays were later republished in *Skyscrapers and Other Essays* (London, 1931).

of the outrages committed by its Government on its non-German nationalities, and also because that is necessary for the good of Europe in general. The disruption of Austro-Hungary will go far towards limiting German influence to German territory.'[21] 'If Austria-Hungary continued to exist', he wrote a year later, 'we should have gathered a defeat.'[22] Any hint of a compromise peace brought forth a violent reaction. He recognized the dismantling of the Empire as a primary war aim of the allied powers.[23]

It was, however, the Polish question which gradually came to monopolize his time. And this had important consequences, for the excesses of Polish nationalism, apparent well before the end of the war, drove him back along the path which had first led him to Tredegar as a young student. It was not that he questioned the right of the Poles to national self-determination. Quite the contrary, he strongly upheld that principle which was indeed a focal point for European liberal thought. But he deplored its violently chauvinistic spirit which casually trampled underfoot the national rights of other communities, in particular those of the Jews. By the end of the war anti-Semitic horrors perpetrated by the Polish forces were too well authenticated to be denied by any but the most prejudiced.

Namier plunged into Polish *émigré* politics with an enthusiasm that almost proved his undoing. His views were modestly, though pungently, expressed. Initially at least, they coincided with those of Pilsudski,[24] the hero of his school-days. Pilsudski's sober policy

---

[21] See his *Germany and Eastern Europe* (London, 1915), xvi.

[22] See his articles in the *New Statesman*, 28 Oct. 1916, 19 May and 2 June 1917.

[23] Namier told the following story to Sir Isaiah Berlin. 'I remember the day in 1918 when the Emperor sued for peace. I said to Headlam-Morley [then deputy head of the Political Intelligence Department of the Foreign Office]: "Wait". Headlam-Morley said to Balfour: "Wait". Balfour said to Lloyd George: "Wait". Lloyd George said to Wilson: "Wait". And while they waited, the Austro-Hungarian empire disintegrated. I may say that I pulled it to pieces with my own hands.' Sir Berlin, op. cit.

[24] Joseph Pilsudski (1867–1935): Polish revolutionary statesman and soldier. The architect of Polish independence after the First World War, he served as head of state from 1918 to 1922. Although he had flirted with socialism in his youth, in 1926, disillusioned with the workings of the parliamentary system, he seized power at the head of a military insurrection, and, until his death, ruled with dictatorial powers. Namier wrote of him: 'Pilsudski was the last, and the most successful of these revolutionary knight-errants; his "socialism" was a modern variant on the creed of the Polish "democrats" of 1848 and 1863. But as early as 1907 he tried to establish a para-military dictatorship within the Polish Socialist Party; and after 1918, and still more after 1926, he entered Napoleon's path without Napoleon's power or justification.' (See Sir Lewis Namier, *1848: The Revolution of the Intellectuals* (London, 1971; first published, 1946; delivered as the Raleigh Lecture in 1944), 14.)

regarding Poland's eventual frontiers, together with his ideas on social reform, appeared to Namier as the only effective way of avoiding a war, or even wars, of *revanche* in eastern Europe and of saving Poland from Bolshevism. Predictably, Pilsudski did not live up to Namier's expectations. Despite his immense prestige, he collapsed before the pressure of the extreme nationalists. From acting as a bulwark against Polish chauvinism, he now appeared as its most illustrious prophet.

Namier had no doubt as to where the main responsibility lay for Pilsudski's lapse. In his eyes, the chief culprit was his *bête noire* from his student days, Roman Dmowski, now president of the newly formed Polish National Committee. This Committee, set up in Warsaw with Tsarist approval on the outbreak of war, claimed to represent Polish public opinion, and the British Government felt unable to publicly denounce its programme or to abandon its leaders. Since November 1915 Dmowski had been conducting his activities from London. He represented everything most abhorrent to Namier: he was both violently anti-Semitic and imbued with an inflated sense of Poland's imperial destiny. 'M. Dmowski', Namier wrote, 'has repeatedly preached the doctrine that there is neither right nor wrong in international politics, only force.'[25] From the outset, these two vastly contrasting personalities clashed, and they viewed each other with absolute and undeviating hostility and suspicion.[26]

Namier neglected no opportunity to point out the follies of the Polish leader's policy. In a long memorandum in September 1917 he argued vehemently against Dmowski's extravagant claims to extend Poland's frontier as far as the eastern extremity of Galicia, thereby including the larger part of Minsk and Volhynia.[27] Support for Polish demands would not only undermine the political integrity of the allies, it would also weaken their anti-German policy. This remained the core of his campaign against the Dmowski–Pilsudski factions. He penetrated to the root of the problem in his usual, incisive manner:

Poland is like a photographic plate with two impressions on it: there is one Poland, the country of the Polish people, and there is another, the country of the Polish land-owning gentry, and more often than not the two do not coincide. In Upper Silesia and in the eastern part of the duchy of Teschen, on the Kasubian coast north-west of Danzig, in many parts of West Prussia, the workmen and miners, the peasants and fishermen, are Poles, but the big landlords, the

---

[25] See *Manchester Guardian*, 11 June 1919.
[26] See Julia Namier, 123–9, for the running feud between them.
[27] See his memoranda of 14 Sept. 1917, FO 371/3016 no. 19476.

mineowners and manufacturers, are German (in Teschen also Czechs), and all the main towns, Kattowitz, Beuthen and Teschen, Danzig, Thorn and Bromberg, are overwhelmingly German. In the east, over more than 200,000 square miles, an area equal to that of the German Empire in its pre-war frontiers, most of the big landed estates, comprising about 40 per cent of the country, are owned by a small group of Polish nobles, and in the towns of Lemberg and Vilna the Poles form about half the population. But of the total population of thirty millions inhabiting Lithuania, White Russia, East Galicia, and the Western Ukraine only three millions are Poles; the remaining twenty-seven millions are Lithuanians, Letts, White Russians, and Jews.[28]

Condemning the Polish invasion of White Russia in February, a campaign, according to the Polish Government, to mark 'the beginning of a Polish–Russian war for the territory of the old Grand Duchy of Lithuania', he asked:

Will it strengthen the hands of the anti-Bolshevik Russians if the international Bolshevik hordes are turned into champions of Russian national rights? Will a war against Russia strengthen the position of Poland in the territories recovered from Germany? Will it make Poland an asset to the Allies or a liability? Is this the beginning of a League of Nations or the prelude to fresh bloodshed and utter anarchy in Eastern Europe?

This was the mainspring of the new Polish imperialism whose ambitions encompassed the eastern border lands from the Baltic to the Black Sea. In a series of articles and official memoranda he denounced these unjust claims and the brutal methods employed to realize them.[29] Under no circumstances, he warned, should the allies contaminate themselves by lending their support, moral or otherwise, to Poland's acts of international violence. 'A very sharp line must be drawn', he cautioned, 'between their [the Polish nationalists] attitude in Poland and their attitude with regard to Lithuania, White Russia and the Ukraine, and most of all with regard to Great Russia, which alone can serve as a pivot for British policy in eastern Europe. It is hard to see how a policy of aggression on the part of Poland towards its neighbours in the East can ever square with our anti-German policy.'[30]

The Poles, perhaps encouraged by anti-Bolshevik opinion in the West, remained impervious to any pleas for moderation. Although by

---

[28] *Manchester Guardian*, 21 Apr. 1919.

[29] Apart from those memoranda already cited, see also his paper, 'The Political Situation in Poland', 25 Apr. 1918, FO 371/3281 no. 02347; and his notes to Sir William Tyrrell, 15 Nov. 1915, FO 371/328 no. 22347.

[30] See 'The Political Situation in Poland'.

1921 an uneasy truce had been imposed on East Europe, the newly reconstituted Poland had succeeded in antagonizing all of her neighbours. Namier's crusade against Poland never slackened. In 1926 he opposed awarding Poland a permanent, or even temporary seat on the Council of the League, citing her illegal conquests of 1920-1 as undeniable evidence of her lack of moral practice and authority.

Although Namier's sentiments were laudable, his methods of persuasion were open to question. Abrasive to an extreme, he seemed to derive positive enjoyment from battering his listeners, or readers, into submission. He simply refused to let his victims off the hook. One of his teachers at Oxford, Professor Oman,[31] commented: 'He is quite sincere, but very self-centered and disputatious: he used to consider himself the only authority in England on the Ruthenian question, and to resent anyone else having an independent point.' Not that Oman disputed Namier's basic assumptions; it was only that they were expressed in 'a spirit of exaggerated hostility, making the worst of the Polish case whenever it is possible to do so'.[32] William Tyrrell[33] also had occasion to employ similar language. On the original draft of what was probably Namier's swansong to the Foreign Office, a lengthy and violent essay on 'Polish Peace Terms to the Bolsheviks', he noted: '[This] paper would be improved if it were more compressed and less hostile in tone.'[34] Namier had advised Tyrrell that

It would be utterly intolerable were the Poles allowed to retain, e.g. East-Galicia and Vilna and thus use the territories under the League of Nations as a cover for their Imperialist conquest and forcible Polanisation of non-Polish territory . . . They are the best hated men in the country and hated not merely by their specially chosen victims, the Jews, but by White Russians, Little Russians and Lithuanians alike.

His habit of knowing everything and of conveying his knowledge by ponderous pronunciamentos which brooked no argument did not endear him to his Whitehall colleagues, nor indeed, at a later date, to

[31] Charles (William Chadwick) Oman (1860–1946): historian; Fellow of All Souls, 1883; Chichele Professor of Modern History, 1905–46; MP for Oxford University, 1919–35. Kn. 1920. Oman served as one of Namier's examiners for the All Souls Fellowship.
[32] See his comments on Namier's memo. of 14 Sept. 1917, FO 371/3016 no. 194676.
[33] William George Tyrrell (1866–1947): entered Foreign Office, 1889; précis writer to Grey, 1905–15; Assistant Under-Secretary of State, 1919–25; Permanent Under-Secretary of state, 1925–8; Ambassador to France, 1928–34. Kn. 1913. Created Baron, 1929.
[34] For the memorandum, dated 20 Mar. 1920, and comments, see FO 371/4287 no. 02379.

)-workers, or 'co-racials' as he preferred to call them, at the Jewish ncy.

Accounts of Polish anti-Jewish atrocities in eastern Europe figured prominently in the reports reaching the Foreign Office.[35] There can be no doubt that the Jewish experience in Poland had the most profound effect on Namier's attitude towards Zionism. He saw no hope of a reconciliation between the Poles, intoxicated beyond control by their chauvinistic fervour, and the Jews, the helpless victims of their megalomania. If the Jews had no place in the violently nationalistic Europe of the post-war era, then perhaps they would have to look elsewhere, to Palestine.

One month after the Balfour declaration, Namier was afforded the opportunity of expressing his thoughts on the nature of Zionism and its political goals. He did so, in a joint memorandum with Arnold Toynbee,[36] in reply to an assessment of the 'Zionist Movement' written by the United States vice-consul in Geneva, Mr Edelmann, an American, anti-Zionist Jew. After strongly defending the Jewish agricultural settlers in Palestine who 'are inspired by a definite live idea', they continued:

The objection raised against the Jews being given exclusive political rights in Palestine on a basis that would be undemocratic with regard to the local Christian and Mohammedan population is certainly the most important point

[35] See for example, FO 371/3277 no. 11050/3363; FO 371/3281 no. 8065; FO 371/4385 no. 793.

[36] Arnold Joseph Toynbee (1889–1976): historian; Fellow and Tutor, Balliol College, 1912–15; employed by Government, 1915–19; member of Political Intelligence Department of Foreign Office, 1918; of British delegation to Paris peace conference, 1919; Koraes Professor of Byzantine and Modern Greek Language, Literature, and History, London University, 1919–24; Research Professor of International Relations, London University, 1925–55; Director of Studies at Royal Institute of International Affairs, 1925–55. Author of *A Study of History*, 10 vols. (1934–54).

Soon after this joint *œuvre*, the authors parted ways, intellectually and politically. It was Toynbee's pro-Arabism which most riled Namier. Periodically he would savage Toynbee's scholarship as expressed in the chapters on Palestine in the *Survey of International Affairs* [see *Conflicts*; and a letter to *Manchester Guardian*, 30 June 1943]. As Toynbee remarked: 'If you crossed Lewis on some issue which, for him, was of importance, he was capable of declaring total war, however old and close a friend of his you might be.' Curiously enough, Toynbee's controversial historical method provoked little animosity from Namier; one might even conclude that it bound them together professionally in a kind of superior historians' trade union. Namier once told him: 'You try to see the tree as a whole, I try to examine it leaf by leaf. The general run of historians try to take the tree branch by branch; and you and I agree that this last approach, at any rate, is an unpromising one.' Despite their differences, Toynbee retained a great admiration for Namier, and wrote a most generous sketch of him after his death. See *Aquaintances* (OUP, 1967).

which the anti-Zionists have hitherto raised, but the difficulty is imaginary. Palestine might be held in trust by Great Britain or America until there was a sufficient population in the country fit to govern it on European lines. Then no undemocratic restrictions of the kind indicated in the memorandum would be required any longer. Meantime the Zionists are completely satisfied with obtaining the security which Turkish rule failed to give them and with full possibilities for cultural and national self-government on a personal and not territorial basis—the Jews in Palestine would rule themselves for the time being as churches do in organized states and not on a territorial basis, which would imply dominion over other races. . . . The new Palestine developing under British and American patronage, and therefore also being in the first place dependent on English and American enterprise, is certain to take the imprint of the communities from which it originates.[37]

In April 1919, Ignacy Jan Paderewski,[38] who was attending the Paris peace conference, invited Namier to Paris to discuss with him Polish affairs and in particular the Jewish question.[39] Namier's chief, James Headlam-Morley,[40] agreed, and in several notes to him Namier formulated his current views on the Jewish question.

The Jews' demands for educational and cultural autonomy, he wrote, were reasonable and just.[41] A composite nation is an organic entity whose components can only develop to the benefit of all within their proper setting. The new Poland, he claimed, would never thrive 'by chopping off an arm from one component body to use elsewhere as a third limb'. Jews could be good and loyal citizens only if no attempt were made to 'Polonize' them and to deny them their own ancient national tradition. Polish leaders who talked of allowing individual Jews civil rights while ignoring their right to a gregarious life of their own were living in cloud-cuckoo land: they had simply no conception of the mainspring of Jewish life. Perhaps in countries—England, or France, or Italy—where the Jews formed tiny minorities such a solution

---

[37] From a memorandum by Namier and Toynbee, 19 Dec. 1917, FO 371/3054 no. 237630.

[38] Ignacy Jan Paderewski (1860–1941): Polish pianist, composer, and statesman; persuaded President Wilson to include Polish independence among the 14 points; served for a short, though unsuccessful, period as Prime Minister of Poland in 1919.

[39] See FO 371/4379, no. 364.

[40] James (Wycliffe) Headlam-Morley (1863–1919): historian; Fellow of King's College, Cambridge, 1890–6; Professor of Greek and Ancient History, Queen's College, London, 1894–1900; historical adviser to propaganda and information department of Foreign Office, 1914–17; to Foreign Office, 1920–8. Kn. 1929.

[41] This passage is based on his letters to Headlam-Morley, 16 and 18 Apr., and 2 July 1919, from Lady Namier's Notes.

was tenable. But to deny a corporate existence to four million Jews[42] would be a denial of basic human rights, particularly as the criterion of national self-determination had recently been universally adopted as a cardinal principle in the post-war world.

Jewish assimilation, he went on, would cripple both communities and is desired by neither. The Poles would prefer the Jews to emigrate rather than risk being 'verjudet à la Esmé' [infected by the Jewbug in Esmé's way].[43] The intensely patriotic spirit which now pervaded Poland, egged on by a bigoted Catholic priesthood, had distinguished itself by the worst pogroms in modern Europe and by day-to-day outrages against the Jews. Under these circumstances assimilation was a pipe-dream. Nothing but a substantial measure of autonomy would suffice. 'These are some of the things', he concluded, 'that I would like to talk of with Paderewski.'

In early May he met the Polish leader several times. No official record remains of their discussions. But twenty years later, Namier remember the following episode:[44]

In May 1919 I had in Paris a long talk with Paderewski, then Polish Premier. The Jewish problem naturally figured largely in it.

'The Jews in England speak English,' started off Paderewski, 'French in France, German in Germany. Why do they not speak Polish in Poland?'

'But do you want them to speak Polish?' I asked in reply.

'Please consider,' I said, 'In Germany the Jews form about one per cent in a highly educated population; and yet this has sufficed for them powerfully to influence German literature, science, the press, and the theatre. If you want the Polish Jews, who form ten per cent of the population, to give up Yiddish and learn Polish, you will have to educate them. And then *you* will have to adopt a different language if you want to think your own thoughts.'

After a moment's reflection Paderewski said: 'You may be right. But let them at least speak Hebrew and not Yiddish, which jars on us.'

'As a Zionist I certainly should wish the Jews to adopt Hebrew,' I replied. 'But you must allow me to say that once you give up your demand that the Jews in Poland adopt Polish, what language they speak is an internal affair of ours.'

It is safe to assume therefore that Namier pressed his views in his

[42] Namier clarified this point. In a purely ethnic Poland there would only be two million Jews; but within the boundaries of a greater Poland, as claimed by Dmowski and his adherents, there would be four million. This did not substantially alter Namier's argument; it merely doubled its intensity.

[43] Sir Esmé Howard, a senior British diplomat, then a member of the British delegation to Versailles, was concerned with Polish affairs. He had advocated assimilation as a solution to the Jewish problem.

[44] *Conflicts*, 166–7.

customary fashion. Nothing of consequence emerged from these parleys. In Poland, anti-Semitism continued unchecked. It eventually struck at his own family. Two months after his meetings with Paderewski, Namier learned that his parents' home at Koszylowce had been plundered and razed to the ground.[45] Although Ukrainian irregulars were responsible for this outrage, Namier directed his anger at the Poles.

. . . the responsibility rests with the Polish jingoes and those Allied statesmen who, lacking adequate energy, bungled. The last decision of the Peace Congress foredooms worse to come. All the massacres in Macedonia will seem as nothing compared with those coming to Eastern Galicia . . . If the horrifying excesses reported by the Poles are true, they only prove the intensity of the Ukranians detestation of them. The instigators, the Poles, will now retaliate in kind with Allied open support. Where can such folly lead?[46]

He was fully aware that his solution to the problem, a neutralized East Galicia under the aegis of the League, was painfully inadequate. Nothing, apparently, could rescue the Poles from their own folly. The Polish empire in the East would be a graveyard for all other national minorities.

Namier's fears were soon vindicated. In the summer of 1919, General Haller, inspired by Dmowski's Committee, and in direct contravention to the instructions of the Allies, struck deep into the Ukraine. Crushed between the Poles in the West and the Bolsheviks in the East, the Ukrainians soon broke. The Allies, seemingly with little deliberation— they were preoccupied at the time with concluding the Versailles treaty as expeditiously as possible—meekly surrendered to the Polish coup. Namier viewed this betrayal of the Ukrainians as 'scandalous'. 'I am flabbergasted,' he wrote, 'The political system has broken down completely.'[47] He hoped to salvage something from this wreckage. From now on his efforts were concentrated on securing Jewish cultural rights in the Polish treaty. By early 1920 he admitted failure. 'The treatment of Polish Jews', he concluded, 'is contrary to the provisions of the Minority Treaty with Poland.' Everywhere in Poland the Jews were 'suffering immediate and serious hardship'.[48]

Having reluctantly abandoned hope of an autonomous Jewish cultural existence in Poland, he turned his attentions elsewhere. On 6 September 1919 he addressed a letter to his closest contact in the Prime

[45] Julia Namier, 142–3.   [46] Ibid. 144.   [47] Ibid. 144–5.
[48] See his memorandum of 12 Feb. 1920, FO 371/4385 no. 793.

Minister's entourage, Philip Kerr,[49] Lloyd George's influential private
secretary:

You may be relieved if I tell you at the outset that his letter does not deal with
Polish affairs but with a 'cleaner, greener land'—with Palestine and Zionist
matters.

I take it the British mandate is now a certainty; anyhow, the Jews of the entire
world are agreed on this point, and there is a Presidential election on in America
pretty soon. So we should get help from there. I also take it that this is the only
solution from the British point of view, not merely because of the pledges
contained in the Balfour Declaration, but also from the point of view of British
interests. We need not therefore wait till the political problems of Palestine are
finally settled, but on the contrary must prepare beforehand for the work which
will await us. The colonists who are to enter Palestine once it is opened up,
ought to be a disciplined force composed of well-trained men and not an
unorganised mob of unskilled refugees. The training by which we have to
prepare these men must consist of military and technical instruction and
general education.

The settlers must be capable of defending themselves and ought as soon as
possible to relieve the British army of occupation. Also for moral reasons some
time spent under proper military discipline will do good to the future Jewish
settlers of Palestine.

By technical education I mean in the first place instruction in agriculture and
in the work done in the army by the Royal Engineers. We need ready cadres of
men who would reclaim our land—the new Jerusalem has to be reclaimed by us
ourselves. New England would never have become the moral force which it has
had Negro slaves done the work for the first Puritan settlers. Lastly it would
seem essential that the future settlers of Palestine should be taught Hebrew and
English and be welded by common training into a unit and given a British
Connection.

Now all this could in my opinion be best done by getting the recruit settlers
from Eastern Europe into military camps of which any number is available at
present; and there are thousands of Jews impatiently waiting in Eastern Europe
for the day when they could leave that House of Bondage, that torture-chamber
which Poland has now become for them. Their life in Poland is a daily round of
insult and oppression. They are complete outlaws, and there is neither justice
nor legal protection for them anywhere, and they are not even allowed to
defend themselves. Their economic position is equally hopeless. The trade and
commerce by which they used to live are at a complete stand-still, and they have

---

[49] Philip Henry Kerr (1882–1940): journalist and imperial statesman; co-founder of
Round Table; Private Secretary to Lloyd George, 1916–21; Chancellor of Duchy of
Lancaster, 1931; Under-Secretary of State for India, 1931–2; ambassador to United
States, 1939–40. Succeeded as 11th marquess of Lothian, 1930.

to rely for their livelihood on relief from America and Western Europe. The position is hopeless and demoralising. Were we to call for recruits we could get any number we wanted, and we should moreover get recruits of the best quality—idealists and men who cannot stand life in Poland under the present degrading conditions. If the British Government provided the camps and supplied a certain number of instructors, the Jewish organisations would pay for the rest—most of these men in Poland have anyhow to be supported from outside. I see many reasons for adopting this plan, and I fail to see any reason against it. I know there are people who have the 'Arab Question' on the brain and who think they will get further by procrastination and passive resistance. But the policy as laid down in the Balfour Declaration is a step which cannot be retraced, *ce sont des mots sur lesquels on ne revient pas*. It will not make the position any easier if on the opening-up of Palestine the Jewish immigration comes as the in-rush of an undisciplined mob, incapable of defending itself and out of control; surely it would be far preferable if it came as an organised, disciplined force under British command, capable of holding the land which they occupy and of developing it. I take it nothing would be more dangerous for our prestige than the mismanagement of Palestine colonisation. All the world over people get most easily reconciled to a successful *fait accompli*; in the East, I understand, this is the case to an even higher degree. Our aim ought to be to realise the policy laid down in the Balfour Declaration in the most efficient and quickest manner, and with the least friction possible. For this a military organisation of the Jewish colonisation seems to me essential.

One more word about a point on which I am particularly keen. The first training camps for these Jewish colonists should be in England and not in Egypt, as some people might suggest. Palestine under a British mandate ought to become a link between the East and the West within the British Empire. In time it ought to become a British self-governing dominion. If successful our scheme may yet mark a turning point in the development of Great Britain's Eastern Empire. It is with a very different feeling from that of the Gentile Westerners that we approach the East. We are determined to work for a good understanding with the other Eastern nations and for a wider regeneration and rehabilitation of the East. All these, however, are problems of the future which will gradually be solved by the course of events in Palestine alone, but at the outset the Jews who go out to Palestine ought to receive a British connection. Let England be for them the gate through which they emerge from their East European torture-chamber, and you can rely on their remembering this country—for the last 3,300 years we have celebrated even an exodus into the Desert merely because it meant the end of the Egyptian bondage.

Yours ever,

P.S. I have talked to Toynbee about the training of Jewish colonists and the Arab Question, and he agrees with my scheme. Weizmann too is keen on our starting to train the future colonists for Palestine, and he will, I believe, talk to you about it during his coming visit to Paris. I do hope you will see your way to support this scheme—do give it careful consideration! Besides other advantages it will relax a bit the terrible tension which now prevails in Polish–Jewish relations, and by opening up more vistas and hopes to the Jews will enable them to hold out. Also remember of what enormous value such a conscientious and active policy will be in our relations with America—the American Jews are a power, they are extremely pro-British, they can be made even more so. In the present hopeless inertia an active step will work better than discussions and propaganda.

Nothing of substance came of the scheme Namier had proposed. His indiscriminate use of 'we' for himself and the Zionists, or for himself and the British, confused, even disconcerted, his friends in both camps. His belief in the British–Zionist connection was absolute. Each side, he contended, needed the other. Although both Kerr and Lloyd George were highly sympathetic to Zionism, the British Government had to reconcile its Zionist commitment to its over-all Middle East strategy. Clearly Namier was asking for too much too soon, a practice he developed to a fine art in the coming years. Yet despite its lack of any positive response, the letter marked an important stage in Namier's development. From it he emerges as a fully fledged, dyed-in-the-wool Zionist. The Polish experience, that 'torture-chamber', had tipped the scales irrevocably towards Palestine. It would not be an exaggeration to conclude that the excesses of Polish anti-Semitism constituted the catalyst for Namier's final conversion to Zionism.

It is from this period that his friendship and working partnership with Weizmann took root. He had met the Zionist leader fleetingly in Oxford during his Balliol days, but according to his own recollection had found him unimpressive.[50] In the autumn of 1918 they met again, no doubt to discuss Polish–Jewish affairs.[51] But again no lasting political contact was made. 'I really don't know why I didn't take an interest in Zionism affairs when I had been a theoretical Zionist for years; nor why the Zionists did not make the least use of me when I would have gladly helped them.'[52]

All the evidence indicates that Namier wrote to Kerr spontaneously, without any prompting from the Zionist Organization. But its contents

[50] Lady Namier's Notes.

[51] During this period many well-documented accounts reporting the pogroms in Poland were being sifted in the Political Intelligence Department. They had been earmarked for Weizmann's special attention, and it is inconceivable that Namier was ignorant of them or unware of their destination.

[52] Lady Namier's Notes.

soon came to the attention of Weizmann, and it alerted him to the obvious fact that here was a well-placed official, highly articulate, at least on paper, whose views closely coincided with his own, and who was not in the slightest way embarrassed from pushing those views in the very highest circles. Nor was Weizmann slow in exploiting Namier's position. Within a short period of time he had briefed Namier on Zionist policies over a wide range of outstanding issues, including the vexed question of Palestine's northern borders and her eventual water supply.[53]

Weizmann's respect for Namier's ability deepened. At the end of September 1919 he asked Namier if, after leaving the Foreign Office, he would care to join the Zionist Organization in an official capacity. Namier took the offer seriously. But in the subsequent negotiations Weizmann revealed a casualness towards his intended aide which did not augur well for their future relationship. Owing to the pressure of his timetable, he had asked two of his closest associates, Julius Simon[54] and Harry Sacher,[55] to ascertain in what capacity and on what terms Namier would be prepared to join the Organization. Neither approached him: 'And again, for years, I forgot about Zionism, and the Zionists forgot about me.'[56]

This was only partially true. His interest in Zionism did not flag. Occasionally his advice was sought; and he never failed to respond:

With regard to the question of approaching the League of Nations Council about the Mandate:

I entirely agree (with what seems to be the general feeling and obviously is yours) that any such appeal would be unwise, even disastrous, and moreover *disloyal*. From my knowledge of the F.O. I would consider it suicidal on our part, and I say it openly, I myself would take *a very grave* view of it. No one has done anything seriously for Zionism except our Government. And then the Zionists are to appeal—to whom? To *France* and that motley crowd, Belgium, Brazil, Japan, Greece, with our ardent friends Poland and Rumania in the back-

[53] See Weizmann to Namier, 18 Sept. 1919, CZA A312/47

[54] Julius Simon (1875–1969): prominent German Zionist, later resident in United States; member of executive of Zionist Organization, 1920–1; a founder of Palestine Economic Corporation, 1925, President, 1931–51, director of operations in Palestine, 1933–49. Broke with Weizmann in 1921 over differences regarding economic policy to be pursued in Palestine.

[55] Harry Sacher (1881–1971): journalist and barrister; prominent English Zionist; member of editorial staff of *Manchester Guardian*, 1905–9, 1915–19; practised law in Palestine, 1920–30; member of executive of Zionist Organization, 1927–31; director of Marks & Spencer.

[56] Lady Namier's Notes.

ground! This would be nothing short of scandalous and would alienate our best friends. I think the matter should not even be considered. It would give any opponent of Zionism a chance to plead *for refusing the Mandate*.[57]

Namier's remaining months in Government service, he left the Foreign Office in April 1920 to return to Balliol, were monopolized by his work on behalf of Jewish refugees fleeing eastern Europe. He himself had only recently been the subject of a loaded question in the House of Commons which stressed his foreign origins and hinted that perhaps, as a consequence, he was politically unreliable.[58] It was an experience which conceivably strengthened both his sense of compassion and his feeling of insecurity. His interventions on behalf of his 'poor co-religionaries' were entangled with his flair for the dramatic. It would have been out of character had he not succeeded in irritating his would-be partners in these ventures, both in the Anglo-Jewish establishment and the relevant Government committees. But his tenacity paid off. On the whole, his endeavours were crowned with success.[59]

*   *   *

Namier did not remain at Balliol for very long. He quickly realized that no matter how many young men he tutored, his book on the eighteenth century would exact more time and money than teaching or lecturing would allow or give him. In the autumn of 1921 he decided to invest his talents in business and journalism in the hope of amassing enough capital to buy the years of leisure he needed for his historical work. Once again, his Oxford friends came to the rescue. He 'went into cotton' as the sales representative in Prague of various English cotton interests. At the same time, he contracted to act as correspondent for central

[57] A note to L. Stein, 15 Feb. 1921, CZA, A312/9. Negotiations between the JA and the Government leading to the final formulation of the Mandate for Palestine were prolonged and often acrimonious. In despair, the Zionists played with the idea of appealing to a higher body, the Council of the League, for justice. Luckily for them they followed Namier's, and others', advice, and did not do so.

[58] A Mr Alfred Baldwin Raper, Unionist MP for East Islington, asked the question; Namier's position was defended by the Government spokesman, Capt. Guest, and by two other friends, Mr A. Shaw and Maj. McKenzie Wood (PD Commons, v. 120. c. 1648–9, 6 Nov. 1919). See also FO 371/4383 no. 642.

[59] In Lady Namier's Notes, three examples are cited of his refugee work. The first concerned 22 Poles who had landed penniless in France and were threatened by the authorities with repatriation; the second, involved some Lithuanian Jews who had fled to England before the war and now wanted to bring their families over to join them; the third, related to a group of Jews in Riga who were unable by the normal channels to obtain British visas to enter South Africa.

European affairs for the *Manchester Guardian* and other journals.[60]

He lived chiefly in Vienna. It was here, a year earlier, that Namier, now clearly under Weizmann's spell, had 'declared himself a Zionist' to his father.[61] His relationship with his father, at the best of times shaky, took a sharp turn for the worse. Two years later, Namier learned that his father had dispossessed him of his rightful inheritance, the estates at Koszylowce. The break with his family was complete.[62] His last physical link with his former life in eastern Europe had disappeared.

His travellings throughout central Europe revived his interest in Jewish affairs, and in particular the age-old problem of those Jews 'who had grown up in the discoloured and discolouring surroundings of Central European town life',[63] his picturesque description of the assimilated Jew. Namier disposed of this species in his own way.

On my first visit to Vienna after the war, I happened to engage in a discussion about Jewish Nationalism and Zionism with one of those high-minded, broad-minded, open-minded, shallow-minded Jews who prefer to call themselves anything rather than Jews. 'First and foremost', he declared in a pompous manner, 'I am a human being.' I replied (and this was twenty years ago): 'I, too, once thought so; but I have since discovered that all are agreed I am a Jew, and not at all that I am a human being. I have therefore come to consider myself first a Jew and only in the second place a human being.'[64]

In the summer of 1925 Namier arrived at Vienna to attend his first

---

[60] Some of his articles from this period appear in *Skyscrapers*.

[61] Julia Namier, 163–4.

[62] As is well known, Namier slowly lost the use of his right hand until finally he found it almost impossible to write with it. There was nothing organically wrong; the complaint was purely psychosomatic in origin. Namier traced the cause of his complaint, he referred to it as 'acute writer's cramp' (Namier to Moyne, 24 Mar. 1941, CZA A312/16), to his 'dispossession'. 'For ten years he had longed for Koszylowce as an outlet where—with a very special joy—he would once again ride out to *his* neolithic obuj [tumulus], and organize on *his* land shoots of wild boar and other game. His right hand having become of no pleasurable use to him, he had let it die.' His psychoanalysts differed. They believed it resulted from 'his unrealizable desire that Hitler should be killed, by him'. (See Julia Namier, 182.) Lady Namier had earlier recollected that 'He had this cramp—paralysis— in his right arm. It wasn't just writer's cramp, and doctors told him that the cause was not physiological but psychological. That was the beginning of his psychoanalysis. In the twenties, his cramp wasn't so bad, but in the thirties, with the mounting mistreatment of Jews, his arm became almost useless. Indeed Lewis was so terrified of the idea of a German occupation of England that he had his doctor friends give him a bottle of poison which he always carried in his waistcoat pocket, so he could kill himself in case the Germans came. Not until after the war was over could I make him throw the tablets away.' (See Mehte, 219–20.) All this remains a topic for inspired speculation. Perhaps his complaint resulted from a combination of all these causes.

[63] *Skyscrapers*, 140–1.   [64] *Conflicts*, 163.

Zionist congress, ostensibly as correspondent of *The Economist* (the editor, Walter Layton, was a friend of his), but in fact to observe at close quarters the deliberations of the elected representatives of Zionism. No doubt the quality of the delegates failed to impress him: their speeches were too long, too turgid, too ideological. There was one notable exception: Weizmann. His much publicized organic approach to politics appealed both to Namier's sense of practical politics and to his sense of history:

There is no *Derech HaMelech*, no 'royal road' to Palestine. He who prefers an easy road, who believes that there is somebody who can show him an easy road, should go to Uganda or the Crimea or anywhere, or stop at home. We shall have to fight this difficult, drawn-out, hard daily fight. Sometimes we shall win, sometimes we shall be defeated. We shall put stone upon stone in Palestine, until a time will come when again a tribunal will sit, to which we can again present our demands in the same atmosphere—though, I hope, not on the same basis. Your future leader will step before this tribunal and will be in a position to reply on the work done, which, though small, is sound and honest and valuable. For this time you will have to wait patiently and courageously, as it becomes an ancient race and an old, cultured nation. Do not press for quick success, which is a boomerang turning back against your work later on. I can but go this one way, which my faith and my experience have taught me.[65]

This was how genuinely great statesmen acted. Visionaries certainly, yet they freed themselves from ideological encumbrances, resolving each particular issue on its specific merits. They were the supreme practitioners of the apophthegm 'politics is the art of the possible'. For his part, Weizmann was determined that Namier's unique talents should be harnessed to the Zionest cause. In several face-to-face meetings he exerted all of his considerable charm to realize this aim. And he succeeded admirably. Namier came away captivated by Weizmann's personality and carried away by his grandiose vision. Namier was now firmly under Weizmann's spell.

On his return to London, Namier decided the time was ripe to put into effect a plan he had long contemplated: to arrange a meeting between Weizmann and one of his closest friends, Mrs Edgar Dugdale, known to all her acquaintances as 'Baffy'. Mrs Dugdale later recorded

---

[65] From Weizmann's speech to the 14th Zionist Congress, Vienna, 23 Aug. 1925, see P. Goodman, ed., *Chaim Weizmann. A Tribute on His Seventieth Birthday* (London, 1945), 191. For further emphasis of his step-by-step approach, see his speech to 17th Zionist Congress at Basle, 1 July 1931, ibid., 205–30.

the incident which reveals much about Namier's habits and his relationship with 'Baffy':

When Lewis Namier was working on *The Structure of Politics* he lodged in two rooms on the top floor of a tiny house in Chelsea—21 Glebe Place. These were not the most auspicious surroundings for giving even a small dinner-party, but it is truer of nothing than of hospitality that 'where there's a will there's a way', and Lewis is a born host. Put him down at the North Pole and he would invite some Polar bears to share his supper. But he would do it with discrimination mixing his guests with care even among those he likes. As for the others (and they would be numerous) they might eat him before he would so much as throw them a frozen lump of pemmican.

In the autumn of 1925 he determined to be the means of bringing me together with Dr. Weizmann, the Zionist leader. Certainly it was high time. Dr. Weizmann's name had been a household word in the Balfour family for years, and A.J.B. [her uncle, Arthur James Balfour] had gone that spring to Palestine to open the Hebrew University. But it was my sister Joan Lascelles and her husband who went with him on that journey, not me.

The evening before the dinner party, Joan Lascelles, who was in London on a chance visit, invited herself. Namier, after some hesitation, agreed. He then made a psychological error:

He thought the best way to break the news to her [his housekeeper] would be to tell her that the extra guest was the Princess Royal's sister-in-law. The effect of this upon the Celtic temperament was immediate and disastrous. Mrs. O'Grady retired to her room, had a nervous breakdown, and announced herself quite incapable of cooking the dinner!

Plans were remade, resources pooled:

In the evening I set out from Roland Gardens in a taxi with a cold chicken in aspic on my lap, while Joan Lascelles, who wore a silver gown and diamonds, nursed a bowl full of salad. When we reached Glebe Place, the light of a street lamp fell on somebody getting out of another taxi and opening the gate of the little front garden. Joan thrust the salad bowl into my hands, and sprang out with a joyful cry of recognition. I heard a deep voice, with a strong Russian accent. The door opened, and the eyes of the little maid grew globular at the sight of my sister—I imagine such a sparkling apparition had seldom floated up the narrow staircase of 21, Glebe Place. Dr. Weizmann stood aside and let me pass. He looked with curiosity at the bowl I was carrying and tried to relieve me of it, and the salad. But he was too tactful to insist. I carried the dishes upstairs, and deposited them in Lewis's bedroom, according to plan, verifying the presence there of the fruits and ices which were his contribution to the dinner. Then I joined the others in the sitting room, where Joan and Dr. Weizmann were already exchanging the 'Do you remembers?' of fellow travellers, and our host was beaming through his huge spectacles, assured that his party was going to be a great and memorable success.[66]

It was. Namier never again lost touch with the Zionist movement. 'Baffy', for her part, succumbed to Weizmann's charm. Following in the family tradition, she became the most ardent Gentile Zionist of her generation. Within a short time she began to work for the Zionist organization, at first as an adviser on a voluntary basis, later in an official capacity. Namier and she worked in close harness. It was the beginning of a most powerful intellectual partnership, one that has scarcely been equalled before or since in the history of Zionism. For Namier, it also cemented his deepest and most lasting friendship. No one else revealed such compassion, understanding, and sympathy for this truly idiosyncratic man. 'No Baffy,' he murmured upon hearing of her death in May 1948, 'I can't believe it, I can't take it in.'[67]

*   *   *

This period witnessed Namier's coming of age as a full-fledged Zionist. In two major essays he laid bare his Zionist creed. In the first, his main proposition was clear. He postulated that the ancient bonds which had held the Jews together for eighteen hundred years—'the Messianic miracle and the return to our land'—were disappearing:

This faith is now dying fast, and Israel has to face the practical problem of its existence and of its uncertain future—a stupendous process of reorientation in the oldest and most tenacious of races. Some of us find the solution in dissolution, others are determined actively to work for the 'miracle' for which we have hitherto waited. Orthodox Jewry is a melting glacier and Zionism is the

---

[66] Quoted from Lady Namier's Notes. This was intended by Mrs Dugdale for an unidentified publication.

[67] See Julia Namier, 275. In the Preface to *The Structure of Politics at the Accession of George III* (2nd. ed., London, 1965), xiii, Namier singles out Mrs Dugdale for special mention: '. . . were I to choose one person to whom to dedicate this book I should have no doubt to whom that was due. Mrs. Edgar Dugdale has helped at almost every step; with her I discussed every chapter before it was written, and she patiently read through the successive drafts down to the proofs, and advised me in things big and small. There was many a moment when without the encouragement and help which she gave me, I should have had to drop the work altogether. How much I can owe her, only her friends can understand.'

river which springs from it; evaporation and the river result from the same process, and are both its necessary results.[68]

Assimilation, or 'evaporation', was a distinct possibility in the Jewish communities in western and central Europe. Nor should such a process be condemned out of hand: 'if community with us has no meaning for them, why should they remain with us?' He asked only that it be carried out without the self-abasement and insult inherent in the denial of their origins. He added: 'these are the fringes of the glacier from which no river can spring and by which one must not judge the nature and future of the glacier itself.' That would be judged in relation to the fate of the two largest, most important communities in world Jewry: those of eastern Europe and the United States. Regarding the latter, it was too early yet to form any lasting judgement. It was apparent, however, that as a result of the war the centre of gravity in Jewry had moved from the German to the English-speaking countries. Yet already a great paradox had emerged: 'the main body of Jews, whose existence forms the real Jewish question, remains in eastern Europe; the Jews primarily called upon to deal with the problem live in America and in England.' He saw no hope for the masses of Jewry in the East, particularly for those trapped in Poland. 'Where will this end if no outlet is found in time for a new Jewish emigration?'

With the loss of the Messianic hope the passivity of orthodox Jewry breaks down. We have to find our place on earth and live as other people do. Where the Jews live in dense masses, speak their own language, and form a distinct community, they have their own 'nationality', whether they profess it or not; anyhow, they are treated as strangers by their neighbours. It is not true that it is the rise of a conscious Jewish nationality which raises a bar between them; the bar exists anyhow, and a national consciousness merely gives the Jews a backbone and relieves them of the feeling of moral inferiority, which some of their neighbours like to inflict on them however much they may loathe its natural consequences—aggressive cringing and pushing. Zionism, whatever possibilities it may open up in future, cannot alone within measureable time solve the economic problems of East European Jewry which cry out for solution; but it can even now help to create an atmosphere in which other remedies will

---

[68] This article, entitled 'Zionism', first appeared in the *New Statesman* on 5 Nov. 1927 (republished in *Skyscrapers*). It had a profound effect upon Sir Isaiah Berlin, then a young Jewish scholar. 'It was the most arresting piece on that subject that I or, I suspect, anyone had ever read . . . Much was being written on that topic then. For the most part it was competent journalism . . . This essay was of an altogether higher quality. In reading it one had the sensation—for which there is no substitute—of suddenly sailing in first-class waters.' op. cit.

become more effective. A consciousness of nationality, of national purpose and responsibility, of the duty to work for a common future and the duty to become normal after eighteen centuries of abnormal life, are in themselves of imponderable value, for along the whole line, in matters economic, national or communal, an end must be made to that nondescript character which the endless detached waiting has produced in great masses of our people.

Possibly a majority of national Jews will have to remain for ever in the Diaspora, but, even so, there must be somewhere a National Home to give them normality—every nation must somewhere have its own territorial centre . . . Our very survival was inherently bound up with the hope of a return to Palestine. The passive hope has now changed into an active will; those of us who still adhere to the idea which for eighteen hundred years stood in the centre of our thinking, have to work for that which we no longer expect to come to us in another way. No one who looks with an unprejudiced eye at the road which the Jewish people has covered, at the sufferings which it has patiently borne, at the spiritual strength it has shown, and lastly at the desperate position in which a large part of it is now placed, can doubt the driving force which there is behind the Zionist movement.

. . . If Palestine is to be our National Home—and we can see no other on the globe nor in all our history—we must not even ask the price at which we can achieve it.

Namier did not deny that the creation of the Jewish National Home was still in its experimental stage, despite its undoubted achievements. He concluded

Should the enterprise in which the British Empire and the Jewish nation are partners fail, to our friends in Great Britain, perhaps the best we have had since Cyrus and Alexander (we can use quaint comparison, as our memory is long), this would be a disappointment, for ourselves a catastrophe of truly immeasurable consequence. And perhaps even the outside world would then find that spiritual catastrophe in Jewry cannot remain a matter of indifference to other nations.

His commitment to Zionism, now on public record, was absolute. Rarely had its case been put more persuasively or with greater intellectual vigour and clarity. For all that, he was beset by a nagging doubt. What would be the fate of Jewry should the experiemnt fail? He had no clear-cut answer to the quandary. But in the second of his essays he perceived an option, which if acted upon, would secure the future of the National Home. His idea, first hinted at in his letter to Philip Kerr, was that Palestine should eventually become 'The Seventh

Dominion'.[69] Although this was a distant goal it was a realizable one, for it would secure not only British strategic interests but it would also provide a constitutional framework in which to resolve the Arab–Jewish conflict. For Namier, as for Weizmann, the British connection was basic. Here, for the first time, he stressed the importance of a fusion between Palestinians, both Arabs and Jews, which could only be obtained under the benevolent umbrella of the British Empire.

What more can we Jews offer the Palestinian Arabs than complete equality, safeguarded by a British connexion and, if need be, placed under a guarantee of the Imperial Parliament? If the Arabs sincerely and unreservedly accept such a symbiosis, all serious difficulties between us are at an end—even the question of which side is in the majority becomes unimportant, once we are sure that they will not use theirs to keep us out of our National Home or to force us into a Pan-Arab union, and they are sure that we shall never use ours to drive them out of the country or reduce them to an inferior position. What 'grievance' then remains?

. . . Palestine as the common home of Jews and Arabs, associated with the British Commonwealth as the Seventh Dominion, would supply a cover to the Suez Canal, better than any naval base or military garrison, and would, at the same time, become the foremost cultural and economic outpost of Europe in the Near East. If the Arabs join with us on this basis, so much the better; but if they refuse, from the very nature of the situation the Jews will still adhere to the British connexion, with or without the mandate.

At present the programme of the Seventh Dominion is no more than a distant goal; it would not be within the power of the Zionist Executive to endorse it, nay, even a Zionist Congress could not take any binding resolution concerning the future of Palestine. Such a resolution cannot be taken outside Palestine, and in Palestine itself it can be taken only when the time has come for the termination of the mandate, which will not be until the National Home is safely established and the country is ripe for self-government. Only as an idea can it be put forward at present; but time and circumstances work for that idea, which alone can harmonise British, Jewish and Arab interests in Palestine.

In retrospect we can see these years as the decisive ones in his

---

[69] The title of his second essay, undated but written some time in the later 1920s (1927?). For original draft, see CZA A312/6. Namier was among the originators of this idea. It was first publicly launched by Col. J. C. Wedgwood in his book, *The Seventh Dominion* (Feb. 1928). A year later, Wedgwood was instrumental in founding the Seventh (Palestine) Dominion League. In November 1936 Namier returned to this topic in a memorandum he wrote for private circulation entitled 'Palestine and the British Empire' (see CZA A312/17); it was later published in *In the Margin of History* (London, 1939). This question has been examined in the author's *The Gentile Zionists* (London, 1973). See also p. 76.

development as a conscious Zionist. His interest in Palestinian affairs deepened. A one-time pupil of his, 'Nebi' Samuel,[70] corresponded regularly with him, keeping him *au courant* with the latest political developments and gossip. He was even involved in some way, possibly fund-raising, with the establishment of a horticultural department at the agricultural research station in Rehovoth.[71] In the winter of 1928 he contemplated a visit to Palestine, though nothing came of it. The stage was set for his next move into Zionist politics. Within a year he would be at the centre of the severest crisis yet to emerge in Anglo-Zionist relations.

[70] Edwin Herbert Samuel (1898–1978): eldest son of Herbert Samuel; educated at Balliol College, Oxford; served in British army in Palestine during First World War; member of staff of Zionist Commission to Palestine, 1918; high official of Palestine administration, 1920–48; succeeded as 2nd Viscount Samuel of Mount Carmel and of Toxteth, 1963.

[71] For these activities, see Samuel to Namier, 9 Dec. 1928, and F. Kisch to Zionist Executive, 25 Nov. 1928, CZA A312/55.

Chapter 2

Political Office

At a Zionist meeting in 1919 Weizmann had described certain Jews whose ultimate support he counted on as 'potential Zionists' in time to become 'completely Zionist'.[1] Namier was in this category, and he remained so for some time. One problem was Weizmann's uncertainty as to the role Namier could best serve by his side. During the Vienna congress in 1925, Weizmann had confidentially spoken to him about taking over the political secretaryship of the Zionist Organization, the present incumbent of that office, Leonard Stein,[2] having recently intimated that he wished to leave:

Chaim asked me if I would take his place. I said I would but had history work to finish which could not take me less than a year even if I devoted all my time to it; and that to finish in that time, I would need from the Zionist Office a loan—to stop wasting myself on free-lance journalism, etc. and to be repaid out of my future salary. Weizmann readily agreed. His only worry was over Stein having already announced that he'd leave at the New Year.[3]

Shortly afterwards, Namier drew the first instalment of the loan—£100. However the scheme to regularize his position in the Organization soon came unstuck. For one thing, he discovered that his academic timetable was quite unrealistic, and that he would be unable to complete his researches in the stipulated twelve-month period. More to the point, Stein decided at the last moment to continue as political secretary. I took no more of the £500 promised me in Vienna; and when in the autumn of 1925, I received a loan from Jack Wheeler-Bennett[4] and also some money from the Rhodes Trust, I repaid the £100 with £6 interest. Miss Lieberman

[1] He made this statement at the Cannon Street Hotel on 21 Sept. 1919. Namier, apparently, was a witness to these proceedings which were held *in camera*. See *Jewish Chronicle*, 26 Sept. 1919; and Lady Namier's Notes.

[2] Leonard Jacques Stein (1887–1973): barrister; served with British army in Palestine, 1918–19; political secretary, with brief interval, to Jewish Agency, 1920–9; legal adviser to Jewish Agency, 1929–39; president of Jewish Historical Society of England, 1964–5; author of *The Balfour Declaration* (1961).

[3] Lady Namier's Notes.

[4] John Wheeler-Bennett (1902–76): historian and author of many works on contemporary international relations; official of League of Nations Union and Chatham House; employed in British propaganda programme in United States, 1941–4; in Political Intelligence Department of Foreign Office, 1944–5; attached to British prosecuting team at Nuremberg trials. Kn. 1959.

[Weizmann's secretary] told me that to her knowledge such a thing had never yet happened in the Zionist Office.[5]

Further attempts to draw closer to the Zionist bureaucracy terminated in failure: 'I went once or twice to see Stein in the Office, but for some reason did not find him friendly, and stopped going. I should have liked to enter into a closer touch with him and the Organization at that time, but failed; possibly through some misunderstanding, though with no conscious fault on my side.'[6]

It was not until the early autumn of 1928 that the offer to Namier was renewed. Stein had finally decided to quit his post. Although, during the preliminary discussions, questions of salary—a sum of £80 per month was mentioned—and his exact position and functions in the Office hierarchy were touched upon, they were by no means finalized. Later, Namier bitterly regretted having omitted to make crystal-clear at these meetings details personally so important to him. Perhaps his reborn enthusiasm distracted his attention from such mundane considerations. Whatever the reason, the oversight was to cost him dear in the coming years.

His intention to join the Organization was an open secret. News of it crossed the Atlantic where it stimulated an enquiry from the Rosenwald family of Chicago, who, unknown to Namier at the time, had generously endowed his historical research since September 1927. 'Are you not making a great mistake to abandon your work before you have finished it?', they asked, clearly hinting that they would much prefer him to continue with his academic pursuits.[7]

Namier fashioned his reply carefully, not only out of politeness and gratitude, but because their query struck at the very heart of his dilemma. In a quite extraordinary letter he laid bare the agonizing choice before him; in it he revealed for the first time the tremendous upheaval that had occurred in his scale of priorities. It is worth quoting extensively:

Let me in the first place thank you most sincerely for what you have done for me—both for your share in the endowment and the initiative which, seeing the circumstances, I do not doubt was yours. Without this help it would have been very difficult for me to do what I have done, and to achieve the success which I can now frankly say, I have achieved. This was a 'whole time job' and could not have been done in any other way.

But now to pass to the question raised in your letter to me—whether, or rather how far and when, I should continue the work? My next book, covering

[5] Lady Namier's Notes.   [6] Ibid.
[7] Correspondence in CZA A312/53. It consists of: Rufus Rosenwald to Namier, 12 Feb. 1929, and Namier's reply, 4 Mar. 1929. Extracts from these letters were first published by Julia Namier, 205–7.

approximately the period 1760–64, and containing a good many of the fundamental points I have to make about the 'Imperial Problem during the American Revolution', will be ready in a month or two (it must not surprise you that those fundamental points should come in so early, but I find them in the political structure of the period, rather than in mere incidents of the later years). If I possibly can, I should still like to write the history of the Rockingham Government of 1765–6, for which I have a considerable mass of material in hand; and in any case I plan (together with a friend, Romney Sedgwick)[8] to edit the Bute and Sandwich MSS., doing that work even after having joined the Zionist organisation. But the question is: should I try to complete my work till 1783 now, before joining the Organisation?

I confess once more, what I have openly admitted in the introduction to my book, I lack a sense of time, and often imagine that I shall be able to finish a certain piece of work much sooner than it is possible in reality.[9] I now see that if I wanted to finish the work up to 1783, in the way and on the scale on which I have done the earlier part, it would be the work of a good many years, in fact, by the time I should have finished, I should be much nearer fifty than forty. This I cannot afford to do, and I shall give you my reasons.

1. My own primary aims were not to build a monument for myself 'aere perennius' and to write the history of that period, but rather to acquire a position which would enable me to work effectively for the Jewish cause, and to make certain experiments in history writing which would be interesting and important, quite apart from the specific subject of my book. I believe, and I am assured by others, that I have achieved these two things, and whatever more I want in that direction, I trust I shall obtain in my second book.[10] I do not mean

---

[8] Richard Romney Sedgwick (1894–1972): Fellow of Trinity College, Cambridge, 1919; Assistant Under-Secretary of State, Commonwealth Relations Office, 1949–54; among the editors of *History of Parliament*.

[9] See *The Structure of Politics at the Accession of George III*, xiii.

[10] The two books were of course *The Structure of Politics at the Accession of George III* (London, 1929), and *England in the Age of the American Revolution* (London, 1930). These works firmly established Namier's reputation as a historian. The 'certain experiments in history writing' inaugurated 'Namierism' as a distinct methodological approach to historical research, described kindly by one critic as 'structural analysis', less kindly by another as having taken 'the mind out of history'. The 'specific subject' matter of his books did however finally shatter conceptions, still widely held even though challenged earlier, regarding the development of British constitutional history in the early years of George III's reign, the so-called Whig interpretation. Needless to say, Namier's academic reputation proved erratic. At times it soared to unprecedented heights; on other occasions, it took severe knocks. This is not the place to assess him as a historian. An extensive literature has emerged which discusses at length the *pros* and *cons* of Namierism. The interested reader may care to pursue the argument in the following works. The most balanced and serious criticism of Namier was penned by Sir Hubert Butterfield in his *George III and the Historians* (London, 1957); see also his article, 'Sir Lewis Namier as Historian', *The Listener* (May 1961). For a succinct and effective defence of Namier see J. Brooke, 'Namier and Namierism', *History and Theory*, 3 (1964), also John Owen, 'The Namier Way', *New Statesman and Nation*, 26 Jan. 1962. See also for some fascinating recollections of Namierism, Ved Mehta, *Fly and the Fly-Bottle*.

to say therby in the least that I would not love to go on with the work and finish it completely; were I not a Jew and had I private means of my own, I would unquestionably do so. But as things stand, I have to consider how the urgency of this task compares with that of others, and what are my own circumstances. 2. Once, in 1914, I broke off my history work for ten years because of a British war. Our own race is now in an infinitely more dangerous and difficult position than Great Britain was in 1914; for on a very moderate estimate half the world makes war on them, and they are practically helpless. I know working for them is neither enjoyable nor remunerative—every one of us can do better for himself by working for, with, and in more prosperous and more honoured communities. Still I consider that for a Jew who sees our position as I do, it is an absolute duty to go and work with and for the Jews as soon as he can do so to *their* best advantage. I have, I think, reached this point now. Anyhow, the Zionist Organisation will have to wait for me for about half a year, with the post which I am to take practically unfilled. I can hardly make them wait longer. In 1914 I broke off my history work leaving it in a perfectly rudimentary condition, without knowing whether I should ever be able to return to it. Now I have laid very clear and firm foundations; I cannot tell how long I shall remain with the Zionist Organisation; changes may occur in it which may compel me to go out soon. I may prove not altogether well fitted for the work. I may stay in it till the end of my life. There is no way of forseeing or determining these matters beforehand. But as I consider it my duty to take up the work now, I have to leave the rest 'on the knees of the gods'.

Of his own ability to contribute to the cause, Namier had no doubt. He was, after all, joining the Organization as 'an absolute duty'. Egocentric to an extreme, he envisaged no other policy but his own. Yet, like all star performers, he could never quite be confident of his audience. Would it applaud him or howl him down? He suffered no illusion as to the vast differences in temperament and style between himself and the run-of-the-mill Zionist functionary. Their eyes saw only the 'infidel', while his detected 'the Kosher gang' in every corner. Pedantic, inflexible to the point of political suicide, repelled by the factionalism endemic in Zionist politics, supremely knowledgeable in the ways of English politics, above all, an outsider brought in by Weizmann, he possessed few if any of the attributes necessary for a Zionist clerk. He would make his way by the sheer weight of his intellectual armour, not by bowing and scraping before a Zionist electorate or their elected representatives. Inevitably, he was repaid in his own coin. He was never elected to the Zionist Executive, the highest political office he sought, even though Weizmann backed his candidature. Politically, he existed by the grace of Weizmann. Whenever he stepped out of the protective shadow of the Zionist leader, he was pitifully vulnerable. He was Weizmann's man, though not his tool, and his political future was inextricably entwined with that of his chief.

Namier must have been aware of these hazards. They did not deter him. He was by now totally hypnotized by his own conception of Zionism and his role in it. In contrast to his much-vaunted method and order, and his over-publicized abhorrence of all things ideological, his Zionism was a curious hodge-podge of romanticism and *realpolitik*, swinging, disconcertingly for his admirers, from the vision to the vested interest. Sir Isaiah Berlin has put it most graphically:

I am not sure that he did not indulge in day-dreams in which he saw himself as a kind of Zionist D'Annunzio riding on a white horse to capture some Trans-Jordanian Fiume. He saw the Jewish national movement as a *Risorgimento*; if he was not to be its Garibaldi, he would serve as the admirer and champion of its Cavour—the sagacious, realistic, dignified, Europeanised, the almost English, Dr. Weizmann.[11]

But the most accurate reflection of Namier's state of mind can best be gauged by the manner in which his re-found faith intruded into his academic work. In 1929 he was working on the final draft of *England in the Age of the American Revolution*. He opens with a passage on the social foundations of eighteenth-century England where he discusses the relationship between peoples and land. In a moving and striking excerpt he abandons his academic detachment for a passionate reminder of his own people's plight:

The relations of groups of men to plots of land, of organised communities to units of territory, form the basic content of political history. The conflicting territorial claims of communities constitute the greater part of conscious international history; social stratifications and convulsions, primarily arising from the relationship of men to land, make the greater, not always fully conscious, part of the domestic history of nations—and even under urban and industrial conditions ownership of land counts for more than is usually supposed. To every man, as to Brutus, the native land is his life-giving Mother, and the state raised upon the land his law-giving Father; and the days cannot be long of a nation which fails to honour either. Only one nation has survived for two thousand years, though an orphan—my own people, the Jews. But then in the God-given Law we have enshrined the authority of a State, and in the God-promised Land the idea of a Mother-country; through the centuries from

[11] Sir I. Berlin, op. cit.

Mount Sinai we have faced Arets Israel, our land. Take away either, and we cease to be a nation; let both live again, and we shall be ourselves once more.[12]

This cry, dramatic and powerful, from the inner depths of his soul, was a vivid manifestation of the emotional conflict which would not relinquish him.

*   *   *

Namier was due to join the Zionist Organization as political secretary on 1 October 1929. To gain more detailed first-hand knowledge of the political cross-currents within the movement, which, he believed, would allow him greater freedom of criticism, he decided to attend the forthcoming Zionist Congress at Zurich. It was an historic gathering. Weizmann, after many years of effort, had finally succeeded in constructing his enlarged Jewish Agency. It would now include Jewish grandees from both sides of the Atlantic, those who had hitherto held aloof from any organized Zionist framework; 'hesitant men with half-avowed sympathies,' as Namier called them.[13] By any reckoning, this was a momentous achievement, though, like any compromise, it pasted over countless inherent difficulties. But it was also the prelude to the gravest crisis yet known in Anglo-Zionist relations. Namier wrote, in a somewhat rambling fashion, his own impressions of these events.[14]

In July 1929 I went . . . to Zurich, to the Zionist Congress at which the new Jewish Agency for Palestine was constituted. It was of cardinal importance that I should get into personal touch with the people, who, from all over the world, gathered for that most important session, and get acquainted with our affairs in the debates which took place over the problems of the Agency. The discussions at the Zurich Congress were passionate and impressive. There were sincere

---

[12] See *England* . . . (2nd ed., London, 1961), 18. Elsewhere, explaining his decision to forsake his historical work, he wrote: 'Pious Jews in Eastern Europe, when building a new house leave one place unfinished; it is called in Hebrew *'zekher lekhurban'* ('the memorial of destruction'), and commemorates the destruction of the Temple. I had concluded researches for the rest of this book, but not on the complex subject of the Colonial agents, when the Arab attack in Palestine, in August 1929, compelled me to relinquish my historical studies earlier than I had planned, and to take up work in the Jewish Agency for Palestine. After that I could do no more than complete the parts for which the material was ready; this unfinished chapter has to be the *zekher lekhurban* of my book.' Ibid., 251.

[13] See his essay, 'Leadership in Israel: Chaim Weizmann', in *Facing East*, 154.

[14] The 1929 crisis has been examined in detail in Lady Namier's biography of her husband and in the author's *The Gentile Zionists*. It would be tedious to repeat again all the twists and turns of the story. This account relies mainly on two papers that Namier wrote: 'Notes on Zionism II' (CZA A312/2, written some time in 1934); and 'A Historical Summary of Discussions Leading up to the Prime Minister's Letter of February 13th, 1931 to Dr. Weizmann' (copies in WA and CZA A312/11, dated 27 Apr. 1931).

misgivings—not merely of the oppositionist character—on the part of the old Zionists and democrats with regard to the junction with the rich and luke-warm Jews who . . . even now would not fully accept either our name or our programme. I remember the tension in the theatre in which our meetings took place . . . and next the extraordinary tension of the nominal vote when the roll-call was taken.

. . . Vera [Weizmann] felt that night like a Queen in Israel. I myself felt rather depressed, something great seemed to have happened, we seemed to stand at the parting of ways or at least at the end of one period and the beginning of the next, and could not say as yet what the meaning of the change would be. Both Chaim and Vera were much annoyed at me because I did not respond to their joy. Shmarya Levin[15] was the only one who understood me. He agreed that when great things happen, even if they seem favourable one cannot rejoice because these things are too great, too mysterious and uncertain for human feelings.

As a matter of fact this great gathering and start was to be the beginning of a trail of our misfortunes. Louis Marshall,[16] the one man of absolutely first class ability among the non-Zionist makers of the Jewish Agency never left Zurich. He died there some ten days after the close of our Congress. The reverberation of *Knesseth Israel* undoubtedly had a great deal to do with the Palestine pogroms, ushered in by the Teschebov riots of August 16th and resulting in the massacres of August 23–31.[17] The Arabs were exasperated and thought that the time had come to deal the decisive blow. September ushered in the American financial crash from which neither the United States nor the world had recovered even five years later; any number of fortunes from which we expected help for our work, disappeared as if they had never been. The Agency was a bride of doubtful beauty; and her dowry was gone. Nor was the political influence of people such as Felix Warburg[18] altogether advantageous. If they had had a few years of education in our movement, they might have been equal to a crisis, but the crisis caught them before they had even started their apprenticeship.

[15] Shmarya (Halevy) Levin (1867–1935): Zionist leader; Hebrew and Yiddish author; outstanding orator; member of first Russian Duma, 1906; member of Zionist Executive, 1911; settled in Palestine, 1924.

[16] Louis Marshall (1856–1929): lawyer; American Jewish leader; president of American Jewish Committee, 1912–29; member of Jewish delegation to Paris peace conference, 1919.

[17] Tischeb'av—(9th Av)—the Hebrew date for the destruction by the Romans of the Second Temple in AD 70. These riots inaugurated the bloodiest communal disorders seen in Palestine since the British occupation in 1917–18. In all, some 472 Jews and 268 Arabs were either killed or wounded. The background and course of the riots were the subject of a Government enquiry. Their findings are in 'The Shaw Report on the Disturbances of August 1929', Cmd. 3530 (March 1930).

[18] Felix Moritz Warburg (1871–1937): scion of German banking family; partner in father-in-law's [J. Schiff] investment banking firm, Kuhn, Loeb and Co., New York; chairman of American Jewish Joint Distribution Committee, 1914–32; noted for philanthropic activities.

On Sunday morning came the first news of the Jerusalem outbreak. Even now hardly anyone had returned to London. Baffy came up and I met her at old Lady Rayleigh's[19] . . . The next few days were a time of strenuous or even desperate work. Weizmann had not yet returned and Rutenberg[20] took the lead. Melchett[21] was in London and saw the Prime Minister with very poor results. He seems to have been highly tactless while his secretary, Naamani (a bouncing bounder), made things infinitely worse. I remember Rutenberg suggesting that Melchett should send a certain message to the Prime Minister; he thought I should convey it to Melchett through Naamani. When I telephoned that fellow (not more than 30 years old) he told me cheerfully that he would 'phone up the Prime Minister. I nearly screamed: 'What! you? nothing of that kind. You will transmit my message to Melchett.' All this would be unimportant did I not suspect that the incomprehensible difficulties we afterwards had, when Weizmann tried to get an interview with the Prime Minister, were due to the annoyance which that very vain and rather inexperienced man felt over the communications from Melchett and his secretary.

Stein was still away, somewhere in Baden, and I for the time being acted as political secretary. It was a terrible time when every day news was coming in of new massacres, S.O.S. messages from our people in exposed and endangered places, news of the British authorities disarming our people and thus rendering self-defence impossible, and all endeavours and pleas in London were met by non-commital answers of the highly official type and expressions of confidence in the man on the spot. Rutenberg, not given as a rule to epigrams or witticisms, coined in those days a very true phrase: 'A pogrom we could have had cheaper in Russia.' There were even difficulties in our communicating with our people in Jerusalem and we suspected the Administration of exercising a censorship. We were afterwards assured that this had not been the case, though possibly Arab officials in the Post Office were conducting a quiet sabotage. Anyhow the only way in which we could quickly communicate with our people was by their telephoning to Cairo, and our representative from Cairo sending the message by cable.

Much as I loved and admired Weizmann, I suffered severely from his indiscretions, and Baffy and I would sometimes withold from him even important things if the danger of their being repeated exceeded the possible loss from their being withheld. One day I was telling Weizmann a part of a very delicate secret and urged him to be careful not to repeat it. It was raining hard.

[19] Kathleen Alice Cuthbert. She had married Mrs Dugdale's cousin, Robert John Strutt [Lord Rayleigh], the well-known physicist.

[20] Pinhas Rutenberg (1879–1942): Russian revolutionary; settled in Palestine, 1919; established Palestine Electric Corporation, 1923; Chairman *Vaad Leumi*, 1929–30, 1939–42.

[21] Alfred Moritz Mond (1868–1930): industrialist and politician; Liberal MP, 1906–23, 1924–8; First Commissioner for Works, 1916–21; Minister of Health, 1921–2; Chairman of Imperial Chemical Industries; of Economic Board for Palestine. Created Bt. 1910; 1st Baron Melchett, 1928.

He looked through the window and said: 'Next you will tell me that it is raining and that this is a secret.' 'No, Chief,' I replied, 'if it were a secret I would not tell it to you.' As I spoke I realised with a pang the contradiction between my work and my having told him of the matter at all.

But, as if to compensate for that inability to keep a secret, Chaim had the strange habit of always keeping some corner dark even from his closest friends and collaborators. I don't think there ever was anyone he trusted more than me; and yet there were certain things which he did not tell me but about which I learned because he would tell them to Baffy. One of our close friends said to me: 'You who know all Weizmann's secrets.' I interrupted him, 'Oh no, if Weizmann was in partnership with the Almighty he would try to keep some small thing secret from him and then tell it to the first American journalist who happened to come along.'

It is an odd and annoying weakness in this truly great man.

It is very difficult for me now, after more than five years, to remember any details of these very exciting days at the close of August. As usual, or even worse than usual, I then suffered of insomnia and the great excitement and strain was not conducive to good sleep. I had frequently to take drugs and work under extreme pressure. When concentrating hard on achieving something, one has not got one's mind free to take in impressions and register them for future remembrance. All I can now recall is our endeavours in those days to obtain for Weizmann an interview with the Prime Minister.

Had there been a Conservative or Liberal power in office, Weizmann could never have had the least difficulty in obtaining an interview with the Prime Minister, or any other Minister, nor had he any after Geneva, even with the Labour Government of the day.[22] Ministers more accustomed to office would not have been cowed as these labour men were by the officials, in the Colonial Office and Palestine. In 1930, when I was at Geneva for the second time, Bob Cecil[23] said to me about the Labour Government with whom he was co-operating as one of their delegates to the League of Nations Council: 'People say that these men are revolutionary. I wish to God they were! but they are entirely in the hands of their officials.'

Although these reminiscences continue for another eight pages, they

[22] There is an element of exaggeration in these complaints. Weizmann first heard of the riots on 25 August while on holiday in Switzerland. He returned immediately to London and met Passfield on the 28th. Approximately a week later, on 5 September, he obtained an interview with MacDonald who was then in Geneva on League business. These dates do not suggest great reluctance on the part of ministers to meet with Weizmann. Namier, perhaps more than most Zionists, believed that the British Government had no other problem of consequence on its mind.

[23] Lord Edgar Algernon Robert Cecil (1864–1958): 3rd son of 3rd Marquess of Salisbury; Conservative MP, 1906–23; Under-Secretary of State for Foreign Affairs, 1915–18; Minister of Blockade, 1916–18; Lord Privy Seal, 1923–4; President of the League of Nations Union, 1923–45; Chancellor of Duchy of Lancaster, 1924–7; Nobel peace prize, 1937. Created Viscount 1923. Lord Cecil was another of Mrs Dugdale's cousins.

are devoted almost entirely to castigating the various officials, both Government and Zionist, with whom he had to deal. This is one of the most fascinating aspects of his narrative: his total incapacity to co-operate with anyone other than those whom he considered his intellectual equals or who at least acknowledged his superior powers— and they were few and far between! The prime minister's private secretary, Herbert Usher,[24] a vital contact, was a 'swollen-headed upstart', a 'miserable Labour journalist suddenly risen to what seemed to him and ought to have been an important post'. His own colleague, Victor Jacobson,[25] an important Zionist official, was a 'ridiculous person', a 'giggling, chattering little fool' who exasperated Namier to such a degree that 'For one moment I saw red, I felt that I could have raised both my fists and banged them down on the head of that grimy little creature.' Even Sokolov,[26] second only to Weizmann in the Zionist pecking-order, reminded him of a 'little Jewish "faktor" [commercial agent] now raised to the level of pseudo-statesmanship'.

But his most violent invective was directed against the members of the British delegation to the League of Nations. Contemptuously, he compared their frivolous, parvenu antics—'An atmosphere of such bank-holiday buoyancy about it,[27] that Hugh Dalton and Irene Noel-Baker[28] went all "native"'—with the modesty, style, and dignity of other British politicians he had known and admired, Balfour and

[24] Herbert Brough Usher (1892–1969): Assistant Editor, *Westminster Gazette*, 1919; Labour candidate for South Leicester, 1924, 1929; Private Secretary to Ramsay MacDonald, 1929–35.

[25] Victor (Avigdor) Jacobson (1869–1934): representative of Zionist Organization in Constantinople, 1908–15; member of Zionist Executive, 1913–21, 1933–4; director of Zionist Bureau, Copenhagen, 1916–18; representative of Zionist organization to League of Nations, Geneva, 1925–35.

[26] Nahum Sokolov (1861–1936): Hebrew journalist and author; member of Zionist Executive from 1911; head of Jewish delegation to Paris peace conference, 1919; Chairman of Zionist Congresses from 1921; president of Zionist Organization, 1931–5; president of *Keren Kayemeth* [National Fund].

[27] 'It' referred to a picnic-excursion on Lake Geneva which, unfortunately, for its participants, Namier witnessed. His original draft read: 'There was such a lower middle-class atmosphere about it.' But he obviously thought better of it and altered the text accordingly.

[28] Hugh John Neale Dalton (1887–1962): lecturer at the London School of Economics, 1919–36; Labour MP, 1924–31, 1935–59; Under-Secretary of State for Foreign Affairs, 1929–31; Minister of Economic Warfare, 1940–2; President of Board of Trade, 1942–5; Chancellor of Exchequer, 1945–7. Created life peer, 1960.

Philip John Noel-Baker (1889–1956): Labour politician, academic, and inter-nationalist; member of Secretariat of League of Nations, 1919–22; Labour MP, 1929–31, 1936–70; ministerial posts, 1945–51; advocate of world disarmament; awarded Nobel Peace Prize, 1959. Created Baron 1977. Irene, daughter of Frank Noel, a British landowner, of Achmetaga in Greece, married Philip Baker in 1915, when they took the surname Noel-Baker.

Curzon for example: 'had these people on the lake been carried to the top by no very clear merit of their own? I see a resemblance between them and some of the new states during the post-war period. These thought they were bringing new ideas and a new mood to Geneva; yet their contributions in real terms was nil.'

These observations reveal great spirit of character, but they are serious flaws in a would-be diplomatist. Also, as we have seen, he was unable emotionally to cope with the stress and strain of a crisis situation. Attacks of insomnia and the frequent use of drugs must have impaired his effectiveness as a negotiator. He aspired to play a role for which he was temperamentally unsuited. Despite his love of political wheeling and dealing at a high level, he acted in a kind of vacuum of his own invention, never really in tune with those whom he sought to convince, and often achieving the opposite results from those intended.[29] Whatever his intellectual virtuosity, his political influence could only have been marginal. There is a bitter truth to the story that whenever he intruded too vigorously into the realm of decision-making, his Zionist associates would sharply remind him that he was merely a secretary and should know his place.[30] Of course, he never did. He told Philip Noel-Baker and Hugh Dalton in Geneva that he had already written the first chapter in the history of the Labour Government's disarmament policy. 'The Arabs said that there would be no peace unless the Jews were disarmed. They were disarmed by the British authorities. They were massacred by the Arabs. They died wrapped in their prayer shawls and the warm sympathy of his Majesty's Government.'

After this initial flurry, the crisis developed slowly but always to the Zionists' disadvantage. More than anything, they feared that a vulnerable Labour Government would capitulate to Arab demands to rescind the Balfour Declaration and to abrogate their rights as guaranteed under the terms of the mandate. Adapting himself to the exigencies of the situation, Namier became not only Weizmann's political adviser, but also his spokesman, courier, and, on occasion, his comforter. He wryly dubbed himself 'Figaro'.[31]

[29] Sir Isaiah Berlin (op. cit.) recounts the following revealing episode. 'Sir John Shuckburgh, then Permanent Under-Secretary [*sic*] at the Colonial Office, was a not infrequent target for Namier when he was on the warpath. I was once present when Namier, in his soft but penetrating and remorseless voice, addressed Shuckburgh who made every effort to escape; in vain. Namier followed him out of the room, on to the steps, into the street, and so on—down the Duke of York's steps, probably to the door of the Colonial Office itself.'

[30] See J. L. Talmon, 'The Ordeal of Sir Lewis Namier: The Man, The Historian, The Jew', *Commentary* (Mar. 1963), reprinted in *The Unique and the Universal* (London, 1965).

[31] Lady Namier's Notes.

As the autumn turned to winter, work at 77 Great Russell Street moved into top gear. Namier and Mrs Dugdale, aided by Leonard Stein, drafted minutes, memoranda, briefs, reports, letters to the press, any document that could underpin the Zionist position. Throughout 1930 they laboured under immense pressure. In March the findings of the Shaw commission were published.[32] Even Ramsay MacDonald, when nailed to the wall by Weizmann, was compelled to admit that the report was 'very bad' and that it would 'depress the Jews and elate the Arabs'.[33] Namier's verdict that it was 'a most unsatisfactory document of plainly anti-Jewish character',[34] accurately reflected the Zionist position as well as a wide body of opinion in British political circles.

Worse was to follow. At the end of May 2,350 immigration certificates were suspended pending yet another government investigation.[35] This was to strike at the Zionists' most sensitive nerve. Already reeling from the effects of the new immigration policy, they received yet another body-blow when the government issued an official statement which in effect endorsed the Shaw report.[36] No amount of goodwill on the part of the Jewish Agency could withstand this kind of pressure. Relations between the Zionists and the Government plunged sharply. Personal contact between Passfield[37] and Weizmann was sporadic; and when they did meet the tension in the air was noticeable. Passfield was a recognized failure as Colonial Secretary. It was widely

[32] See Cmd. 3530. The report was overwhelmingly critical of Zionist methods. Only in one aspect was it favourable: that the outbreak was an attack by Arabs on Jews for which there was no excuse. It found no ground for serious complaint against either the Palestine Arab leadership or the Palestine administration. It did however hint broadly that immigration and land purchases might have to be severely restricted. In short, it concluded that the fundamental cause of the riots was in Arab frustrations consequent upon the disappointment of their national aspirations and fear for their economic future. Only Mr H. Snell [later Lord Snell] disputed these conclusions in a minority report. For the Zionist rebuttal, see L. Stein's memorandum (Jewish Agency, May 1930).

[33] From notes of a meeting with MacDonald, 28 Mar. 1930, WA.

[34] Namier to Kisch, 8 May 1930, WA.

[35] The decision to suspend immigration was ostensibly taken by the Palestine administration; but of course the Government was privy to the decision and approved it. The new Commission was intended to supplement, or, as the Zionists hoped, to supersede the Shaw report. After some dithering, Sir John Hope Simpson, a colonial administrator with no experience of Palestine, was appointed to head the investigation. His appointment was opposed by the Zionists who had hoped that Smuts, a committed Zionist, would fill the post.

[36] See Cmd. 3582.

[37] Sidney James Webb (1859–1947): social reformer and historian; author of *The History of Trade Unionism* (1894), *Industrial Democracy* (1897), *Soviet Communism: A New Civilization?* (1935), etc.; launched the London School of Economics, 1895; founded *New Statesman* (1913); Labour MP for Seaham, 1922–9; President of Board of Trade, 1924; Secretary of State for Dominions and Colonies, 1929–30; for Colonies, 1931. Created Baron, 1929.

believed, by his wife among others, that he was run by his officials. Ramsay MacDonald said of him: 'He was old, in some ways efficient, but he has the mind of a German professor and an indestructible belief in the experts who sit in the C.O.'[38] Namier compared him to 'a man who feels himself coming off the log and tries to keep his balance by wildly waving his arms.'[39] He dubbed him 'Lord Passover'.[40]

Neither Weizmann nor Namier placed any trust in the officials—whether they sat in the Colonial Office in London or in Government House in Jerusalem. On balance, they were hostile to Zionism and out to sabotage the National Home. Their prejudices were so deep-rooted, their influence so widespread and pernicious, that further co-operation between the Jewish Agency and the Government, the foundation-stone of Weizmann's policy, had become virtually impossible. There is some truth in this hypothesis as well as some exaggeration. But the precise historical truth is less important than how the Zionists' perceived their position. They believed they were under siege, and they acted accordingly.

By early October 1930 the Government's new proposals for Palestine had been approved by cabinet. Weizmann, renewing a threat he had made earlier in the year, informed Passfield that he would have no option but to resign if the government persisted in its policy. Passfield was not impressed. In the event, it was too late for the government to draw back. On 17 October the statements[41] were delivered to 77 Great Russell Street. Namier was on hand to receive them:

[38] From notes of a meeting between MacDonald and Weizmann, 6 Nov. 1930, WA.
[39] Namier to Kisch, 27 May 1930, WA.
[40] See K. Middlemas, ed., *Thomas Jones, Whitehall Diary* (OUP, 1969), ii. 254.
[41] There were two papers, Cmd. 3686, 'The Hope Simpson Report on Immigration, Land Settlement and Development' (Oct. 1930) and Cmd. 3692, 'A Statement of Policy' (Oct. 1930). The latter document achieved fame, or notoriety, as the Passfield White Paper. Both these statements, which envisaged drastic restrictions in land purchases and the scale of immigration, were extremely damaging to the Zionist cause. The Passfield White Paper in particular was formulated in a manner to cause offence. Beatrice Webb, no friend of the Zionists, commented: 'The statement . . . is a badly drafted, a tactless document.' (Beatrice Webb diaries, 26 Oct. 1930, Passfield Papers, LSE). The Hope Simpson report was of crucial importance because it was chiefly on its figures and conclusions that the Government formulated its policy. Namier lost no time in demolishing the foundations of the report. Hope Simpson's figures were based 'on doubtful assumptions, on hastily compiled statistics, and on a misreading of material submitted to him'. He had written his report, covering 185 printed pages, in three weeks. 'This may account for some of its shortcomings. But he has pronounced a verdict upon the work, the dreams, the last hope of a suffering people. He had no right to hurry, or allow himself to be rushed. Shortage of time is no excuse in a judge. He has not done justice to his mission, to our work, or to the people who received him with trust and respect which his previous record commanded. He has not done justice to himself.' See Namier's notes of 30 Apr. 1931, CZA A312/10.

I sat in the office, 77 Great Russell Street, to receive the document. It came very late; I read it in the wretched light of a taxi lamp and saw what it was like. Passfield was probably afraid that we might get at Ramsay MacDonald and therefore delayed delivery until he knew the P.M. had gone off for the weekend. When I came to the office [Lord Melchett's office at the ICI building, Millbank] I gave it to Weizmann and told those present [Lord Reading, Lord Melchett, and James de Rothschild] what I thought of it. Reading looked at it, and remarked despondently something to the effect that there was nothing more to be done. Baffy afterwards remarked: 'And he for one did nothing more.' Leaving ICI with Weizmann I said to him in his car, 'We have reached rock bottom; must stop . . . [illegible] . . . say our political 'Shema Israel'. And then I quoted to him Kelvin's words to King Francis I: 'Nous conservons nos âmes et attendons la main forte du Seigneur.' . . . [Illegible] . . . and Baffy were the only non-Jews who came to see us and sat with us that night; it was as if we were sitting in mourning. Next day we started work at the office . . . Then Baffy got in touch with Leo Amery[42] and decided that something must be done to express public sympathy with our case and Weizmann.[43]

I was against Weizmann's appeal for a last interview with Passfield and stopped him from writing the letter which would point out patent weaknesses and mistakes. I said that the worst the White Paper the better for us if we had to fight to remove the most blatant absurdities. When I once told Malcolm MacDonald[44] how Passfield had cheated us, MacDonald said that he did the same to Snowden[45] and himself. Snowden who was Chairman of some kind of Committee to deal with Palestine, had told Passfield that he must not publish his White Paper before having come to some understanding with Weizmann. Passfield misrepresented the two conversations, completely inconclusive as they were, as 'consultative'. Malcolm told me that the picture he had given him of the White Paper was equally misleading.[46]

[42] Leopold Charles Maurice Stennett Amery (1873–1955): journalist; prominent Conservative politician; First Lord of Admiralty, 1922–4; Colonial Secretary, 1924–9; Secretary of State for India, 1940–5.

[43] Mrs Dugdale's lobbying resulted in a letter to *The Times*, published on 23 October, signed by Amery, Baldwin, and Sir Austin Chamberlain. The letter, drafted by Mrs Dugdale, contended that the new policy 'appears to conflict with the intention of the mandate, and the whole spirit of the Balfour declaration'. Churchill later associated himself with this protest.

[44] Malcolm John MacDonald (1901–   ): son of Ramsey MacDonald; Labour MP, 1929–31; Nat. Lab. 1931–5; Nat. Govt., 1936–45; Secretary of State for Dominions, 1935–8; for Colonies, 1935, 1938–40; Minister of Health, 1940–1; High Commissioner for Canada, 1941–6; various high administrative positions in Commonwealth.

[45] Philip Snowden (1864–1937): chairman of Independent Labour Party, 1903–6, 1917–20; Labour MP, 1906–18, 1922–31; Chancellor of Exchequer, 1924, 1929–31; Lord Privy Seal, 1931–2, Created Viscount, 1931. MacDonald was referring to the cabinet committee which discussed the Government statements before publication.

[46] Namier's Notes, CZA A312/2.

Various explanations, ranging from the machiavellian to the naïve, have been put forward to explain the Government's handling of the situation. We probably do not have to look any deeper than lack of experience. This would satisfactorily account for the Government's fumbling and dithering during the coming months.[47] Uncertain as to the probity of their policy, they allowed themselves to be manœuvred into one concession after another. They were, of course, terribly vulnerable. An embattled, minority Government, dependent for survival upon Liberal goodwill, combating the grave domestic effects of the world economic crisis, they were exposed to political flak from all sides. Naturally, the Zionists exploited their weakness to the utmost, canvassing support from every available quarter in an orchestrated campaign designed to break Passfield's policy. Weizmann resigned from office as President of the Jewish Agency, followed by other top leaders, thereby magnifying the intensity of the crisis. Support was drummed up among the parliamentary opposition and within the Labour party itself. Public opinion was mobilized, both at home and abroad. Anti-British demonstrations were organized throughout the Jewish world. In New York, rumours were current that plans to bring economic and political pressure to bear on the Government were under consideration.

MacDonald could not remain indifferent to this 'Jewish hurricane', as the Webbs referred to it,[48] for long. Not only was it threatening to strain Anglo-American relations, a corner-stone of his foreign policy, but it had already destroyed the national consensus, which had hitherto dominated the Palestine issue, and transformed it into a topic for acrimonious inter-party bickering, a development his administration could ill afford. Some form of compromise was inevitable; and the first gesture came from the Government, a sure sign of weakness.

Namier played a leading role in these events. They were in fact tailor-made to suit his talents, and he rightly came to regard the achievements of these months as his greatest triumph. He was never as close to Weizmann as he was during this period. On familiar terms with the

---

[47] The same could not be said for the Palestine administration. The new High Commissioner, Sir John Chancellor, held decided views concerning the future of Palestine. Throughout the crisis he stressed the need for drastic changes in the structure of the mandate, changes which envisaged the termination of British rule in Palestine and consigned the *Yishuv* to the status of a permanent minority. See P. Ofer, 'The Role of the High Commissioner in Britain's Policy in Palestine; Sir John Chancellor' (unpublished Ph.D., London, 1972).

[48] See Beatrice to Sidney Webb, 21 Oct. 1930, Passfield Papers.

chief protagonists on both sides, his prize catch was Malcolm MacDonald, the Prime Minister's son, 'who is really a very decent and sensible fellow'.[49] The younger MacDonald proved to be a most profitable and sympathetic channel of communication into 10 Downing Street. If Namier was not the architect, he was certainly the master-builder in the reconstruction of the bridges between the Jewish Agency and the Government. After all, in the final analysis it was a matter of redrafting the policy papers in a manner and style more acceptable to the Zionists. No one was more competent than he to fulfil this task proficiently.

One factor which must have boosted his confidence, if not his academic ego, was the totally unexpected offer of the Chair of Modern History at the University of Manchester. This occurred in November 1930. In many ways, this solved the most acute of his problems, though he never fully reconciled himself to his banishment to a provincial university.[50] No longer would he be dependent financially on endowments or on that 'absurd and stingy group', the Zionist executive, which had persistently treated him as 'a labourer not worthy of hire'.[51] His independence secured, he could devote himself entirely, without fear or favour, to Weizmann and his policy of revising the Passfield White Paper.

In the past, both Namier and Weizmann had suggested that a Round Table Conference might profitably be called to work out a joint statement of policy. By now, this was clearly impracticable: the Arabs would have none of it; and the British wished to avoid unnecessary complications, not create them. But at luncheon on 6 November, Ramsay MacDonald told Weizmann that he proposed to convene a mini-conference, to include the Zionists and a cabinet sub-committee, the purpose of which would be to discuss the Palestine situation in general and the White Paper in particular, though it was made quite clear that there could be no abrogation of the Government's docu-

[49] Namier to Kisch, 29 May 1930, CZA A312/12.
[50] Although he remained at Manchester until his retirement in 1953, he refused to accept his tenure there as permanent. His gaze was always focussed on greener academic pastures. He wrote to Mrs Dugdale in August 1943; 'Practically all my books I have brought to this office and put them at the bottom of the cupboard where certainly the greater part will rest till I go to Manchester, or if fate is kind to me, till I move to Oxford or Cambridge, or *faute de mieux*, to London University.' See CZA A312/44.
[51] Lady Namier's Notes.

ment.[52] In due course, Arthur Henderson[53] was appointed the committee's chairman and Malcolm MacDonald, in deference to Weizmann's request, his personal assistant.

The Anglo-Zionist conference met from mid-November until the end of January; in all six sessions. Namier left an account of these involved and, at times, highly technical discussions:[54]

The draft of the first part of what was originally called 'the Henderson letter' reached us on Saturday, November 29th, 1930.

So far the only document which had been handed in by us was Stein's memorandum,[55] i.e. our criticism of the White Paper; and this first part of the Henderson letter was a reply discreetly meeting our contentions on certain important points, but controverting them on others with considerable, and often excessive, emphasis. As we had not yet put forward our positive demands, the Henderson letter did not deal even with the subjects of land and immigration in a positive manner, and was admittedly an incomplete document. Its chief weakness lay in that it pursued two, to some extent contradictory, purposes: it tried to correct the mistakes of the White Paper, but at the same time to defend it. Consequently, the document, which aimed at reassuring Jewish public opinion, in appearance engaged in a certain amount of acrimonious controversy against us.

We have no certain information as to the way in which the letter was drafted, but I understand that its groundwork was supplied by the Colonial Office, and that this was revised and considerably pruned by the Lord Advocate.[56] I believe that originally it comprised some 28 points, which by the time it reached us, had been cut down to 20; and that originally its tone had been even more controversial.

After a preliminary examination by Stein and myself, I decided to divide the subject matter of the 'H.L.' into three parts:
i) Matters which did not involve questions of principle were to be dealt with in a separate memorandum (which was afterwards colloquially referred to as 'the

---

[52] During the discussion, MacDonald made the revealing remark that 'There is no white paper,' but for reasons of Government prestige there was no possibility of 'retracting the document'. 'We cannot be expected to do that,' he remarked. Minutes of meeting in WA.

[53] Arthur Henderson (1863–1935): Labour MP, 1903–31; 1933–5; Secretary of Labour Party, 1921–34; Member of War Cabinet, 1916–17; Home Secretary, 1924; Foreign Secretary, 1929–31; President of World Disarmament Conference, 1932–4; awarded Nobel Peace Prize, 1934.

[54] See L. B. Namier, *A Historical Survey* . . . Also his letter to Mrs Dugdale, 11 Jan. 1931, WA in which he recounts in detail some aspects of the negotiations.

[55] See L. Stein, *The Palestine White Paper of October 1930* (Jewish Agency, London, 1930).

[56] Craigie Mason Aitchison (1882–1941): barrister; Labour MP for Kilmarnock, 1929–31, National Labour, 1931–3; Lord Advocate for Scotland, 1929–33; Lord Justice-Clerk of Scotland, 1933–41.

flea-catching memorandum'), but which I shall refer to here as the 'Drafting Memorandum', or for short, as 'D.M.'

ii) The paragraphs of the letter interpreting the Mandate, being of a technical legal character, were to be dealt with by experts.

iii) Problems involving questions of policy, i.e. land, immigration, the Development Commission, etc.—were to be dealt with by Dr. Weizmann at the next meeting of the conference.

These procedures were agreed upon. But the pace of the negotiations soon slowed down owing to an easily foreseeable development:

. . . When in reality merely a convenient *'note verbale'* was required as a basis and guidance for further discussions, the various members of the Zionist Executive and the Political Committee, who had no share in the work of the negotiations and no real idea of what was required, wished to go record for ages to come in a 'historic memorandum' etc. etc. Precious time was wasted to no purpose whatsoever . . . These ten days (December 6th to 16th) of endless, incoherent, irrelevant discussions in the joint meetings of the Z.E. and P.C. were, looked at from a distance, a defensive battle fought by us with a view to preventing certain members of that assembly from burdening the negotiations with impracticable demands, and from dragging points already stated in the D.M. into the main memorandum, which would merely have endowed them with undue importance, and rendered a satisfactory settlement more difficult. Even so, the Memorandum in its final form, added a number of petty, impractical, unnecessary demands, which we had to withdraw shamefacedly when they came up in the negotiations.

On the other hand, the delay caused by the discussions in what I shall in future for shortness call 'Y', rendered our further work in connection with the negotiations infinitely more difficult and came very near to endangering the results. The memorandum having been handed in only a week before Christmas no further progress could be made before the House adjourned. But after the House had risen, the L[ord] A[dvocate] had to spend most of his time at the Crown Office at Edinburgh, Mr. Henderson was only exceptionally in London and on January 12th left for Geneva. Henceforth the negotiations during the short intervals when the necessary people were available, had to be carried on under severe pressure, and points which would have required more careful enquiry had sometimes to be dropped by us merely because such delay would have endangered the result of our work.

Until the beginning of February Namier participated in a series of official sessions and private meetings, often lasting until the small hours of the morning, ironing out the last details of the letter. Its fifth and final draft was submitted to the Cabinet on 4 February. The following day, Malcolm MacDonald informed the Jewish Agency that the letter had been ratified by Cabinet and that the Prime Minister would sign it.[57]

The MacDonald letter was an important milestone in the history of Anglo-Zionist relations, even if it only repaired the breach caused by the Government's inconsistency of policy. Although it did not abrogate the White Paper, it constituted in fact the legal basis for the administration of Palestine until the May White Paper of 1939. But it also heralded a period of unprecedented growth and expansion. Immigrants and capital flowed into Palestine on a scale undreamt of before. In a very real way, the economic and political future of the National Home was secured during those years. Of course, outside factors contributed; in particular the triumph of anti-Semitism in Germany and eastern Europe. But without the letter, without the change in the psychological atmosphere, personified not least by the appointment of Sir Arthur Wauchope as High Commissioner, Palestine would have been unable to absorb either the immigrants or the capital in such quantities. In short, it provided the *Yishuv* with a sufficient breathing space. When the moment of supreme crisis came, almost a decade later, neither the British nor the Arabs were able to reverse the process.

*   *   *

Namier's friendship with the Weizmanns deepened. He was a valuable, possibly unique, asset. He relieved the Zionist leader, not always in the best of health, of much of the minutiae of the day-to-day work in the office. His loyalty was absolute. He was completely trustworthy; he was also efficient. Lacking political guile himself, he was admirably suited to play counterpoint, perhaps unwittingly, to his chief's political manœuvrings. Moreover, he was not imprisoned in any rigid Zionist ideology. Pat answers, so popular with the ideologues, were repugnant to him. Free from the whims and dictates of any faction or party, except for Weizmann's, he rarely indulged in high-flown discussion or thought. Always to the point, he kept the matter-in-hand under review until its conclusion. The last two years had given him a wide yet detailed knowledge of Zionist and Jewish affairs which added zest and punch to his contributions. As his self-confidence rose, so too did his tactlessness. His unparalleled gift for the offensive phrase earned him many enemies. Weizmann did not restrain him. Perhaps, secretly, he felt very much as Namier did; or perhaps he was using Namier as a sounding-board in his own inter-party battles. Whatever the reason, the rumour spread that

---

[57] For text, see appendix 1, PD Commons, v. 248, c. 751–7, 13 Feb. 1931.

Weizmann had a devastatingly clever *éminence grise* by his side, the President's evil genius.[58]

Weizmann's leadership had been under heavy attack since the onset of the crisis. Opposition mounted with the approach of the seventeenth Zionist Congress in July 1931. Even before the letter was signed, it appears as though Weizmann had decided to leave office, and Namier would go with him: 'Weizmann and I mean to withdraw from this office as soon as the first part of our work is concluded[59] . . . [He] is determined to leave. Most of the Executive are determined to stop him from leaving. If he leaves, I of course, leave with him.'[60]

In late February, Weizmann left England for the Continent and Palestine. Namier remained in London, tying up the loose ends. Without Weizmann's protective and conciliatory presence, his clashes with those left in charge became more frequent and more violent. Exasperated, and in any case having to prepare for his professorship, he loosened his links with them. Even when in London, he spent most of his days alone, writing his *Historical Survey* of recent events. Crisis point was reached when, without his knowledge, a communiqué was issued to the press that the Zionist Executive and the Political Committee would meet 'to consider the outstanding problems yet to be discussed in the course of further negotiations' with the Government.[61] Namier exploded. Yet it is difficult to perceive in the statement anything other than a minor indiscretion. Given the goodwill it could surely have been smoothed over. But this is precisely what was lacking; and Namier escalated this trifling incident into a crisis of major proportions. In a circular to the Jewish Agency Executive, the Zionist Executive, and the Political Committee, he flung down the gauntlet. 'I am not prepared to stay one day longer in this office', he ruled, 'if political decisions of this nature and importance are taken without my knowledge.'[62]

Brodetsky[63] tried in vain to persuade him to the contrary. But his

[58] Lady Namier's Notes.

[59] It was widely believed that after the immediate issue of the Passfield White Paper had been settled, both sides would continue to meet in order to clarify the terms of reference of a proposed Development Commission for Palestine, in some ways a topic of no less importance than the Passfield White Paper.

[60] Namier to Malcolm MacDonald, 1 Jan. 1931, CZA A312/12; see also Namier to Mrs Dugdale, 11 Jan. 1931, WA.

[61] See *Jewish Chronicle*, 27 Feb. 1931.

[62] From his circular of 23 Feb. 1931, CZA A312/12.

[63] Selig Brodetsky (1888–1954): Professor of Mathematics at University of Leeds, 1920–49; member of Executive of Zionist Organization, and head of Political Department of Jewish Agency in London, 1928–49; President of British Zionist Federation, 1949; President of Hebrew University, 1949–52.

decision was final, and 'it would serve no purpose ever to raise that question again'.[64] However, if his co-operation was genuinely desired, he did not want to refuse it if he could be 'of any real service'. He continued:

what I feel most concerned about is that I should not find myself with a whole crowd of people trying to impress me with their views, or to make me take special care of their particular—often ill-informed or absurd—desiderata. The two years of my Zionist experience have taught me that the fundamental tendency here is towards 'charabanc' solutions. When Congress does not know whom to elect to the Executive, the four seats in a taxi are changed to thirteen seats in a charabanc; and when the Z.E. plus the Political Committee cannot agree on the demands to be put to H.M.G., they agree to ask for anything anyone can ask of. Now that charabanc method is impossible.

Having thus demolished in the most abrupt terms the techniques of Zionist diplomacy, Namier authoritatively listed nine conditions which would ensure the independence of the negotiating body from factional rivalries and hence allow, perhaps, his continued participation in the talks. Adding insult to injury, he concluded: 'I wish to repeat that all I say here is said on the assumption that Dr. Weizmann is going to America, that he will therefore not be in a position to assume the supreme direction of the work himself; and that consequently the work will, in a way, have to be carried on by a Committee.'

The contents, style, and presentation of his circular guaranteed that future co-operation between himself and his erstwhile colleagues would be minimal. In fact, there was much justice in Namier's complaints, as Weizmann appreciated, though, unlike Namier, he was conscious of the limitations of his own office. Namier's criticism had undoubtedly struck a raw nerve. But there was no chance of his ultimatum ever being accepted. Zionist functionaries everywhere must have regarded it as preposterous, as an extreme manifestation of his unbridled arrogance. He did, however, unknown to himself at the time, receive mild support from an unexpected quarter. Felix Warburg, no friend of his and a maverick in his own right, commented:

Namier's attitude, while a little prima donna-ish in laying down his conditions regarding how he would be willing to continue the negotiations, is not unreasonable, and butting-in from the outside from everybody is surely enough to drive a saint wild. I am not an admirer of Mr. N., as you know, but if anybody

---

[64] Namier to Brodetsky, 15 Mar. 1931, CZA A312/12.

has to say it to the Zionist Organisation people, he might just as well be the one.[65]

Warburg, a man of immeasurable wealth and therefore, in his estimation, of extensive influence, was not averse from playing his own version of Namier's game. As far as Namier was concerned, such praise was akin to the kiss of death.

Namier's 'prima donna-ish' attitude was a reflection of Weizmann's crumbling position. Ever since the crisis broke, his leadership had fallen under relentless, at times vitriolic, attack from those who sought to replace him.[66] He received no help from the British Government which should have been keen to maintain him in office. The Colonial Office and the Palestine Administration went their own way, blocking the path to full implementation of the agreement. Only weeks after the letter was published, the Zionists were complaining bitterly at official indifference.[67] Weizmann desperately needed some gesture from the Government to buttress his position at Congress.

In a roundabout manner, MacDonald responded. On the eve of Congress he invited representative Zionists to meet him at Chequers. His precise motives remain unclear. Possibly his conscience troubled him; conceivably his son Malcolm, throughout these months in continuous contact with Namier, was pressing for such a confabulation. At any rate, it was decided that Namier and Ben Gurion[68] would meet the Prime Minister. They flew from Basle, where the delegates were gathering, to London, and from there drove to Chequers, arriving on 12 July. Namier was an odd choice as one of the emissaries. Distrusted intensely by most Zionists, he was certainly not one of their representatives. Clearly he went at Weizmann's behest. His personal loyalty was beyond doubt, while his friendship with the MacDonalds was an extra bonus. These were powerful arguments for any objective observer, but they could have hardly raised Weizmann's credibility as a leader with the oppositionists. In this sense, Namier was a liability. That Weizmann did not jettison him is a striking indication of his utter

[65] F. Warburg to Dr M. Hexter, 27 Mar. 1931, WA.

[66] The opposition included the Revisionists, the General Zionists 'B', and the Mizrachi. The American General Zionist leader, Rabbi Stephen Wise, taunted Weizmann: 'You have sat for too long at English feasts.' Weizmann could muster support only from the General Zionists 'A' and the Labour Zionist group.

[67] See Notes of an Interview between Ramsay MacDonald, Ben Gurion, and Namier, 12 July 1931, WA.

[68] David Ben Gurion (1886–1974): Sec.-Gen. of *Histadruth*, 1921–35; chairman of Zionist Executive and Jewish Agency, 1935–48; Prime Minister and Defence Minister of Israel, 1948–53, 1955–63.

confidence in him.[69] This was the high-tide mark of their partnership.

The discussions, which lasted the best part of the day, ranged over a wide field of Anglo-Zionist problems, with particular emphasis on 'the principle of parity between Jews and Arabs as national entities' in any future constitutional arrangement.[70] From Weizmann's point of view, the mission was a resounding success. But it did not save him at Basle. His key speech to Congress, which mentioned 'the great services rendered to our cause' by Namier, Mrs Dugdale, and Leonard Stein, was a memorable piece of rhetoric.

I have endeavoured to face, honestly and squarely, the position which confronts us. My respect for our people, my belief in the justice of our cause, and a grave sense of responsibility, do not permit me to indulge in fantasies or to suggest adventurous policies, which can only lead to heartbreaking disappointment. Instead of chasing a mirage, and wasting our energies on futile internecine strife over shadows, let us concentrate our efforts on what is within reach of a reasonable possibility—and first of all on the consolidation of the work that has already been begun in Palestine . . . We are the sons of a people whose history is a long record of hardship and suffering. Our ancestors survived them because they believed in the fate of the Jewish people. Their mantle has fallen on us; we may sometimes become oppressed by the great responsibility, but we shall not falter. There is an indestructible force in our Movement, and it will, I am confident, emerge renewed out of the present crisis. May this Congress show the right way towards it, and thus become an important milestone on the road to fulfillment.[71]

The majority of delegates, however, remained unimpressed by his oratory. Rejected, Weizmann walked out of the hall into the political doldrums.

Namier's reaction to his chief's defeat was characteristically violent, and he climbed to new heights of vituperation in his anger:

Dear Brodetsky,

I have to thank you for the courtesy of your letter of the 16th. I am sorry, however, I cannot congratulate you either on your new chief, or on some of your new associates, or on your decision to join the new Executive. I consider that

---

[69] Of course, it might be argued that at this point Weizmann, irked beyond measure by an ungrateful movement, was weary of leadership and deliberately searching for an excuse to rid himself of a tiresome burden. Namier's mission might therefore be interpreted as an act of bravado. This is an attractive theory but it flies in the face of whatever evidence we possess regarding Weizmann's struggle to maintain power, and even more to his reaction to losing it.

[70] The full text of the agreement, in the form of a telegram, has been published in *The Gentile Zionists*, 52.

[71] From P. Goodman, ed., *Chaim Weizmann*, 205–30.

Weizmann was extremely ill-advised to have in any way connived at its formation, and that, while not securing our present, it is calculated to compromise our future. The political apprenticeship of our opponents might have been expensive, but would have been welcome. The rule of Sokolow, Farbstein,[72] and Co., under the mantle of Weizmannism, is a sight which I, for one, cannot bear. They have killed him, and at the last moment succeeded in making him bequeathe to them his clothes, with which they now open a second-hand clothes shop. And we and our cause have not even a shroud left in death.

As an afterthought, he added a postscript:

This letter is not meant to be unfriendly to you, but you must understand, you have placed yourself—or let yourself be placed—in a false position, in which I cannot help you; and I fear that in time you will not be able even to help yourself—among those frogs born of the slime of the Seventeenth Congress.[73]

In vain did Brodetsky protest that Weizmann's pressure had been crucial in his decision to join the new Executive. He had succumbed to the lures of office and placed himself beyond the pale.

Namier's tactics were clear. He wished to force the new leadership to its knees by denying it any form of co-operation with his—i.e. Weizmann's—group, except on his own terms. Even Mrs Dugdale earned his displeasure by refusing to endorse his intransigent attitude. In all this, Weizmann maintained a discreet silence. From his viewpoint, Namier's advice must have been a great nonsense. A leader of Weizmann's calibre cannot simply opt out of politics. Every conversation he holds, every letter or article he writes, every meeting he addresses, even his physical presence at an informal gathering, has a political connotation. Together with Mrs Dugdale he managed to tone down Namier's rage. By mid-September Namier was thinking about meeting the new leadership to discuss the terms of Weizmann's co-operation.[74] Despite this turnabout, his attitude had not fundamentally altered. He had bowed to Weizmann's and Mrs Dugdale's wishes out of friendship and respect, not out of conviction. 'I am afraid', he clarified

---

[72] Sokolow had succeeded Weizmann as President. Joshua Heschel Farbstein (1870–1948) was a member of the new Executive and a leader of the Mizrachi, the religious bloc.

[73] The correspondence is in CZA A312/12.

[74] It was typical of Namier that he laid down strict conditions for this concession. First, that Mrs Dugdale should participate in the discussions. Brodetsky had wished to exclude her because the Executive were 'astonished' at the extent of her influence with Weizmann. Secondly, Namier objected to the presence of Michael Marcus, a Jewish though non-Zionist MP, as party to the preliminary talks, particularly after Mrs Dugdale had been so conspicuously cold-shouldered. See Namier to Weizmann, 14 Sept. 1931, CZA A312/12.

to Mrs Dugdale, 'that my advice at Basle was right, even though it seemed merely an expression of my bitter and violent nature. . . . I shall always absolutely oppose any further political action on the part of "C" [Weizmann]'.[75] Yet he was perceptive enough to realize that Weizmann in opposition needed more pliable advisers than he: 'I think he should take your [Mrs Dugdale's] advice rather than mine', though he could not resist adding 'that sooner or later he will come round to my intransigence.'[76]

Despite these political differences, Namier and Weizmann strengthened their personal relationship. In defeat, Weizmann craved more than ever for the company of his most trusted supporters. That autumn he wrote to Namier, already teaching in Manchester: 'we are quite alone, rather longing to see you'. On the following day: 'I hope to hear from you soon. Baffy is not here and London is not the same without both of you.' And the day after: 'I'm delighted you are coming to town. Will you dine with us on Friday? If you cannot dine (I hope you can) come round for tea, in fact any time; only let me know. You could possibly stay the night here.'[77] He undertook, at Namier's request, a delicate task: the upkeep of Namier's father's grave in a cemetery just outside Merano.[78] In a different context, he asked Namier to recommend some history texts for his youngest son, Michael, who was then studying for his School Certificate. 'You know that Michael considers you firstly as the highest authority on all subjects including Zionism (the only sensible man who takes preference over his father!).'[79]

By now Namier was firmly ensconced in Manchester, coping or not with the multifarious details of academic life.[80] Even so, he was slowly drawn, as was Weizmann, into greater participation in Jewish and Zionist affairs. He had advised Weizmann to 'keep well away from things for the next year or two',[81] a principle easier to espouse than to uphold. Events outside his control ensured that he would not bury himself in scholarly work. His idyll ceased when the phenomena of anti-Semitism and Hitler erupted into Jewish and world affairs.

[75] Namier to Mrs Dugdale, 2 and 9 Nov. 1931, CZA A312/44.
[76] Ibid.
[77] See his letters of 19–21 Oct. 1931, CZA A312/12.
[78] Weizmann to Namier, 18 Oct. 1931, WA.
[79] Weizmann to Namier, 13 Nov. 1931, CZA A312/12.
[80] A junior colleague of his at the time, Mr A. J. P. Taylor, recollected that he displayed little enthusiasm for university administration: 'What have the others got to do with their time?' he proclaimed. He spent less and less time at Manchester. (Interview, 20 Sept. 1976.)
[81] Lady Namier's Notes.

Chapter 3

The Approaching Storm

Namier had read *Mein Kampf* when it first appeared and had immediately recognized its author to be in deadly earnest. Unlike some of his contemporaries, he did not consider the Hitlerian phenomenon to be an accidental eruption on to the German scene. 'In reality', he wrote after due consideration, 'Hitler's unparalleled rise is due to the fact that he has given expression to some of the deepest instincts of Germany. His creed follows the pattern of German national crystallisation. "He has spoken from their soul." He is probably one of the most representative Germans that ever lived.'[1] Nor did he wait upon the events of the 1930s before forming his opinions about the Germans and their national traits. These were already firmly set before and during the First World War. 'It did not require either 1914, or 1933, or 1939 to teach me the truth about the Germans. Long before the last war I considered them a deadly menace to Europe and to civilization.'[2] He may truthfully be said to have belonged to the school which enunciated the dogma of 'original German sin'. 'Even the cruelty of a Tartar', he proclaimed in 1915, 'does not approach that of a German.' 'In almost every Jewish pogrom in Russia', he added as further proof, 'the moving spirit has been a person of German extraction.'[3] Hitler, that 'mountebank dictator', was merely the latest and most conclusive demonstration of 'how deep Nazism is rooted in the German nature'.[4] Three months after Hitler's appointment as chancellor, Namier reflected on the essence of his revolution:

The present German revolution has dreamt no dreams, has made terrorism and suppression precede resistance, and, with regard to the rights of the individual, to Parliamentary Government, the Press, education, etc., has, by its free and deliberate choice, adopted from the outset all that was most ruthless in the advanced stages of other revolutions . . . the persecution of the Jews, who have

---

[1] From his article 'National Character' in the *Spectator*, 28 Feb. 1941, reprinted in *Conflicts*.
[2] See Namier's correspondence with Kingsley Martin, Aug. 1942, CZA A312/55. See also pp. 136–38, for another slant on his views on Germany.
[3] See his monograph, *Germany and Eastern Europe*.
[4] From 'National Character', op. cit.

fought and worked for Germany, is its only original contribution. History supplies no analogy for that lifeless but horrible counterfeit of revolution.[5]

His hatred of Nazism was intense and personal. When the children of his 'counterfeit revolution' began to devour themselves, he was overcome with glee. A. J. P. Taylor has recalled:

On 30 June 1934, when Hitler murdered Roehm and many others of his early associates, Namier visited me in the country. As his train drew into the station, he put his head out of the carriage window, waved his newspaper, and cried joyfully: 'The swine are killing each other! The swine are killing each other.'[6]

At times, he effected a detached, intellectual understanding of anti-Semitism:

Nor is there anything necessarily and inherently wicked in anti-semitism. Nations do not like each other and they dislike strangers in their midst; but what others can bear with comparative, or even cheerful indifference is made painful for us by our defenceless, helpless condition, and by the fact that we Jews frequently do not feel 'strangers' where we are looked upon as such.[7]

But there can be no doubt that the barbaric nature of German anti-Semitism resulting in the virtual extermination of European Jewry sharpened his sense of Jewish-Zionist identity and intensified his detestation of Germany. After the war, when Anglo-German relations were on the upswing owing to the exigencies of the Cold War, he was invited to address a Foreign Office Summer School on German–Russian relations. A number of Germans had been invited to attend the seminar. Without hesitation, he rejected the invitation:

I am a Jew by race, and the Germans have tortured to death or exterminated six and half million Jews. Hundreds of thousands of Germans must have participated in these atrocities, millions approved of them and rejoiced in them, while the vast majority of the German nation acclaimed Hitler, and would still be doing so had he been successful. I prefer not to meet any German unless I can be certain of his having been an active anti-Nazi at the time, and not merely now in his own fruitful imagination.

Even from a wider point of view I can merely deplore activities such as described in your letter. I quite realise the very serious difficulties presented by

[5] See his article, 'Pathological Nationalisms', *Manchester Guardian*, 26 Apr. 1933, reprinted in *In The Margin of History*. Also his letter to *Manchester Guardian*, 6 May 1933.

[6] See A. J. P. Taylor, ed., *Off The Record. Political Interviews 1933–1943* (London, 1973), 45.

[7] From his introduction to Dr A. Ruppin's book *The Jews in the Modern World* (London, 1934), republished in *In The Margin of History*.

the problem of how to deal with the Germans; but I am certain that associating with them as if nothing had happened—and this is the attitude with which they would like to 'innoculate' the world, for their crimes do not way [*sic*] with them in the least—will do no good but a great deal of harm. We are entering the old path which rendered the sacrifices of the First World War nugatory, and enabled the Germans to engineer the Second. If we proceed along it the Third is in the offing.

The last thing in the world I would do is to talk to these people about any of our late allies and fellow sufferers however perverse and atrocious their present behaviour may be. The only aspect I would be prepared to speak about would hardly suit your purpose: the poisonous effect which Germans always had, and are probably having now, on Russia.

In case you might think that what I say is merely the effect which the German crimes against the Jews have had on my mind and attitude, I add that even forty years ago I looked upon the Germans as a deadly menace to the world: I for one did not need to change my views about them either in 1914 or in 1933.[8]

His views regarding the aims of German foreign policy were equally unyielding. Analyzing the notion 'that a straight fight between Teuton and Slav would not have concerned us', he pronounced at the outset of the First World War that 'German Imperialism is "one and indivisible" in its spirit, and a victorious German advance in eastern Europe would have soon been followed up by German aggression in the West.'[9] During the 1930s he modified his assessment as to the immediate thrust of German policy, though not as to its basic aim, expansionism, which he continued to regard as a fundamental tenet of German nationalism. Thus Hitler's primary aim would be to absorb 'any solidly German territory' within 'the framework of the "totalitarian State"'. The establishment of a Greater Germany, which would include Austria, which 'has been in the forefront ever since he assumed office', the Sudentenland, and finally the lost territories in the East, would constitute only the first step towards confrontation with the West. Although he overestimated the ability and the will-power of the smaller European powers to oppose the German menace, he accurately predicted that the most effective barrier to resist German aggression would be to resurrect and strengthen the Russian connection.[10]

---

[8] Namier to Mrs Reeve [of the German Section of the Foreign Office], 30 May 1949, CZA A312/55.

[9] *Germany and Eastern Europe*, 58.

[10] See his essays, 'German Arms and Aims', *Manchester Guardian*, 28 June 1935, reprinted in *In The Margin of History*, and 'After Vienna and Versailles', *The Nineteenth Century and After* (Nov. 1940), reprinted in *Conflicts*. Also his letter to Walter Elliot, 28 Oct. 1938, published in *In The Nazi Era* (London, 1952), 177.

'Berchtesgaden', he gloomily forecast, 'is now the centre of an incalculable German policy, and the storm which is brewing threatens Vienna. When it breaks it will not be a merely local disturbance.'[11]

But it was the fate of the Jews now under Nazi rule which gave rise to his most immediate concern. In Hitler, anti-Semitism had found a passionate believer whose ruthless devotion to his twisted cause heralded a tragedy without parallel in recorded history. The steady growth of Nazism in Germany encouraged anti-Semitic movements elsewhere. From the early 1930s Jewish, and other, refugees sought safety in the more liberal West, the trickle swelling into a flood after Hitler's accession to power in January 1933. Unlike some Jews, Namier did not remain indifferent to their plight. Indeed, his genuine concern for their welfare reflected one of the more attractive features of his personality.[12] In a very literal sense, he held in his hands the destiny of scholars, their families, often of their entire academic establishments. And with every month, the number of destinies requiring outside help increased. This was a cause which he promoted with his usual enthusiasm. It was also the beginning of a new kind of partnership with Weizmann, a more equal one, based no longer on a purely master–servant relationship. Inevitably, this too was not without its hazards. These years were punctuated by minor personal squabbles which, at times, gravely strained their friendship.

By March, Namier had succeeded in putting together a Manchester Academic Society. Its prime aim was the placement of German academic refugees in British universities and institutes of higher learning; its most acute problem, a dire shortage of funds. Namier proposed to overcome this obstacle, partially at least, by tapping the resources of certain trust funds, the Bernard Baron and Alfred Beit funds were mentioned; and also by relying on a committee of prominent Manchester businessmen, mainly Jewish, to finance his schemes. He was more successful in the first of these enterprises than in the second.[13] Fund-raising, as Namier soon discovered, is an art-form in its own right. Enthusiasm rapidly flagged; the number of worthy causes multiplied at an alarming rate; and the circle of potential contributors, in any case

[11] From 'German Arms and Aims'.

[12] 'I have always had a certain grudge against Grant Robinson, who, as examiner, had preferred Crutwell to myself', Namier told Sir Isaiah Berlin in the late 1930s, 'but when I think of what he has done for the German Jewish refugees—I forgive him.' Sir I. Berlin, op. cit.

[13] See Namier to Weizmann, 2 May 1933, and Namier to Sir Harold Hartley, 15 May 1933, CZA A312/15.

restricted, shrunk as time progressed. 'All the different appeals always tap more or less the same local source,' he complained to Weizmann, 'none of which is really great.'[14] It was, he concluded, like robbing Peter to pay Paul.

Namier put his prize scheme to Sir Harold Hartley, a director of LMS and head of its coal research department:

A committee of prominent business men in Manchester intends to raise a fund which proposes to offer to the University with a view to giving one year's 'shelter' to distinguished scientists or literary refugees from Germany. No permanent appointments are intended—all we mean to do is to give time to these poor fellows, who suddenly have had the roof burnt over their heads, to look around and see where to turn.[15]

Though an encouragement, the 'one year's "shelter"' was also an anxiety. The university authorities, while quite prepared to grant a year's grace, understandably had no desire to be saddled with an ever-growing reservoir of foreign academics whom they could not possibly hope to absorb on a permanent basis. If Namier could guarantee them employment elsewhere, after the year had elapsed, it would considerably ease his task with the University Senate. Among other possibilities, he considered Weizmann's project in Rehovoth, the Daniel Sieff Research Institute, then in its final planning stage. But however attractive this prospect was, and Weizmann certainly encouraged it, lack of personal contact with Weizmann, or vexed questions such as allocation of funds and job priorities, intervened to ensure that it barely left the ground and, incidentally, soured their relationship.

Much of the mounting tension between them—'Frankly I was sick of writing to you time and again about business matters on which I had to make decisions here without having received a reply'[16]—was due to neither man being able to work smoothly unless aided by an adequate staff. In this respect, Namier, who delighted in delegating minor jobs to voluntary supporters, was, on the whole, better served during those months than Weizmann, deprived, with the notable exception of his secretary, Miss Doris May, of his Jewish Agency apparatus. Not even Miss May's efficiency, however, could offset Weizmann's embarrassing carelessness in office routine. Letters were mislaid, turning up later in forgotten pockets or other odd places, or often simply disappeared, sunk without trace. It was Weizmann, at his most disarming, who best

[14] Lady Namier's Notes.   [15] Namier to Hartley, 15 May 1933, CZA A312/15.
[16] Namier to Weizmann, 15 Sept. 1933, CZA A312/15.

captured the tedium of these recurrent contretemps: 'I was extremely sorry, but neither I nor Miss May can find any trace of them.[17] Your letter we have filed away, but no enclosures thereto. Please accept my sincerest apologies. We shall have another search for them, going through my accumulations at home.'[18]

By the beginning of 1934, Namier, in despair at Weizmann's antics, was bent on resignation. For some months he had pressed his chief, as he still called Weizmann, to appear before his Committee in Manchester. Weizmann hedged, pleading overwork. After much shilly-shallying he finally confessed to being 'guilty of negligence', and added, on a note of resignation, 'you will be thinking that I am a rather disagreeable customer to deal with'.[19] Namier agreed.

Now I look a perfect fool towards them [the Committee], and they themselves look foolish towards the people whom they have made to join the Society and who have expected some return for their precious gunieas . . . [to] have to beg you, with no effort, to come to one meeting, is more than I can take on with all the other work I have on my hands . . . I quite understand how overworked you are; I have been with you probably through the worst time, and I know what it means to be overworked. Still, some consideration is also due to me in the matter. . . .

These futile exchanges continued throughout the year. The visit never materialized. Early in 1935, Namier informed Weizmann that his Society was 'practically in *statu mortis*'; even the most dedicated of his supporters had refused to renew his subscription.[20] But by then a new political situation was engulfing them and absorbing the acrid fumes of these over-long, rancorous, and somewhat inconsequential clashes.

*   *   *

After his defeat Weizmann tried hard to follow Namier's advice 'to keep well away from things for the next year or two'. But as he later admitted, he found it impossible, even in the isolation of his laboratory, to ignore the harsh realities of Jewish life.[21] Refugee work and fund-raising in South Africa and America occupied much of his energy. At the same time, he accepted the presidency of the British Zionist Federation, no doubt anxious to retain some kind of political power-base. His position within the Zionist movement, desperate in 1931, materially improved

---

[17] 'Them' being the *curricula vitarum* of some unfortunate academics.
[18] Lady Namier's Notes.   [19] Weizmann to Namier, 3 Nov. 1933, CZA A312/15.
[20] Lady Namier's Notes.   [21] See *Trial and Error* (London, 1950), 424.

in the coming years as key members of the Labour group, *Mapai*, Weizmann's chief political support, became more prominent in Jewish Agency affairs. Despite their pleas, he adamantly refused to attend the 18th Congress at Prague: 'I ain't going',[22] he finally informed Namier. But by virtue of their increased political leverage, he began to act again, with official sanction, the role of the elder statesman, conferring with leading cabinet ministers at home and important political personages abroad. This renewed activity affected Namier's position. There was no question of Weizmann excluding him from his political rehabilitation. Quite the contrary, he appeared more keen than ever to retain Namier's services.

The early 1930s witnessed a sharp rise in Jewish immigration into Palestine,[23] accompanied, predictably, by a heightening of Arab–Jewish tension. By way of skirting round the essential issues, the British resurrected an old scheme of theirs, long since discarded by both sides: a Legislative Council for Palestine. The question had first been mooted in 1921–3, but had been abandoned owing to the almost unanimous opposition of the Arabs and the lukewarm support of the Jews.[24] Fresh life was breathed into this battered idea as a result of the 1929 crisis. By the end of 1934 the plan was in its final stages of preparation, vigorously solicited by the Palestine Administration and backed by the Cabinet in London. Namier had no doubt that an untimely Legislative Council would cripple, perhaps fatally, the National Home. He was not even enthusiastic about the idea of 'parity', a formula widely accepted by the Zionists, whereby Jews and Arabs would be represented on the Council in equal numbers. He argued that any kind of Council, but particularly one based on proportional representation, would create a dangerous precedent which the Arabs would exploit and which neither the British nor the Jews would be able ultimately to control: a kind of Frankenstein's monster manipulated by Arab chauvinism. Namier wrote for Weizmann two memoranda in which he expounded his views in full:[25]

Palestine belongs to two nations: the Arabs resident within its borders, and the Jews, desirous of making it their National Home. A Legislative Council in

[22] Lady Namier's Notes.
[23] For the years 1933–5, authorized immigrants numbered 134,640. This was a truly dramatic rise when compared with the over-all immigration figure of 247,404 for the years 1921–35. See Peel Report, Cmd. 5479, 279.
[24] See *The Gentile Zionists*, 43–4.
[25] Dated 28 Aug. 1934, and 5 Feb. 1935, CZA A312/15.

Palestine would have to deal with a multiplicity of subjects intimately affecting the Jewish National Home, and the Jewish representation in it would unavoidably tend to displace the Jewish Agency in advising the Palestine Administration on such matters[26] . . . We cannot admit a Jewish representation in the Legislative Council based exclusively on Jews who are citizen or residents of Palestine. . . . The problem can, however, be solved by means of two separate Chambers, one for the Jews and one for the Arabs. The Jewish Chamber would consist of representatives of the Jewish population of Palestine and of the non-Palestinian branches of the Jewish Agency, in proportions to be determined by the parties concerned in an understanding with the Mandatory Power. This proportion would have to be periodically adapted to the change in balance between Palestinian and World Jewry. Delegations from the National Chambers, joined by an official representation of the Mandatory Administration, would constitute the Legislative Assembly.

This was too hard a line for Weizmann to uphold, even though he could not fault Namier's verdict on the inherent dangers of a Council. Like any politician, Weizmann did not act in a vacuum. By totally rejecting a Council he ran the risk of being condemned, both by groups within his own movement and perhaps of more importance in the eyes of world public opinion, as being unnecessarily intransigent and even undemocratic. He stuck to his formula of parity. From Weizmann's viewpoint, it was a reasonable compromise: it preserved, perhaps enhanced, the democratic nature of the movement, and in fact did allow a large degree of manœuvrability in the field of constitutional change. Fortunately for the Zionists, the Arabs proved even more intransigent than they, and steadfastly refused to consider any form of Council unless it was the prelude to a Palestinian state based on an Arab majority.[27] This issue dragged on until the spring of 1936, with Namier in the thick of the battle to win parliamentary support,[28] when the outbreak of the Arab general strike and rebellion drove all other questions from the stage.

* * *

The completion of Namier's second memorandum had coincided with a most pessimistic letter from Weizmann, written on his return journey after a long stay in Palestine:

[26] By article 4 of the mandate, the Jewish Agency was designated as the advisory body to the mandatory power on all matters appertaining to the National Home, see Cmd. 1500.

[27] See their memorandum of 25 Nov. 1935, printed in *Survey of International Affairs, 1936* (London), 722.

[28] See *The Gentile Zionists*, 60–1.

I am most anxious to see you as soon as ever possible. I must unburden myself and we must come to some practical conclusions. We are in mortal danger of ruining everything and unless some of us are ready to stake all, we shall certainly go down unsung and unwailed. Even greater sacrifices—the supremest—may be of little avail, but we are in honour bound to try.[29]

Despite the differences which had recently emerged between them and which had, to a certain extent, tarnished Weizmann's previously immaculate image, Namier still believed him the only Jewish leader capable of negotiating with the mandatory power on a basis of equality and of advancing their still precarious cause. His response was brief and generous: 'Its contents come as a surprise, even as a shock . . . I am at your disposal any time.'[30]

Of the meeting that followed he gave a detailed account to a friend, Marie Beer, who was only marginally concerned with Palestine but greatly interested in Namier's preoccupations:[31]

You asked what happened with Weizmann. I saw him for an hour on Friday, and shall see him again during the coming week-end. He is much depressed, and even alarmed, by the situation in Palestine. To put it in a nutshell: things as experienced by living there look different from what they seemed to a visitor. He said to me: 'We have made a mistake. We ought to have gone to live there ten years ago.' I replied: 'It was not for me to tell you so, but [T. E.] Lawrence said to me fifteen years ago, 'One does not build the National Home by living in a villa in Addison Road.'[32]

During his visit Weizmann had been mainly concerned with his work at the Sieff Institute, including the building of his new house nearby. He had also travelled extensively throughout the country, often un-accompanied and unheralded. What he saw had appalled him: grossly inflated land-prices; shoddy standards of workmanship; the selfish pursuit of material benefits. He was witnessing the emergence of a *petit-bourgeois* society devoid of all the old pioneering values. To break this drift, he considered launching a scheme remarkably similar to one Namier had proposed to Philip Kerr in 1919:[33]

What Weizmann really wants more than anything at present is to work for some internal executive for a better schooling of labour immigrants in the *Galuth*; for

---

[29] Lady Namier's Notes.   [30] Ibid.

[31] For Namier's complicated relationship with Marie Beer, see Julia Namier, 48–57, 177–9, 194–5, 198, 233–5.

[32] Namier to Marie Beer, 30 Jan. 1935, CZA A312/15.

[33] See pp. 22–24.

some soundness in it all. He is a really great man. I said to him: 'Do you remember when, after my return from Paris at the end of September, 1933, I suggested that we should use that German Jew in Paris, Sommerfeld, to teach our *Haluzim* building, you said they had better go to Palestine because in half a year they are builders?' He replied 'Yes, and I talked nonsense'. It requires a great man to give that answer. He now sees that over there blind leads blind.[34]

Weizmann then turned to Namier's future:

Weizmann finally said to me: 'If things in the [Hebrew] University are set right, would you take a professorship?' I said 'No. My work is on 18th century British and 19th century diplomatic history. There is no possibility of doing research on either in Palestine, nor much point in teaching them.' Weizmann: 'But you are a historian; could you not teach other branches of history?' N. 'You are a great chemist. If someone told you that you must not touch your own special branch but could teach the rudiments of other branches of chemistry, would you do it?' W. 'No, you are right.'

Then he thought for a moment and said: 'If I become President again will you come with me into the executive?' N. 'Yes, I shall.' But after a moment's consideration, I told Weizmann that I could do so only on one condition: That the right men—I do not care who they are, and do not even care to know—put down £10,000 as an endowment for me for life. If I go into the Executive I not only give up my chances here but any I may have at Oxford, a sacrifice sufficiently big for one man to make. But if I have an assured life rent of £500 a year, then should I leave the Executive and the Palestine work after a few years I shall have at least a certain minimum which will enable me to take up research again.

The question was left open. But Namier was clearly under the impression that Weizmann would leave no stone unturned to retain him as his adviser in some official capacity; and Weizmann did nothing to disillusion him. It was not to be. At the Lucerne Congress, held in August 1935, Weizmann, though re-elected as President of the movement, was unable to fulfil his promise. Owing to the exigencies of internal Zionist politics, Namier was excluded from any arrangement. He was understandably bitter at this setback. When Weizmann returned to London he presented Namier with an alternative. A new committee was to be formed—to conduct political work in London—and Namier would certainly be a member, possibly its chairman. It would render him a firm standing in the movement; and a handsome monetary reward was implied. By late October it was apparent that even this compromise was unacceptable to the Zionist establishment.

[34] Namier to Marie Beer, 30 Jan. 1935.

Namier, by now thoroughly incensed, 'sacked' Weizmann. Weizmann replied in as restrained a manner as possible:

I was distressed to receive your short note 'giving me the sack'. It was—in spite of a sincere desire—not possible to form a committee and it would have been no good. We can do some work together and we can prepare something for the future. But with Brod [etsky] & Goldmann[35] there can be no committee in which you or Stein or both should be members. I cannot help myself. If you still care to go on with the work of seeing people and talking to them I would feel deeply grateful.[36]

But instead of appeasing Namier, Weizmann's reply roused him to even greater fury:

To sum up the situation in one sentence: you dropped me at Lucerne, and you let me down in London. On your return you started the idea of the Committee, which you said was desired by the Executive. I talked over the matter with Baffy and Eder,[37] and reached the conclusion that such a Committee would be useful on public grounds, and indispensable to me in the work which you had asked me to undertake. It would have given me a definite 'locus standi' in the Organisation, and in cultivating what in eighteenth century language would have been called our 'parliamentary interest'; also in dealings with Malcolm [MacDonald], if he remains. That basis I now lack.

While you were in London, there were meetings, and conferences, and what not. If you wanted my collaboration, you ought to have had me invited to some of them. From what you told me, there were no strong objections to me on the part of the executive; but if there was, the more was it up to you to show that you insisted on my being given a share in the work . . .

But you never thought it necessary to do anything of the kind; probably you did not think about it at all. It is one of the regular difficulties which your most devoted friends have in co-operating with you that you do not think or seem to care in what position you place them, or how you add, unnecessarily, to their work and troubles. This is wrong towards your friends, and wrong towards the cause; and it is high time someone told you that straight out.

All this is very unpleasant writing and unpleasant reading, but these are facts, and they have to be faced. For years I have been at your beck and call, but now I do not choose to be whistled for and whistled off again, whether the invitation

---

[35] Nahum Goldmann (1895–   ): Zionist statesman; member of Jewish section of German Foreign Ministry during the First World War; representative of Jewish Agency at League of Nations, Geneva, 1935–9; active in diplomacy leading to establishment of State of Israel; President of World Zionist Organization, 1958–68.

[36] Weizmann to Namier, 4 Nov. 1955, CZA A312/15; see also Weizmann to Namier, 1 Dec. 1935, ibid.

[37] David Montagu Eder (1885–1936): medical doctor; English Zionist leader; member of Zionist Commission to Palestine, 1918; member of Zionist Executive, 1918–29; President of Zionist Federation of Great Britain, 1931.

concerns the Executive, a Committee, or a talk; and if you want at all times to be able to count *on* me, you must also occasionally count *with* me. Still, I do not refuse collaboration: our position is such that if I can be of any service, we have no right to quarrel, or part company in Zionist work. But regards and loyalty must be mutual.[38]

Despite the shabby treatment he had received, Namier did not retire from Zionist politics.[39] As he had made clear, he did not 'refuse collaboration'; and Weizmann, patient and diplomatic as ever, allowed tempers to cool before drawing him back into his inner circle. Just five weeks after their recent acrimonious exchange, Weizmann cabled from Palestine that Namier should join him immediately 'to discuss political work'.[40] Within a few days Namier was in Rehovoth. The situation was indeed serious. Apart from the contentious question of the Legislative Council, the Zionists had access to accurate information that the Government was contemplating new legislation severely restricting land sales and immigration quotas. They interpreted this all-out attack as a 'studied attempt to crystallize the National Home'.[41] The main purpose of Namier's visit was to co-ordinate a plan of campaign in the media and in Parliament to thwart the Government's intention. Upon his return to London, Namier, ably assisted by Mrs Dugdale, mobilized his wide range of contacts to improve the Zionists' position. In his own words, 'to re-establish our connections in the Cabinet and in Parliament and to see that in future our friends do watch over such matters'. He was not in favour, as were apparently some of the wilder elements in Weizmann's entourage, of an outright confrontation with the Government. Not, he hastened to add, because he had no stomach for battle:

If it comes to a fight, we shall fight like blazes; and you know well that I never shun a fight, and never feel better than in a fight. None the less, I would think it over not ten, but fifty, times before letting ourselves in for it now, if there is any chance of avoiding it . . . with proper work here we may rally in the next month or two some considerable influences; the whole thing may have received a new turn . . . But if we let it come to an open break, it may be very difficult to go back on it, and in any case, it would leave behind considerable bitterness and resentment.[42]

[38] Namier to Weizmann, 18 Nov. 1935, CZA A312/15.
[39] At a later date, September 1937, Namier was in fact co-opted on to the London Political Advisory Committee, a committee similar in composition and purpose to the one referred to above. See p. 84.
[40] From Namier's Notes, CZA A312/15; undated, but the beginning of Jan. 1936.
[41] Namier to Weizmann, 27 Jan. 1936, CZA A312/14.
[42] Ibid.

Namier's activities over the coming weeks reflected his definition of 'proper work'. He buttonholed Cabinet ministers, exerted pressure on political leaders, harassed Government officials, canvassed support in the press.[43] Once again he was in the thick of events; and he clearly enjoyed his return to politicking. Those on the receiving end of his assaults were less enthusiastic. 'He is a most tiresome person', a Foreign Office official noted, 'and we already know he is not to be trusted.'[44] Namier soldiered on, happily unaware of the violent feelings of disapprobation his lobbying engendered. If nothing else, he had proved to himself his indispensability to Weizmann in a moment of crisis.

The other aspect to his visit was equally profitable. Although he travelled extensively throughout the country, he stayed chiefly with the Weizmanns at Rehovoth. Relations between them naturally improved. 'Both Vera and myself were extremely happy to have you', Weizmann wrote later.[45] Nothing could have pleased Namier more. The tone of his correspondence with Weizmann, always an accurate indication of their relationship, returned to its more intimate style. Both parties had succeeded in bracing up their crumbling friendship.

*   *   *

Namier had agreed to act as Weizmann's representative on the Council for German Jewry, a body set up under the chairmanship of Sir Herbert Samuel to help resettle Jewish refugees from Germany.[46] He was eager and enthusiastic for this cause, but he rapidly discovered that his ideas conflicted with those of his colleagues. The main bone of contention was how best to use the monies raised by the Council. The transfer of Jewish assets out of Germany was an extremely complicated procedure, and although an agreement had been signed with the German Government,[47] its implementation was subject to the whims of the Nazi bureaucracy and would at best account for only a fraction of

---

[43] See Lady Namier's Notes; Weizmann to Lord Melchett, 17 Jan. 1936, WA; Namier to Weizmann, 27 and 30 Jan. 1936, CZA A312/14. Also *Dugdale Diaries* for this period.

[44] Minutes in FO 371/20480, W241Z/172/98.

[45] Weizmann to Namier, 22 Jan. 1936. CZA A312/14; also Lady Namier's Notes.

[46] This passage is based on Namier to Samuel, 17 May 1936, CZA A312/19 and Namier to Samuel, April 1937, CZA A312/55.

[47] The *Ha'avarah* [Transfer] agreement was negotiated between the Jewish Agency and the German Government in August 1933. It allowed emigrants to transfer funds to Palestine by depositing marks with German exporters, ostensibly for the export of goods to Palestine, and receiving from importers in Palestine the equivalent sum in local currency. The agreement held, though its profitability steadily decreased owing to pressure from the German Government, until November 1938. See also, *G.D.*, Series C, v. 1, nos. 369, 399.

Jewish property in Germany. From Namier's point of view, the chief drawback was that the *Ha'avarah* agreement, by definition, applied only to those who had assets to transfer. What, he asked, would become of the poor? How would they escape from Germany? Who would finance their resettlement? In order to answer some of these questions a Liquidation Bank was set up to meet the financial requirements of this complex operation.

Put briefly, the selfish attitude of the wealthy leaders of German Jewry towards their poorer brethren disgusted him. He spoke most strongly for a communal effort, the rich aiding the poor, particularly as the Council, through its Liquidation Bank, was funding the major portion of the repatriation process. There was another point which strongly influenced Namier. The rich, benefiting from the transfer agreement, were able to settle wherever they chose, subject to the immigration quotas of the country of their choice; the poor, deprived of this luxury would, with Jewish Agency support, make their way to Palestine. Although the choice was never as clear-cut as Namier believed, there was some force in his argument. At any rate, he was appalled at the manner in which the rich, who participated in all the relevant committees, exploited their position by diverting funds raised by the Council for the benefit of their own families, thereby depriving the poor of their just rights. In Namier's view, whatever the moral aspects involved, this was tantamount to embezzlement, and he did not mince his words when drawing the attention of the Council to this travesty of justice.

There was, of course, an element of exaggeration in Namier's accusations; but there was also enough of the truth to endow his arguments with a convincing ring. Namier's presence in the Council stuck out like a sore thumb. His interruptions allowed his more staid colleagues no rest. Altercations, mainly though not always on Namier's initiative, blocked the Council's work with persistent regularity. His departure from its meetings was clearly only a matter of time. In April 1937, he composed for Samuel a formidable analysis of the Committee's work and shortcomings all of which left him no option but to sever his 'connexion with the Council' and thereby free himself from 'all responsibility for further developments'. His parting shot was typical:

The rich and educated are like big animals which fill the air with their wailings, while the poor, like insects trodden under foot, die in silence. In future the German Jews must not expect to enjoy such a perfectly disproportionate share in the help of foreign Jewries, especially if, by their importunities and connexions they manage to have large sums of foreign monies misapplied to their internal budget.

His onetime colleagues must have viewed his departure with a sigh of relief.

*   *   *

The year 1936 inaugurated Namier's most prolonged and most active period in Zionist politics. It reflected the general crisis in international affairs and was not to end until the defeat of Nazi Germany in 1945. In Manchester, his academic timetable was gradually adjusted to suit his comings and goings until finally, in 1939, he was seconded to the Jewish Agency for essential war work. The troubles began in April 1936 when Arab riots broke out in Jaffa.[48] On the surface there was little to differentiate this incident from countless others which had periodically disturbed the fragile tranquillity of Palestine. But in fact it set in motion a chain of events which was to prove decisive in the history of that country.

Namier's initial reaction to the riots was not markedly different from that of other leading Zionists. His belief in the 'strong hand' was confirmed by Mrs Dugdale, then in Palestine on a visit. 'You must impress on everybody at home the absolute necessity of no bargaining. Better have some bloodshed than that, in my opinion.' 'Above all,' she concluded, 'let there be no Committee of Enquiry. The facts this time

---

[48] On 19 April serious rioting flared up in Jaffa. The immediate cause of the riots was the murder of two Jews on the Nablus–Tulkarem highway on the night of 15 April. The following night two Arabs were found murdered in a hut outside Petach Tikva, it being generally believed that this was an act of Jewish retaliation. The funeral of one of the Tulkarem victims became an excuse for anti-Arab demonstrations, and some Arabs in the Tel Aviv area were assaulted. As a result, the riots of the 19th followed and Arabs, incited by false rumours that the Jews were killing their brethren, ran riot in Jaffa, killing and wounding several Jews. A curfew was imposed on the area and emergency regulations brought into force. The next day an Arab National Committee was set up and a general strike declared throughout Arab Palestine. On 25 April a Supreme Arab Committee was established, subsequently known as the Arab Higher Committee. In this manner, the Palestine disturbances, which were to continue intermittently until the outbreak of the Second World War, began. There were, of course, far deeper reasons for the outbreak. The above events were only the culmination of a protracted period of mounting tension between the two communities resulting from the phenomenal growth in Jewish immigration figures during the years 1933–5. This factor, coupled with a more militant nationalist sentiment throughout the Arab world, and which found particular expression in Egypt and Syria, effected also the Palestinian Arabs and produced a potentially explosive situation. Their revived national spirit manifested itself in extreme political demands put forward in November 1935: self-government for Palestine based on the Arab majority; a ban on all land sales to Jews; and the total cessation of Jewish immigration.

are very clear (so far).'[49] The person Namier chose especially to impress was William Crozier, editor of the *Manchester Guardian*. From the beginning of the riots in April 1936 until the outbreak of war, he supplied Crozier with a steady stream of top secret information—'extremely confidential stuff'—which included accounts of interviews with Cabinet ministers and the highest officials in the Government and the Palestine administration.[50] The *Manchester Guardian*, under Crozier's guidance, proved a most valuable friend.

One aspect in particular of the new situation troubled him. He was most concerned that the Jews prove themselves militarily capable of maintaining their position in Palestine and of helping to combat any potential emergency in Europe. He wrote to Mrs Dugdale:

[We have to] work for a real Jewish militarism outside. I have already taken steps to get in touch with the Committee of Imperial Defence. We must talk to the soldiers and see whether we could in some way impress them and get their support. I also think the question of some Jewish regiment of territorials in this country should be seriously considered . . . if the Scots, Welsh or any country group within this island has its territorials, why should we fight shy of having Jewish territorials ('fight shy' being the only fight for which the O.T.I. [Order of Trembling Israelites—Namier's apophthegm defining his Zionist adversaries] are fit!)[51]

If the British wouldn't agree, he would turn to the French and persuade them 'to have a Jewish regiment in the French Foreign Legion'. But however the problem was resolved, he was convinced

that a new chapter starts in Jewish history. If we could get the full number of men into Palestine and train them there, this clearly would be the best. But we cannot—and therefore very much more has to be done in the Galuth in the way of having armed or fully trained forces ready for the next great emergency, when the offer of say 30 or 40 thousand men with military training might impress the general staff and trembling cabinet ministers. In the past most of the Zionist leaders were so damned pacifist and high-minded, and the one who had military inclinations—I mean Jabotinsky[52]—was so damned literary and theoretical.

[49] See Mrs Dugdale to Namier, 23 Apr. 1936, CZA A312/17. The 'no bargaining' referred to the Arab demands first raised in November 1935.

[50] See CZA A312/17–18.

[51] Namier to Mrs Dugdale, 23 Aug. 1936, CZA A312/44.

[52] Ze'ev (Vladimir) Jabotinsky (1880–1940): Zionist leader, journalist, and author; founded Jewish Legion during First World War; organized *Haganah* in Jerusalem, 1920; member of Zionist Executive, 1921; resigned from Executive to found World Union of Zionist Revisionists, 1925; President of New Zionist Organization, 1935; commander of *Irgun Zva'i Leumi* [National Military Organization], 1937.

He expanded on this theme in a memorandum he wrote in November 1936 entitled 'Palestine and the British Empire'.[53] Although it was widely circulated at the highest levels, his paper provoked little positive response. However convincing his thesis might appear on paper, it was clearly out of touch with political reality as viewed from Whitehall. 'No British Government would permit an arms industry in Palestine or elsewhere not in the British Empire', warned Sir Philip Chetwode,[54] 'and if you arm the Jews the Arabs would make similar demands.' The only solution, according to the Field Marshal, was to arm neither, and 'don't frighten the man in the street—who in the end decides these matters at an election'.[55] These arguments proved decisive in all subsequent attempts to foster intimate Jewish–British military co-operation.

Dominating Namier's current idea was his firm conviction that, owing to the deteriorating situation in Europe and in Palestine, 'We shall have to pass to a most intense "radicalism of deeds" '.[56] Everything appeared to substantiate his impression. In Palestine, the Government's response to the riots had been to appoint a Royal Commission. Its terms of reference were 'to ascertain the underlying causes of the disturbances . . . [to investigate] whether they [the Jews and the Arabs] have legitimate grievances . . . and to make recommendations for their removal and for the prevention of their recurrence'.[57] Initially, the Zionists, Namier among them, conjuring up visions of a repetition of the 1930 crisis, viewed this move with deep suspicion. But eventually, realizing there was no viable alternative, they aquiesced in it.[58] The Commission did not begin its inquiries until November. In the interim period—between its appointment and its departure for Palestine—the

---

[53] See CZA A312/17, later published in *In The Margin of History*, 84–93.

[54] Philip Walhouse Chetwode (1869–1950): commanded 20th Army Corps in Palestine Campaign, 1917–18; commander-in-chief, India, 1930–5; Field Marshal, 1933. Kn. 1918, created Baron, 1945.

[55] Sir Philip Chetwode to Namier, 15 Nov. 1936, CZA A312/14.

[56] Namier to Mrs Dugdale, 23 Aug. 1936, CZA A312/44.

[57] See Cmd. 5479, *The Report of the Palestine Royal Committee* (July 1937), otherwise known as the Peel Report.

[58] Although there had been Commissions of Inquiry before, this was the first, and last, occasion that the Government appointed a Royal Commission. A minor point perhaps, but it did endow the Commission with an authority which the others lacked, and appeared to indicate that the Government was prepared to implement fundamental changes in the mandate should it be thought necessary. The composition of the Commission also placed it in a higher league, both politically and intellectually, from its predecessors. The Commissioners were: Lord Peel, chairman; Sir H. Rumbold, vice-chairman; Sir L. Hammond; Sir W. Carter; Sir H. Morris; and Professor R. Coupland.

Zionist leadership was in almost continuous session. Acutely aware that they might be called upon, even compelled, to make far-reaching concessions, their consultations were conducted in an atmosphere of impending crisis. Nerves were on edge and incompatible temperaments clashed.

This was clearly illustrated at a Zionist conference in June when Weizmann proposed that the Jewish Agency should offer 'to suspend immigration for a period in order to help the Government'.[59] This suggestion was violently rejected by all present except Mrs Dugdale. Ben Gurion's opposition was the most vociferous and influential, and he was ably backed by Namier. Namier's 'radicalism of deeds' obviously appealed to Ben Gurion. From the summer of 1936 they began to work more closely together. In the early winter he wrote to Namier:

[Berl Locker[60]] writes about the '*stimmung*' [mood or frame of mind] in London, about our political group—their reactions to our problems and their method of approach—and he writes with concern about yourself. He thinks you are the only person who actually worries about Zionist politics, who is always full of initiative and political devices and 'whose Zionist conscience knows no rest'. He writes with undisguised concern about you leaving London. It is perhaps no secret to you that this question has been occupying me for a long time. . . . It is obvious that we are now in for a 'London season'. On various occasions we discussed the question whether the vital spot was in Jerusalem or London. For my part, I think that one is as important as the other . . . Yet there are times when the decision rests entirely with London, especially in periods of stress and political fluctuations. I do not know at what conclusions the Committee will arrive, but there is no doubt that some changes will be made and that the nature and extent of these changes will be determined only in London. Our position in London fills me with the greatest concern and it is in my opinion not to be thought of that the grave and serious task which confronts us should be carried out without your active assistance and constant cooperation.

I am well aware that you are not the man to be preached to, and that it is not your fault that you are not in a position to devote your whole time to our political work. I admit that the Congress has committed a grave blunder by not electing you to the Executive. If I say 'Congress' I mean, of course, ourselves. We have made a mistake, but I think that it can be corrected, and it is quite clear to me that it *must* be corrected.

[59] '*Baffy*': *The Diaries of Blanche Dugdale, 1936–1947* (London, 1973) ed. Norman Rose; henceforward referred to as *Dugdale Diaries*, 10 June 1936.

[60] Berl Locker (1887–1972): Labour Zionist leader; head of World Union of *Poale Zion*, 1920; member of Zionist Executive, London, 1931–6; head of political bureau of Jewish Agency, London, 1938–48; chairman of Jewish Agency Executive, Jerusalem, 1948–56.

We are now confronted with a new political era. Apart from the Commission, it is obvious that we are on the threshold of a political reorientation in the world at large and especially in England. Our affairs in London must now be watched over by alert and sensitive men who are imbued with initiative and who have freed themselves from obsolete political habits, men who know how to read the signs of the times and who find access to the new trends which creep up in political life.

It is obvious, for instance, that world politics and especially English policy will be determined in the near future by the apprehension of a world war and the military and strategic considerations connected therewith, and it may well be that the Defence Forces will perhaps be given no smaller weight in the decisions upon English policy in Palestine than the Colonial Office. A Zionist policy which does not take into account this new factor will remain sterile. We will not get on with our old political routine and the new era necessitates new men.[61]

Ben Gurion's motives in approaching Namier are clear. His references to 'old routines' and 'new men' were an obvious dig at Weizmann. He feared a recurrence of Weizmann's collapse in morale in June. Convinced that without his presence on the scene Weizmann would have dragged the London Executive with him, he searched for a method to neutralize the ageing leader's influence and stiffen his resolve in moments of crisis. What better choice than Namier? They had co-operated in the 1930 crisis and again, more recently, on the immigration issue. Unlike some of Ben Gurion's colleagues, Namier relished a fight and did not shirk from expressing his opinions, however unpopular they might sound. Moreover, Namier was widely regarded as Weizmann's man; he could therefore speak to the Zionist leader from a position of strength and authority based on many years of collaboration.

If Weizmann suspected Ben Gurion of playing at politics, the same accusation could never be levelled against Namier whose ambitions, in that sense at least, were strictly limited. Ben Gurion's calculations, logical and plausible, did not take into sufficient account Namier's ebullient character. If they agreed on some matters, other issues divided them. Namier proved to be an unpredictable partner for both Weizmann and Ben Gurion.

Nevertheless, throughout the coming months Ben Gurion and Namier worked in close union, much to Weizmann's chagrin. As a result, and as was perhaps to be expected, Namier's standing with

[61] Ben Gurion to Namier, 4 Nov. 1936, CZA A312/19.

Weizmann diminished. His uninhibited criticisms together with his grating personality, quite apart from his 'switch' in political allegiance, roused Weizmann's antagonism. 'Lewis irritates him [Weizmann] frightfully. But it's no good saying anything. It would only hurt Lewis and he can't change.'[62] By December relations between them had not improved. Namier was then in Palestine helping the Jewish Agency prepare its case for the Royal Commission. 'It seems that Lewis's presence is not oiling the wheels between Chaim and Ben Gurion.'[63] Two months later, Namier's immediate Zionist future was decided:

went to Zionist Office for long talk with Chaim about Lewis. Whether he ought to join the Agency Executive if asked. Chaim clear he should do so only if he can combine it with Manchester. On whole Chaim would obviously be relieved if he did *not*. Lewis's faults are much on his nerves. We went into the row with Ben Gurion, which I fear Lewis did *not* soothe in Palestine.[64]

Characteristically, Namier played into the hands of his enemies, erecting insurmountable obstacles to his being co-opted as a member of the Executive. 'He will not join the Executive', Mrs Dugdale noted, 'unless he is made independent and can give up his Professorship. He wants £10,000 (per annum).'[65] This extravagant demand in effect settled his fate. Despite Ben Gurion's promise to regularize his position, Namier continued to serve the movement on an *ad hoc* basis, travelling to London when needed, a member of the Executive in everything but name. Weizmann, despite the differences between them, differences that were to grow with time, refused to relinquish his services and continued to exploit his talents.

*   *   *

The Arab general strike was brought to an end on 12 October. A month later the Royal Commission began its enquiries and continued in session, in Jerusalem and London, until February 1937. By early January it was clear that the Commission was seriously considering partition as a way out of the Palestine impasse. Weizmann's immediate reaction was positive; he accepted the idea in principle.[66] Most of his supporters in London followed suit. Mrs Dugdale believed that 'The Jews would be fools not to accept it, even if it were the size of a table cloth.'[67] Namier was slightly more circumspect. Obviously nothing

---

[62] *Dugdale Diaries*, 13 July 1936.   [63] Ibid., 21 Dec. 1936 [unpublished].
[64] Ibid., 19 Feb. 1937.   [65] Ibid., 26 Feb. 1937 [unpublished].
[66] See *The Gentile Zionists*, 128–9.   [67] *Dugdale Diaries*, 1 Feb. 1937.

could be decided finally until the territorial details of the scheme were known. But he too subscribed to the proposal. He laid out the general lines of Zionist policy for the coming months. On tactical grounds it was essential that the scheme should not be regarded as one inspired by the Zionists, or even favoured by them. This would give them greater room for manœuvre in the forthcoming negotiations with the Government. The general consensus of Zionist opinion during these weeks was that everything turned on what the British were prepared to offer. So far the signs had been encouraging, but no more. Two conditions were considered essential: the continuation of immigration on a large scale—a figure of 50–60,000 per annum was mentioned—together with sufficient territory to absorb such an influx; and 'real sovereignty'. Namier added a touch of his own: 'the Jewish State must have the power to keep the outside Arabs out of Palestine. He referred to the moral and physical value of openly having an army.'[68]

At the end of June the contents of the Peel report were leaked to Mrs Dugdale. 'The boundaries look to me all right. Haifa is all right. Jerusalem a British enclave-Mandate in perpetuity. . . . Nothing in all this that cannot be adjusted by negotiation.'[69] The report was issued on 7 July. Accompanying it was a statement of policy that immigration for the coming eight months would not exceed 8,000 for all categories. This created a tremendous 'uproar' in Zionist circles, and raised serious doubts as to ultimate British intentions.[70] Two days later Namier set forth his views on the situation:

First, about the declaration published on Wednesday [7 July] . . . we meant publicly to state our view that the Mandate has not been unworkable, but was not worked, or rather was sabotaged and that under no conditions would we accept the 'palliatives'[71] which constitute a very serious infringement of the Mandate (and immediately to express our condemnation of the latest piece of the Colonial Office's stupidity and of the illwill of the Palestine administration). By this we secure in a way our retreat to a situation in which the Mandate would still be considered valid, should the partition scheme fall through; it would be a

[68] These developments may be followed in: Namier to Shertok, 23 Feb. 1937, A312/55; Notes of a Zionist Conference, 15 Mar. 1937, WA; Notes of Meeting of London Political Advisory Committee, 14 Apr. 1937, A312/20; *Sharett Diaries* (Hebrew, Tel Aviv, 1968) for this period; and *Dugdale Diaries*.

[69] *Dugdale Diaries*, 22 June 1937.   [70] Ibid., 7 July 1937.

[71] In the event of partition proving unacceptable, the Commission recommended certain 'palliatives' as a second alternative. They included zonal restrictions for Jewish settlement; prohibition of land purchase in some areas; and a 'political high level' of 12,000 immigrants a year for the coming five years. See Cmd. 5479, 366–7.

deplorable position, but every possible safeguard must be retained. On the other hand we were careful to say nothing which would amount either to an immediate acceptance or rejection of the partition scheme.

While I did not want to neglect any possible safeguard, I consider that the Mandate is dead beyond all hope of revival; and that if we hitch ourselves to it, we shall be dead with it. The Mandate may still serve a legal purpose, but it has no political future. We may be right in asserting that it was not inherently unworkable, but the British Administration proved unable to work it . . . There is no other Power to whom, were it possible, we would wish to see the Mandate transferred—France would not take it, Italy we would not trust, America would mismanage it even worse than Gt. Britain; a small country such as Holland or Sweden could not possibly take it on. In short, my conclusion is that if Gt. Britain cannot work it, it cannot be worked at all.

. . . Wherever the fault may lie, people here are as sick of the kicks they have received for the Palestine Administration, as we are of the kicks we have received from that Administration. In the entire press there is not one voice advising the continuance of the Mandate in its old form. Please realise that if we were to reject the partition scheme, or if it failed clearly through our fault, we should lose the support of a great many of our best friends in this country.

This being so, we must make partition and a Jewish State the starting point of our reasoning and policy. The frontiers are certainly unsatisfactory, and so are many other proposals, (e.g., about the common port between Tel Aviv and Jaffa, the temporary and yet indefinite Mandate over the four towns, etc.).[72] All these things, which I hardly need to enumerate or stress in this letter (as I am sure we feel about them alike), we must fight for as hard as we can. None the less, in doing so, we ought to remember that a partition scheme satisfactory to us is the thing which we now must work for, and that a failure to secure such a scheme would leave us in a position more serious than we had ever contemplated in the past.

. . . I think we should stick to the truth and not finesse. I would tell the Government and the Commissioners at the earliest possible date that our group accepts the principle of partition and is prepared to support it before Congress; but that it would be impossible for us to carry it without these corrections, and very difficult if these corrections are only partially conceded.

Undoubtedly our future will be difficult even under the partition scheme; it

[72] The four town specifically referred to by Namier were Haifa, Acre, Safad, and Tiberius, all of which contained large Arab and Jewish communities. It was also proposed to include in the reduced British mandate a land corridor from Jerusalem and Bethlehem to Jaffa, including the towns of Lydda and Ramla, and Nazareth and the Sea of Galilee. It can hardly be doubted that these proposals were fashioned to meet British strategic requirements. The above areas gave the British control over almost the entire transport-communications system of Palestine, including the important Haifa bay area, with its oil installations, the vast supply camp at Sarafand, and the air-staging post to the Persian Gulf and the Far East on the Sea of Galilee.

will be impossible without it. Against one thing I strongly warn you: do not imagine for a moment that the British will wish to hang on to the Jewish State, to boss it, or be responsible for it. Some few officials may try to hang on to their jobs; but the feeling in this country is to shed responsibility for our State as soon as it possibly can. Gt. Britain will not be able to shed it altogether from the military point of view, because of Haifa, the pipe-line, and the British canton of Jerusalem; but otherwise will wish to get rid of the responsibilities, the difficulties, and the unpleasantness of the job. I assert this and I can claim to know the British better than any one of you; and this view is shared by Baffy. Altogether, we shall not get far if we start out with fears and anxieties and dire forebodings, and waste a great deal of time on imparting such thoughts and feelings to each other (when everyone's own imagination is quite equal to supplying them). We have to be severely pragmatic, determined and bold; see the facts, and act accordingly; and if things are unfavourable or difficult, we have to accept unchangeable circumstances as one accepts the weather.[73]

Weizmann had no quarrel with these sentiments. But he was in a sense acting in a vacuum. The British Government had not yet adopted the Peel recommendations. Nor, it must be remembered, had his own political constituency decided wholeheartedly to follow in his footsteps. Much would depend on the extent to which he succeeded in imposing his authority on the forthcoming Zionist Congress. Oppositionist views were loud and influential. Ben Gurion's attitude was of particular concern. He was by no means an enthusiastic adherent of partition, at least not at this stage of the game. While Weizmann and his group were canvassing support for partition in London, Ben Gurion was making 'foolish and intransigent speeches' in Palestine.[74] More than anyone else, he was responsible for the 'uproar' on 7 July when the British statement limiting immigration was received. To his demand that the Zionists break with Government—'We had fought the Romans . . . [and] we were going to fight this bloody British Government,' Namier had replied that 'it was not yet time for *katastrophenpolitik*. Mr Ben Gurion's line would lead to nothing; it would promote no solution for anybody or anything.'[75] Yet Ben Gurion was a difficult man to control. Temperamental, volatile, lacking all sense of proportion, supremely conscious of his position as leader of the Labour group, he was liable to shoot off at a tangent at the slightest provocation, real or

[73] Namier to Shertok, 9 July 1937, A312/21.
[74] *Dugdale Diaries*, 2 Mar. 1937 and 22 June 1937; also Notes of London Political Advisory Committee, 14 Apr. 1937. WA.
[75] Notes of a Zionist meeting, 7 July 1937, WA.

imagined. Even though Mrs Dugdale could write at the end of June that 'Ben Gurion will now stand or fall with Chaim',[76] doubts lingered on until Congress convened in August.[77]

At Congress Weizmann secured a considerable victory. By a two-thirds majority he was empowered to enter into negotiations with the Government to determine the precise conditions for the establishment of a Jewish state. Namier also basked in Weizmann's triumph. He had resumed his old position as Weizmann's adviser, briefing the Zionist leader, writing or translating reports, drafting speeches and lectures, lobbying support for his policies. It was a most gratifying experience, graphically expressed by Mrs Dugdale's ecstatic comments after Weizmann's keynote speech to Congress:

He spoke for two hours. It was not a speech—it was an inspired utterance. He will never rise to these heights again—we shall never hear the likes of it again. I do not know how much he got from the audience—which was swept by gusts of Hush-Hush-Hushing when some few were driven to a burst of hysterical applause. Looking back on yesterday, when Lewis and I were preparing a few poor bones of the skeleton which he brought to glorious life, I think one of the greatest moments of privilege of my life should be that when he came out to the balcony where we were working—apologized for interrupting—and said: 'Children, I shall probably put in a few words about Messianic hopes.' To have been near him, and perhaps a little help to him, in the days when he was preparing this, is an unforgettable thing. All felt like this.[78]

Namier, however, also suffered acute disappointment. Once again, the issue was his standing in the Zionist Organization. He believed that official recognition of his services could no longer be denied. But the same problem remained:

I spent all afternoon talking over with Brodetsky the question of the new London Executive, and the pros and cons of Lewis. He is very unpopular with some people—especially the E(nglish) Z(ionist) F(ederation), and Chaim will

[76] *Dugdale Diaries*, 29 June 1937.
[77] As late as 9 July he wrote in the *Daily Herald*: 'No Jew will accept Partition as a just and rightful solution . . . the proposal of the Royal Commission . . . is to put a drastic limit to the possibilities of a Jewish return, and to condemn the rest of the country to stagnation and desolation.' Of course, he was acting under the shock of the latest immigration proposals; and it can be argued that the article was merely a tactical ploy designed to put pressure on the Government. Even so, the unrestrained language betrayed a depth of feeling that went beyond mere political calculation. Whatever the interpretation, he remained an uneasy bedfellow.
[78] *Dugdale Diaries*, 4 Aug. 1937.

need to exert his influence if he really wants him. I think Henry Melchett,[79] Lewis and Brodetsky would on the whole be the best trio to help Chaim through the forthcoming negotiations—not that B. is much good for that, but he is a popular figure.[80]

Eventually Namier was excluded from the Executive. He accepted his defeat philosophically, no doubt interpreting it as a deliberate act of malice, typical of the petty-minded officials he so despised. He did not refuse to go on serving, 'But', as Mrs Dugdale remarked, 'the position is very difficult.'[81]

Despite this rebuff, he was included in a special Political Advisory Committee appointed by the Jewish Agency. Namier's friends went to some lengths to insist that his position had in fact been regularized.[82] As a member of the Committee he would certainly play a leading part in the formulation of policy in London. But he was perfectly aware that this was a poor substitute for a place on the Executive. After some hesitation he agreed to participate, mainly, it seems, because Mrs Dugdale was also co-opted on to the Committee, the first time she had agreed to serve on an official Zionist policy-making body.[83]

*   *   *

By the end of 1937 it was apparent that the British Government was retreating from its previous commitment to partition. Parliament had deferred judgement on the Report, instructing the Government to take the proposals to Geneva before presenting a 'definite scheme' to both Houses.[84] In September, Eden announced to the League that his Government intended to appoint a special commission to visit Palestine to draw up specific recommendations for partition.[85] This procrastination allowed the anti-partition forces to gather momentum. Particularly vocal among British representatives in the Arab world, they found sympathetic listeners in Whitehall. In November, the

[79] Henry Mond (1898–1949): industrialist; director of Imperial Chemical Industries, Barclay's Bank, etc.; Liberal MP, 1923–4, Conservative, 1929–30; chairman of Council of Jewish Agency, 1930. Succeeded as 2nd Baron Melchett, 1930.

[80] *Dugdale Diaries*, 10 Aug. 1937 (unpublished).

[81] *Dugdale Diaries*, 7 Sept. 1937.

[82] Ibid., 16 Sept, 1937 (unpublished).

[83] Mrs Dugdale was not included in the original list of Committee members [see CZA A312/21]. It was only at the end of September that she was asked if she would serve. She explained: [It is] the first time I have ever accepted a position on any Zionist body—but it seemed silly to refuse now that my advice is so much sought, and Lewis would not have worked without me as things are.' See *Dugdale Diaries*, 30 Sept. 1937.

[84] For the debates, see *PD Lords*, v. 106, c.599–674, and *Commons*, v. 326, c. 2235–367.

[85] See *The Times*, 15 Sept. 1937.

Foreign Office, always susceptible to Arab and Moslem pressure, and backed by the service ministers and the chiefs-of-staff, launched a powerful, and ultimately decisive, attack on partition.[86] The nature and object of this formidable combination were known to the Zionists. On paper they remained faithful to their commitment to partition; but this did not exclude the formulation of alternative proposals should partition eventually be abandoned. It was Ben Gurion who first drafted a substitute programme.[87] The linchpin of his scheme was that 'A sovereign, independent Palestine State' should be established in which 'complete autonomy' would be granted 'to all communities'. In this way 'A Jewish National Home but not a Jewish state' would be guaranteed.[88] Dealing with the delicate problem of immigration, he made an even more radical suggestion. 'The maximum Jewish population of Palestine and later of Trans-Jordan shall not exceed an agreed figure which shall be less than 50 per cent of the total population.' For Ben Gurion this was a natural retreat to the position he had held before the Peel recommendations. We have no evidence indicating how Namier reacted to Ben Gurion's initiative, but the Zionist leadership, Namier included, now began to consider in earnest the possibilities of a federal Palestine with an independent Jewish state as one of its constituent parts. A year later, Namier approached Mrs Dugdale with 'a rather vague plan for a "group" to push the idea of a Jewish State among Federated Arab States'. Mrs Dugdale, 'frightened of "groups" who run policies on their own', poured cold water on the plan; but the federal idea re-emerged later, in the summer of 1939, in vastly changed circumstances.[89]

*   *   *

[86] For details, see *The Gentile Zionists*, 151-2.

[87] See his letter to Namier, with enclosure containing his nine-point plan, 8 Dec. 1937, CZA A312/22.

[88] These linguistic nuances, perhaps incomprehensible to the uninitiated, were an essential, if exaggerated, part of the rhetoric of the dispute. How did Ben Gurion himself define the difference between a Jewish National Home and a Jewish State? In January 1937, he told the Peel Commissioners that the term National Home embraced a conception larger than the term Jewish State. A State, he continued, implied domination over the Arabs which the Jews did not want. It also insinuated a separate political entity which, Ben Gurion clarified, was contrary to the wishes of the Jews who preferred to remain connected with the British Commonwealth. See report of proceedings in *Jewish Chronicle*, 15 Jan. 1937.

[89] See *Dugdale Diaries*, 6 July 1938, 16 Sept. 1938, 5 Dec. 1938 [unpublished]. Namier's 'group' included Capt. Orde Wingate, and the scheme he referred to was in fact known as 'the Wingate plan'. This may well explain Mrs Dugdale's reluctance to become involved. She always distrusted Wingate's political activity and judgement.

Eden's special body, the Woodhead Commission, reported in October 1938. The Zionists had never been happy with its appointment. Despite their efforts to obtain wider terms of reference for the Commission, it had only concerned itself with the technical aspects of partition. Dubbed by them 'the Re-Peel Commission', its report confirmed all their worst expectations. Unable to recommend viable frontiers for either a Jewish or Arab state, it produced three alternative schemes none of which was acceptable to the Zionists.[90] The Commission's deliberations were enacted against a background of increased international tension. In the Far East the Japanese, now involved in a war with China, were threatening vital British interests. In Europe, Austria had fallen to Germany in March, while throughout the summer the Czech crisis simmered until it reached its dramatic conclusion in September. It was not difficult to foresee how these events would affect British policy towards Palestine. Clearly there was an overriding need to avoid either a military or political confrontation with any group which could jeopardize British strategic interests in the area. In this context, the Zionists had little leverage, at least when compared with an Arab and Muslim world which stretched from Egypt to India. Certainly by the summer of 1938 the Zionists were perfectly aware that the Government had in effect abandoned partition. This could only mean a return to the mandate on terms totally unacceptable to them. The general feeling in Zionist circles was that they, like the Czechs, were about to be sacrificed on the altar of appeasement in the name of greater things.

Namier's reaction to these developments was understandably bitter. 'We must not allow ourselves to be patted on the back, and at the same time betrayed', he told a Zionist conference.[91] At the same time, following Ben Gurion's example, he rejected Weizmann's highly emotional response which in all but name called for a break with the British Government: 'We should not emotionally fix our policy at this stage in any final direction. In our dangerous situation we could not afford to do it. Moreover to show a break to-day to the world would be to bring catastrophe upon the Jews even more quickly.' Of course, he was under no illusion as to the direction British policy was taking; nor did he bother to hide his disgust at the lack of backbone his former pupil, Malcolm MacDonald, now Colonial Secretary, displayed. But it was not until the winter months, with the approach of the St. James's Conference, that his policy hardened. By this time, however,

[90] See 'The Palestine Partition Report', Cmd. 5854 (Oct. 1938).
[91] Minutes of the Conference, 26 Sept. 1938, WA.

Weizmann had reconsidered his position, so that once again they found themselves on opposite sides of the fence.

*   *   *

Weizmann still remained the undisputed leader of the Zionist movement. In the field of Anglo-Zionist relations in particular he towered head-and-shoulders above any of his contemporaries or rivals. But time had taken its toll. The wear and tear of so many years of tension had left their mark. He was more nervous, more easily agitated, far more prone to emotional outbursts than in the past. Perhaps also he sensed that his long and distinguished period of leadership was approaching its end. He had led the Zionist movement to its greatest triumphs, could he now save it from impending disaster? All this, compounded by his lack of administrative discipline, reflected on his powers of leadership. Repeatedly he clashed with his closest advisers. Mrs Dugdale, who was in the unique position of universal confidante, recorded the process. At times she had seen Weizmann so infuriated that all work in the Zionist Office had to cease while 'all tried to soothe him'. 'Chaim calmer', she noted later with obvious relief. Deploring his inability to co-operate with any outspoken colleagues, she sadly concluded that he was 'a *bad* team driver. They all feel some grievance.'[92]

Even Mrs Dugdale was not immune from Weizmann's suspicions; and naturally Namier was somehow involved in the incident:

To Zionist Office for a conference. But Chaim spoke to me beforehand in a most extraordinary manner—about 'a cloud' between us. Also declared that Vera had said to him that I had told her that Namier had criticized Chaim as being 'weak' with Malcolm [MacDonald]. There is not one word of truth or substance in this, and I was terribly upset that Chaim should be ready to swallow an allegation that I was making mischief between him and Namier. But what can Vera have said—and *why*? Why Chaim's sudden unmistakeable suspicion and hostility towards me. All this is like a bolt from the blue! At the Conference it was decided not to break on the 10,000 children,[93] but to issue a statement

---

[92] *Dugdale Diaries*, 2 Mar. 1937; 23 Sept. 1937 [unpublished]; 17 Oct. 1938 [unpublished]; 31 Aug. 1939.

[93] This concerned the fate of 10,000 German and Austrian children whom the Zionists wished to absorb in Palestine. An emotional issue at the best of times, it assumed a particular significance after the pogrom in Germany of 8–9 November. Initially, both Weizmann and Namier argued that the Zionists should boycott the forthcoming tripartite conference unless the British acceded to their demands. Weizmann later retracted; Namier held firm to his original position, seeing in it a test of British good faith. Despite Zionist pressure, the Government refused the children entry into Palestine, but they did relent sufficiently to allow them into England.

which Stein will prepare. Chaim's violent animosity against Lewis burst forth in black rage.

On going home, I wrote both to Chaim and Vera, saying I must make it clear for Lewis's sake that he never made any such remark as that attributed to him. I also told them that I thought we had better not try to meet until after I came back from Scotland. I told Chaim I had advised Lewis to withdraw from trying to work with Chaim. It is obviously no good. All this nearly did me in.

Four days later, the situation had improved: 'Had talk with Lewis, who has had long talk with Chaim. This miserable misunderstanding had better be left behind.'[94]

Whatever Vera's motives for relaying this piece of gossip, it was undeniably true that serious differences now divided Weizmann from Namier, differences which they hardly bothered to conceal from the British Government. Malcolm MacDonald, after discussing the future of the London Conference with both of them, reported to the Cabinet: 'I came away with the impression that Dr. Weizmann had been a bit shaken, but that Professor Namier was more firmly convinced than ever that the Jews should wash their hands completely of any responsibility for the London discussions.'[95] Whether Namier was openly critical of Weizmann at this stage is not clear, but it is beyond doubt that in the coming weeks he became increasingly perturbed and vocal at Weizmann's lack of firmness in presenting the Zionist case.

The decision to go to Conference was taken on 16 December, against the advice of Namier and Mrs Dugdale.[96] Weizmann had the last word: 'It was in the Jewish interest to participate in the Conference however terrible the situation was. He was not going to endanger the slender chance of drawing from the Conference what he could by refusing the invitation now.' Namier replied that 'unless Dr. Weizmann would break off with full conviction that he was doing right, he would not try to persuade him. He thought that it was a mistake to go into the Conference, but the man at the wheel must be convinced that we were on the right road.' So the situation stood until, after much hesitation on the Arab side, the conference opened at St. James's Palace on 7 February 1939.

[94] See *Dugdale Diaries*, 16 and 20 Dec. 1938.
[95] See his note of 16 Dec. 1938, FO 372/21869, E.7200/1/31.
[96] Notes of the meeting CZA A312/23. In the recorded minutes only Namier and Mrs Dugdale came out strongly against participation; Brodetsky wavered, while Shertok merely informed those present of the 'anti' sentiments of the *Yishuv*.

The net effect of the conference, which continued until mid-March, was to polarize the existing attitudes of the parties concerned. The Arabs, in a sense, were silent spectators, content to observe the verbal battles fought between the British and the Jews.[97] There was something inherently false about the whole situation. The magnificent setting of the Royal Palace, the punctiliousness of the opening sessions, the stiff formality of the occasion, all served to mark the distasteful fact that the main decisions had in fact already been taken, in principle if not in detail. Throughout the discussions the Jews were on the defensive, though they took 'All the dialectical honours.'[98] Almost from the outset they were debating whether or not to break the conference. Namier too was of this opinion, hoping that the Government would run after the side which broke first. Only Weizmann, who 'looked, and is, tired', was 'unwilling to break, and may easily take a line of his own'.[99] His behaviour caused much concern. Namier told Mrs Dugdale that 'the criticisms of Chaim's conduct of the negotiations were widespread—far too weak, many points going by default, and a subservient manner.'[100] One knowledgeable observer, Peter Rutenberg, remarked that Weizmann 'was "all broken to pieces" . . . but must be preserved in leadership as "there is no other Weizmann"!'[101]

Namier, who had obtained a short leave of absence from Manchester University to attend the conference, was a member of Weizmann's

[97] Delegates from Egypt, Iraq, Saudi Arabia, Yemen, and Transjordan attended the conference. The Palestinians, who were divided by the violent feud between the Nashashibis and the Husseinis, the two main Palestinian factions, only succeeded in presenting a so-called united front at the last moment. As the Arabs refused to talk directly to the Jews, [there were informal talks, though not with the Palestinians] the British by default became the spokesmen for the Arab case. From the Zionist viewpoint this proved disastrous, for they found it increasingly difficult to differentiate between the Arab and the British case. And the Government's final proposals, even though they proved unacceptable to the Arabs, seemed to substantiate this assumption.

[98] *Dugdale Diaries*, 11 Feb. 1939.   [99] Ibid., 20 and 21 Feb. 1939.

[101] *Dugdale Diaries*, 25 Feb. 1939. During the war, Namier told the following story to Lady Namier to illustrate Weizmann's inability to cope with the rapidly changing situation of the late 1930s. 'To me he wrily explained the nature of the catastrophe by telling a Jewish story. A father and son were going to market in a cart. They drove in turns, till an altercation boiled up over what to do with the anticipated proceeds of their sales. To use his hands more expressively in argument, whichever was then driving stopped the cart and dropped the reins. Next both clambered out to gesticulate with even greater abandon. Only after an agreement had been reached did they turn round to remount the cart. But it had long since driven off, unmanned. Father and son missed the great day's market altogether. During World War Two the cart of Imperial and Middle East policies drove off leaving Weizmann stranded.' (From Lady Namier's Notes.)

advisory 'Panel', the chief Jewish deliberative body.[102] This committee acted purely in an advisory capacity. The main political decisions were taken by the Jewish Agency executive which met more frequently than the unwieldy Panel and which co-opted members, Namier being the most prominent example, for the actual conduct of the negotiations. He was therefore intimately involved in all the twists and turns of the discussions, both on an official and unofficial level, and quite convinced, by the end of February, that the Conference had run into a dead end. The day the Conference collapsed, he expressed his revulsion for the proceedings to a former academic colleague:

The Palestine Conference was a downright torture to me; I have suffered as a Jew and felt ashamed as a British subject. It was worse than Munich—a Munich even without the excuse of danger. As for meanness in tactics, it could hardly have been exceeded. They tried to bully and frighten us into accepting their betrayal of promises. It was almost like the Nazis in a concentration camp: when they beat up someone then make him sign that he has been well-treated and that nothing has happened. Thus my dear friend Malcolm wanted us to testify: agreement all round, smiles, good-fellowship, sandwiches and orangeade (and even their orangeade was not made of Palestinian oranges but some nasty Spanish stuff). I have never been so much disappointed in any human being as I am in Malcolm . . .

I don't want to see any more ministers, politicians or anyone of that tribe. Their consciences and their smiles are all made of rubber, and I don't think you will be astonished if I tell you that the Holy Fox [Halifax] who continually turns his eyes to heaven and seems to look to the angels for advice, is no better than the rest . . .[103]

After the war, Namier recalled the atmosphere of futility which had enveloped the proceedings: 'I often wondered why he [MacDonald] did not read out to us *Alice In Wonderland* or *Bradshaw*; either would have made a nice long speech, would have been restful, and for relevancy would have equalled some of his own performances.'[104]

The final session took place on 15 March. Weizmann and Ben Gurion boycotted the meeting; the nature of the Government's final proposals was such as to make their presence undignified. Further co-operation between the Zionists and the Government was now quite impossible.

---

[102] Its official title was the Palestine Conference Discussion Committee. It included representatives of the Jewish Agency, *Aguduth Yisrael* [the religious groups], and Anglo-Jewry, known as 'the Lords'.

[103] Namier to A. J. P. Taylor, 15 Mar. 1939. The author is grateful to Miss Constance Babington Smith for allowing him to use this letter which is in her possession.

[104] See *Diplomatic Prelude* (London, 1948), 3.

Immigration was to be restricted to a maximum of 75,000 for the coming five-year period, and then renewed only with Arab consent; crippling restrictions on land sales were envisaged; and finally, a constitution would be drawn up by a Palestine National Assembly in which an Arab majority was assured. These proposals were refined, though not substantially altered, and published on 17 May, a document which achieved instant notoriety as 'the May White Paper'.[105]

At a meeting of the Jewish Agency executive in April, Namier, in his customary blunt and trenchant manner, expounded on the current situation:

> they should not delude themselves. They did not count as a military force. The government regarded the Arabs as indispensable and the Jews not . . . They were in a bad position just now. There were times when one had to work carefully for a small aim. He would like nothing to happen which was not likely to change afterwards. Everything would work against them if they had no policy . . . He did not think that even Mr Churchill would worry very much about their affairs at the present moment. They must realize that in the present circumstances they were only a small problem, and that the most important thing was the action to be taken vis-a-vis the totalitarian states.[106]

But in fact the Zionists had no convincing policy to offer. The publication of the May White Paper shattered whatever remained of their relationship with the Government. For Namier it personified the 'Drivel, Fuddle and Bungling' which had characterized British policy since Munich.[107] Others viewed the document as a 'sort of mental and moral aberration' brought on by the current international crisis and destined to disappear once that crisis had been resolved.[108] But the

---

[105] See 'Palestine: A Statement of Policy', Cmd. 6079 (May 1939).

[106] From the minutes of the meeting, 13 Apr. 1939, CZA A312/29. These events must be placed in their correct international context. Since Munich, tension in Europe had never slackened. From the beginning of 1939 rumours had been persistent that Germany was about to embark on a new foreign adventure. On 15 March, the same day that the St. James's conference collapsed, the Germans occupied Prague; a week later they entered Memel. On 7 April the Italians invaded Albania. The British Government, searching for an adequate response, had, during these weeks, taken some startling foreign policy initiatives, attempting to construct a diplomatic barrier in eastern Europe against further German or Italian aggression. Naturally, these great affairs of state took precedence over an issue that, however complex, must have appeared, at least in cabinet ministers' eyes, as a marginal problem. This was a perspective often overlooked by some Zionists, weighed down by the enormity of the Jewish tragedy in Europe.

[107] See Sir C. Coote, *Companion of Honour. The Story of Walter Elliot* (London, 1965), 184.

[108] For a fuller discussion of the implications of the May White Paper, see *The Gentile Zionists*, 208–10, and the author's introduction to *The Letters of Chaim Weizmann, 1939–40* (Jerusalem, 1979).

contents of the paper and the manner in which it had been forced on the Zionists prohibited any further co-operation. Nowhere was this more apparent than in their relationship with Malcolm MacDonald, once a good friend but now an utterly despised figure. Namier demolished MacDonald in a style very much his own. The following story, perhaps apocryphal, is nevertheless quite typical.

I spoke to him [MacDonald]. I began with a jest. 'I said that in the eighteenth century peers made their tutors Under Secretaries, whereas in the twentieth Under Secretaries made their tutors peers. He did not seem to understand. I did not bother to explain.'[109] Then I said something he would understand. I said to him, 'Malcolm'—he is, you know, still Malcolm to me—I know him quite well—'I am writing a new book.' He said, 'What is it, Lewis?' I replied, 'I will tell you what it is. I have called it The Two MacDonalds: A Study in Treachery' . . .[110]

In these last months before the outbreak of the war, the main weight of Zionist diplomacy focused on reviving the federal option. The chances of reversing the Government's decision were, in any event, slender. They disappeared entirely with the announcement of the Soviet–German non-aggression pact on 22 August, an event which convinced even the most naïve of observers that war was inevitable. When Namier heard the news he declared himself ready to fly out at once to Geneva, where the twenty-first Zionist Congress was in session, and bring back a declaration of world Jewry's determination to support Great Britain through thick and thin.[111] On 29 August Weizmann sent a letter, drafted by Namier and Mrs Dugdale, to Chamberlain, pledging that the Jews will 'stand by Great Britain and will fight on the side of the democracies'. He continued: '[we] place ourselves in matters big and small under the co-ordinating direction of His Majesty's Government. The Jewish Agency is ready to enter into immediate arrangements for utilizing Jewish manpower, technical abilities, resources, etc.'[112] Chamberlain replied on 2 September, after the German attack on Poland, in a stiff and cool manner which did not augur well for the future.[113] Nevertheless, Namier was convinced that his strategy was

---

[109] Sir Isaiah Berlin clarified this obscure point. 'Only Namier would have supposed that the average educated Englishman (or Scotsman) would realise that he was referring to the fact that the philosopher Locke had been made an Under Secretary by his ex-pupil, Lord Shaftesbury, and that Mr Godfrey Elton, who had been Malcolm MacDonald's tutor at Queen's college, Oxford, had recently been elevated to the peerage.'

[110] Sir I. Berlin.   [111] Lady Namier's Notes.

[112] Weizmann to Chamberlain, 29 Aug. 1939, WA.

[113] Chamberlain to Weizmann, 2 Sept. 1939, WA.

correct, and despite much provocation from the Government, he never
wavered from it throughout the war. Mrs Dugdale recorded: 'Lewis
would subordinate all Jewish affairs now to an allied victory. He would
not resist any measure that brought Arabs to our side though he does not
believe they would be dependable.'[114]

*   *   *

With the outbreak of war Namier decided to put his personal affairs in
order. In mid-September he prepared a will. He requested that, in the
event of his death, all his property should be realized 'and the proceeds
invested in debentures of the Keren Kayemeth [Jewish National
Fund]'.[115] He made one main provision: that any income arising from
the investment should be used to provide for Marie Beer, then
hospitalized in a mental ward in Friern Hospital, New Southgate.[116] It
was an act of generosity somehow out of keeping with his abrasive
public image. But he clearly felt a moral responsibility for Miss Beer's
welfare, and he continued to provide for her until her death in February
1945. Namier now turned his full attention to the war and how best to
utilize Jewish resources in the struggle against Nazi Germany.

[114] *Dugdale Diaries*, 9 Sept. 1939 [unpublished].
[115] Namier to Arthur Lourie, 22 Sept. 1939. The author is grateful to the late Mr Lourie
for allowing him access to a copy of this letter. Namier named Mr Lourie as his executor.
[116] For Namier's relations with Miss Beer, see p. 68.

Chapter 4

War

For the first month of the war Namier remained in London, reluctant to return to his university duties in Manchester. He had no doubt where his duty lay. When summoned back to Manchester he behaved 'like a Prima Donna about our efforts to get him out of it'.[1] It took the hurried intervention of Weizmann and R. A. Butler[2] before the university authorities agreed to release him for 'work of national importance'.[3] His official task was to act as a liaison officer between the Jewish Agency and those Government departments—the Foreign Office, the Colonial Office, the War Office, the Admiralty—responsible for the formulation of Britain's Palestine policy.

No sooner had Namier settled down at 77 Great Russell Street, than he was involved in one of the more outlandish attempts to resolve the Palestine question, the so-called Philby[4] scheme. Namier had known Philby fleetingly for some time. At the end of September they chanced to meet at the Athenaeum. Philby was too committed an Arabist for Namier ever fully to trust him, but he listened attentively to Philby's grandiose vision of future Arab–Jewish co-operation which turned chiefly on granting Ibn Saud a dominant role in a future Arab federation and massive Jewish economic aid to Saudi Arabia. Although sceptical, Namier thought it worthwhile to pursue the matter further, and arranged a luncheon meeting between Philby, Weizmann, and Shertok:

Philby's idea was that western Palestine should be handed over completely to the Jews, clear of Arab population except for a 'Vatican City' in the old city of

---

[1] *Dugdale Diaries*, 4 Oct. 1939 [unpublished].

[2] Richard Austin Butler (1902–   ): Conservative MP, 1929–65; Under-Secretary of State for Foreign Affairs, 1938–41; Minister of Education, 1941–5; Minister of Labour, 1945; Chancellor of the Exchequer, 1951–5; Lord Privy Seal, 1955–9; Home Secretary, 1957–62; Deputy Prime Minister, 1962–3; Foreign Secretary, 1963–4; Master of Trinity College, Cambridge since 1965. Created Baron, 1965.

[3] See Weizmann to Professor John S. B. Stopford, Vice-Chancellor of Manchester University, 5 Oct. 1939, WA.

[4] Harry St. John ('Jack') Bridger Philby (1885–1960): Indian civil servant and explorer; confidant to Ibn Saud, king of Saudi Arabia. Converted to Islam and adopted the name Abdullah.

Jerusalem. In return the Jews should try to secure for the Arabs national unity and independence as, according to him, was promised in the MacMahon–Hussein correspondence;[5] moreover extensive financial help should be given to the Arabs by the Jews. Such unity could be achieved under Ibn Saud alone [6]

Weizmann was prepared to consider the 'economic advantages'—Philby mentioned the sum of £20 million—but he was unable to undertake any binding political promises as 'we had not the power "to deliver the goods" '; nor would he consider any action which 'might conflict with our loyalties towards Great Britain and France'. It was agreed to explore the issue more thoroughly, Weizmann with his supporters in the United States and England, Philby with Ibn Saud in Saudi Arabia.

Nothing materialized from these parleys, although both sides remained in contact until the end of 1943. Throughout, Philby displayed great confidence in his ability to persuade the king of the benefits which would accrue from his plan. But Ibn Saud refused to be drawn into any meaningful negotiations, despite hints of British approval and eventual American intervention in the affair. Finally, at the end of 1943, he withdrew his support, at the best of times lukewarm, from Philby's initiative. The Zionists' attitude was mixed, though not entirely negative: Shertok barely disguised his scepticism, while

---

[5] See Cmd. 5957, *The Text of the Correspondence between Sir Henry MacMahon and the Sherif Hussein of Mecca, July 1915–March 1916*; also Cmd. 5974, *Report of a Committee Set Up to Consider Certain Correspondence between Sir Henry MacMahon and the Sherif of Mecca in 1915 and 1916.*
The tortuous language of the Correspondence invited political and historical controversy, particularly over the Palestine issue, and the argument has raged to this very day. Arab apologists contend that MacMahon 'pledged' Palestine as part of a great Arab state destined to arise at the end of the First World War in return for Arab participation in the war against Turkey. The British, supported throughout by the Zionists, consistently and resolutely denied this interpretation, claiming that it had never been their intention to include 'Palestine' or the 'more northern coastal tracts of Syria' in an Arab state [see Sir Henry MacMahon to J. Shuckburgh, 12 Mar. 1922, CO 733/38/13471]. A close reading of the Correspondence bears out the British version. For the latest, and most convincing contribution to the debate, see E. Kedourie, *In the Anglo-Arab Labyrinth* (Cambridge University Press, 1976).
[6] Records of meetings, 26 Sept. and 6 Oct. 1939, CZA A312/27; also minutes of a meeting 16 Nov. 1943, WA; and meetings in Jan. 1944, CZA A312/39. For Philby's account see *Arabian Jubilee* (London, 1952), 212–13. His biographer, Elizabeth Monroe, refers to an earlier meeting on the same topic in Feb. 1939 during the St. James's conference [see *Philby of Arabia* (London, 1973), 219], although Philby himself makes no mention of this meeting. The Philby episode has been further examined in R. W. Zweig, 'British Policy to Palestine, May 1939 to 1943. The Fate of the White Paper' (unpublished Ph.D. thesis, Cambridge, 1978), 276–80; and M. J. Cohen, *Palestine, Retreat from Mandate* (London, 1978).

Weizmann and Namier were more inclined to grasp at this flimsy straw. Indeed, from their viewpoint, any scheme which promised them 'western Palestine' was immensely attractive, particularly as both Britain and the United States proved receptive of the idea, or at least did not reject it outright. No doubt as a result of these considerations, Namier, together with Mrs Dugdale, drew up a fairly detailed contingency plan which incorporated the chief elements of Philby's original proposal.[7] The Zionists might also have hoped to profit from the long-standing feud between Ibn Saud and the Hashemite kingdoms of Iraq and Transjordan. During the disturbances of 1936, all three countries had intervened in Palestine, though for conflicting reasons, to bring the Arab general strike to an end. This precedent, viewed with the utmost alarm by the Zionists, led to the so-called Arabization of the Palestine question, a development markedly visible at the St. James's conference, and one which worked to the detriment of the Zionists. Allowing Ibn Saud a more decisive role in the question would clearly have had the effect of heightening inter-Arab rivalries, diverting Hashemite eyes, whether from Baghdad or Amman, away from Jerusalem. Saudi Arabia, geographically and politically more remote from Palestine, might conceivably have been a more reliable and moderate partner than the more overtly nationalist and ambitious Governments of Iraq and Transjordan. This reasoning, logical and persuasive to the Zionist mind, found no echo in Ibn Saud's ultimate decision to reject the Zionist overtures.

*　　*　　*

The Philby episode was in fact of marginal significance to the great issue which still divided the Zionists from the British Government. The White Paper continued to poison relations between them. In the early stages of the war, Namier had expressed the opinion that 'all Jewish affairs' should be subordinated 'to an allied victory'.[8] But he found this viewpoint increasingly difficult to sustain in face of the British determination to proceed with the White Paper policy almost at any price. When Namier met Butler at the Foreign Office he made it clear that the Zionists considered the White Paper to be 'in abeyance'. Butler himself hardly reacted, but Namier's turn of phrase provoked a stinging rejoinder from MacDonald who firmly denied Namier's interpretation

[7] See the 'Namier-Baffy scheme', 13 Nov. 1939, CZA A312/27.
[8] See p. 93.

and reminded his colleagues that the Colonial Office, not the Foreign Office, was the correct channel of communication between the Jewish Agency and the Government.[9]

The first major confrontation occurred over the promulgation of the land transfer regulations of the White Paper in February 1940. For some time there had been unmistakable signs that the Government would not hesitate to implement the regulations. Zionist anxiety was compounded by the severity of the Government's immigration policy. Since September the number of immigrants had been drastically reduced, culminating in the cancellation of the Jewish quotas for the six months' period October 1939–March 1940.[10] Although the majority of immigrants tended to settle in the urban conurbations, there was an obvious link between land and immigration policies. The Zionists were already planning in terms of a future mass Jewish immigration of millions,[11] an unattainable aim unless sufficient land was made available. At the end of November Weizmann, on the eve of a trip to the United States, wrote to Halifax:[12]

Is the land law to be promulgated, or is it for the time being to remain in abeyance? Are the Jews in Palestine to be treated as suspects, or as people whose loyalties and readiness to serve deserve to be encouraged? Are political considerations rooted in the White Paper to be allowed to defeat schemes of practical assistance in the conduct of the war, or are British war interests to prevail.[13]

Halifax's reply must have shattered whatever hopes Weizmann had entertained that the Government might nullify its policy. In an abrupt, uncompromising letter he ruled that 'It is not possible to modify or postpone the application of the white paper policy.' He went on:

So far as this country is concerned, we are putting our whole energy into a life-and-death struggle with Nazi Germany, the persecutor of Jewry in Central

---

[9] Minutes of meeting, 6 Nov. 1939, FO 371/23251, E7471/7471/31, E7472/7472/31.

[10] See Namier's minutes of 21 Nov. 1939, FO 371/24096, W.17965/1369/48.

[11] Lord Moyne reported to the cabinet on 2 Oct. 1941 that Weizmann was talking in terms of an immigration of three million Jews after the war, see CAB 65/19.

[12] Edward Fredrick Lindley Wood (1881–1959): Conservative MP, 1910–34; Viceroy of India 1926–31; Lord Privy Seal, 1935–7; Lord President of Council, 1937–8; Foreign Secretary, 1938–40; Ambassador to United States, 1941–6. Created Baron, 1925. Succeeded as 3rd Viscount Halifax, 1934.

[13] Weizmann to Halifax, 30 Nov. 1939, WA.

Europe, and by riding Europe of the present German regime we hope to render a supreme service to the Jewish people.[14]

The logic of Halifax's argument, no doubt soothing to his colleagues' consciences, left the Zionists unmoved. Nevertheless, it highlighted the insuperable dilemma which confronted the Jewish Agency, a dilemma from which they never fully escaped until the end of the war. Strategically, both parties claimed a common goal: the defeat of Nazi Germany. Yet they found little or no common ground to define the Jewish contribution towards the realization of that goal. No matter how much pressure the Jewish Agency exerted, or how convincingly the Zionists argued their case, they were ultimately dependent upon the goodwill of the British Government. Ben Gurion's celebrated slogan— 'We shall fight the White Paper as if there were no war, and the war as if there were no White Paper'—betrayed a fundamental weakness in the Zionist position, despite its inspiring rhetoric.

It was decided to canvass support among those ministers sympathetic to the Zionist cause. Churchill was the obvious target. His speech to the Commons in May 1939 denouncing the White Paper had earned Weizmann's special praise;[15] and he had never concealed his intense dislike of the anti-Zionist policy adopted by the Government. Moreover, since the outbreak of the war his political standing had risen enormously. If anyone could mount a successful counter-attack against the White Paper, it was surely Churchill. As a first move, Namier approached Brendan Bracken,[16] Churchill's aide. By the beginning of January it appeared as though Churchill had intervened decisively:

He [Brenden Bracken] then said that M(alcolm) M(acdonald) had had a 'thorough trimming', but that we must not crow over him—nothing must be known about his defeat. Winston had pointed out the reduced majority on the White Paper,[17] and had reminded his colleagues of the fact that he had opposed

[14] Halifax to Weizmann, 19 Dec. 1939, WA.

[15] Weizmann wrote to him: 'Your magnificent speech may yet destroy this policy, words fail to express my thanks', tel., 23 May 1939, WA.

[16] Brenden Bracken (1901–1958): Conservative MP 1929–51; Parliamentary Secretary to Churchill, 1940–1; Minister of Information, 1941–5; First Lord of the Admiralty, 1945. Created Viscount, 1952. Churchill appointed Bracken as his liaison with the Zionists on 20 Sept. (See *Dugdale Diaries*.)

[17] The Government had clearly suffered a vote of no-confidence. Even though the House divided on a three-line whip, its majority was cut dramatically from 248 to 89. In passing, it is of interest to note that the Government's majority in the White Paper debate was only eight more than in the debate over the Norwegian campaign in May 1940, a vote which led to the fall of the Chamberlain administration.

it. Now no important legislation or administrative action is to be taken in Palestine without the War Cabinet. M.M. had finished by admitting the wisdom of what Winston had said.[18]

Bracken had greatly exaggerated the extent of MacDonald's 'thorough trimming', and the Zionists were only too eager to swallow his optimistic evaluation. Opposition to the Government materialized from two sources: Churchill; and the American Zionists, who had made fierce and untactful representations to the Government. As a consequence of these entreaties, the Cabinet, at MacDonald's prompting, had consented to postpone further action on the land question for about two weeks, sufficient time to enable the Colonial Secretary to marshal his facts and present his case in as convincing a manner as possible. During the Cabinet discussions Churchill vigorously opposed the legislation. He wished, as he put it, to dispel any ambiguity regarding his position; but at the same time he refused to press his opposition to the point of a Cabinet split. This was not the most credible of arguments, and predictably he found no support among his colleagues. Chatfield,[19] with his eye on imperial communications, posited that nothing must be done to upset the stability of the area, while Halifax argued that it would be a positive development to slow down intensive cultivation as there was the distinct danger of over-production of citrus fruits![20] On 12 February the Land Regulations were approved in Cabinet.[21] The comparative ease with which Churchill's challenge had been mastered signalled an ominous portent of things to come.

---

[18] Namier to Mrs Dugdale, 2 Jan. 1940, CZA A312/44; see also *Dugdale Diaries*, 28 Dec. 1939.

[19] (Alfred) Ernle (Montacute) Chatfield (1873–1967): First Sea Lord, 1933–8; Admiral of the Fleet, 1935; Minister for Co-ordination for Defence, 1939–40. Kn. 1919. Created Baron, 1937.

[20] Halifax's point, though put in a perverse way, was perfectly valid. From 1938 until well into the war there had been a catastrophic drop in the export of citrus fruits, the figure falling from $15\frac{1}{4}$ million cases to 4,500 in 1943 (these figures do not include the fruit bought by the Government for the armed services in the area). See *ESCO Foundation: A Study of Jewish, Arab and British Policies* (Yale University Press, 1947), ii, 1056. The root of the problem however was not over-production but lack of markets, particularly in Europe. Perhaps in Halifax's view these were two sides of the same coin, but his emphasis revealed an unfortunate political connotation.

[21] The minutes of the Cabinet discussions for 27 Dec. 1939, and 16 Jan. and 12 Feb. 1940, are in CAB 65/2, 5. For Halifax's memorandum, 20 Dec. 1939, WP (G) 101, see CAB 67/3; for Churchill's, 25 Dec. 1939, WP (G) 163, CAB 67/3; and for MacDonald's answer, 5 Jan. 1940, WP (G) (40) 3, CAB 67/3.

The Land Transfer Regulations were promulgated on 25 February 1940. They constituted a devastating, in theory fatal, blow to Zionist plans. Out of an estimated total of 10,429 square miles only 519 were set aside for unrestricted Jewish land purchases, and these included the large urban areas of Haifa, Tel Aviv, and Jerusalem.[22] The Regulations roused the *Yishuv* to new heights of indignation. For six consecutive days mass demonstrations, often dispersed in the most brutal manner, were held throughout the country. One incident in particular attracted attention, that of a seventeen-year-old youth, Menahem Privas, who had died in Hadassah hospital, Jerusalem, from multiple skull fractures.[23] The Government, upholding the explanations of the Palestine administration, rejected Weizmann's demand for a judicial enquiry 'into the outrages'. No action was ever taken. Weizmann, in a phrase which illustrated the helplessness of his position, reserved the right to publish reports of police brutalities as soon 'as this can be done without injury to our common cause'.[24] These wretched events, according to Lady Namier, 'turned Namier's grief to perpetual gloom'.[25] But they failed to silence him. Responding to MacDonald's defence of the Regulations in the House, he had the last, and quite characteristic word:

There were members of the Government side who by their votes in May and July [1939] had shown that they were doubtful about the White Paper policy. There were others irritated at the pertinacious Jews who would not cheerfully sacrifice their last and oldest hope when requested to do so. Mr. MacDonald soothed uneasy consciences. He earned gratitude. The atmosphere was reminiscent of the days of Godesberg and Munich. Justice had been shown once more to coincide with a supposed British interest. And the scene was dominated by Mr. MacDonald, an artistic, a magnificent skater. With supreme skill he

[22] Although the Regulations had a serious effect, they by no means brought to a halt Jewish land purchases. Legal and other loopholes were discovered which enabled the Jews to continue to acquire land in the prohibited and restricted areas, though on a reduced scale. Various sources estimate that during the war Jewish land possessions increased by approximately 245,000 dunams. See *ESCO*, 940–1; Zweig, 3; B. Wasserstein, *Britain and the Jews of Europe. 1939–45* (Clarendon Press, Oxford, 1979), 19.

[23] MacDonald stated in the House on 13 Mar. 1940 that during the demonstrations 74 Jews and 5 British policemen were seriously injured, and 323 Jews and 18 British policemen were slightly hurt. See PD. C., v. 358, c. 1194–5.

[24] This correspondence, and the reports compiled by the Jewish Agency, including the medical records, are in CZA A312/16. See also a Jewish Agency summary, CZA A312/30.

[25] Lady Namier's Notes.

skimmed over the ice, rounding obstacles and drawing whatever figures he chose. The one thing which the figure-skater cannot do is to walk straight.[26]

*   *   *

On 29 August 1939 Weizmann wrote to the Prime Minister, Neville Chamberlain, declaring that 'the Jews stand by Great Britain and will fight on the side of the democracies', and stating further that '[we] place ourselves in matters big and small, under the co-ordinating direction of His Majesty's Government. The Jewish Agency is ready to enter into immediate arrangements for utilising Jewish manpower, technical ability and resources, etc.'[27] This was the first shot in a campaign to raise an independent Jewish Fighting Force [JFF] which was to continue until the autumn of 1944. Namier was in the thick of it from the outset. His initiative and energy fuelled much of the Jewish Agency's efforts to attain this desperately sought-after goal. He had long been an impassioned advocate of Jewish self-defence. As long ago as September 1919 he had written: 'The settlers [in Palestine] must be capable of defending themselves and ought as soon as possible to relieve the British army of occupation.'[28] It would not be an exaggeration to say that this point obsessed him, that he saw in its fulfilment not only the redemption of Jewish honour in the present but also the key to Jewish survival in the future. The right of the Jews to arm and defend themselves in a war against their most vicious persecutor was, in his judgement, defensible on every imaginable ground. He grew increasingly angry and disillusioned with the British Government's dishonourable attempts to wriggle out of what he considered to be a moral and political right, reinforced by military necessity.

Chamberlain's response was hardly encouraging,[29] and it presaged a protracted and dreary controversy which lasted until the final stages of

---

[26] *Manchester Guardian*, 15 Mar. 1940. See also his letter to *The Times*, 6 Mar. 1940.

[27] Weizmann to Chamberlain, 29 Aug. 1939, WA.

[28] Namier to P. Kerr, 6 Sept. 1919. See pp. 22–24. The following story also illustrates Namier's preoccupation with the need to demonstrate Jewish martial ability: 'I well recollect a meeting to interview candidates for a post in English in the University of Jerusalem, at which Namier would fix some timid lecturer from say, Nottingham, with his baleful, annihilating glare, and say: "Mr. Levy can you shoot?" the candidate would mutter something—"Because if you take this post, you will have to shoot. You will have to shoot our Arab cousins. Because if you do not shoot them, they will you." Stunned silence. "Mr. Levy, will you please answer my question: can you shoot?" Some of the candidates withdrew. No appointment was made.' See Sir I. Berlin.

[29] See Chamberlain to Weizmann, 2 Sept. 1939, 1939, WA.

the war.[30] Even more disheartening were the actions of the British authorities in Palestine. They clamped down heavily on the activities of the *Haganah*,[31] seemingly intent on crippling its operational capacity and destroying its morale.[32] Despite the overtly hostile attitude of the Palestine administration, encouraged no doubt by the more or less open support they received in Whitehall, the response of Palestine Jewry to the war effort was remarkable. By the end of September, out of a community at that time of less than half-a-million, 136,000 Palestinian Jews—90,000 men and 46,000 women—had registered, through the Jewish Agency, for some kind of essential national service, the vast majority of men specifically mentioning their readiness to serve with the British army. The British reaction to this impressive demonstration was niggardly. The figures speak for themselves. By mid-1941 only 9,000 Palestinians, including 70 officers, had been absorbed into the British forces.[33]

The first official call for Jews to join British units came in the autumn of 1939. But the numbers requested were small, and, of more consequence, they were to be enlisted on a basis of strict numerical parity between Jews and Arabs. As the Arabs scarcely responded to this appeal, the Jewish contribution was limited to a bare minimum. In December Weizmann renewed his offer of 'a Jewish division to be recruited in Palestine and elsewhere for service with the British forces in

[30] I have made no attempt here to recount in detail the negotiations which terminated finally in the establishment of the JFF, but have concentrated only upon Namier's specific contribution and views on this topic. The main outline of the story is in any case well known. For its most recent treatment see M. J. Cohen. For the first stage of the negotiations leading to the establishment of a Jewish Fighting Force, see Yoer Gelber's detailed study, in Hebrew, *Jewish Palestinian Volunteering in the British Army During the Second World War* (Jerusalem, 1979), vol. 1, 1939–42.

[31] The underground defence organization of the *Yishuv*. It had been established in 1920 to protect Jewish settlements, both urban and rural, against Arab marauders. Although it represented Palestine Jewry as a whole, apart from the Revisionists, it was firmly under the control of the left-wing, socialist groups based in the kibbutz movement and the *Histadruth* [Trade Union Federation].

[32] Many examples could be cited to illustrate the hostility of the Palestine administration. Perhaps the most glaring case was the arrest and detention in October 1939 of forty-three members of the *Haganah* who were caught in possession of arms by the British authorities. Many of these had served with distinction under Wingate during the Arab disturbances. They were however condemned and sentenced to long terms in prison—ranging from life-imprisonment to ten years. [See Notes on Treatment of 'The 43', 19 Dec. 1939, CZA A312/8]. It was only after a prolonged public campaign that the detainees were finally released, as a gesture of goodwill, in February 1941.

[33] These figures are taken from a long report compiled by the Jewish Agency on the 'War Effort and War Potentialities of Palestinian Jewry', CZA A312/8. The report was unsigned but its formulation bears the distinctive hallmark of Namier's style.

the present war wherever required'. He accepted the fact that the higher command posts would be filled by British officers, but asked that the junior officers should 'include a strong contingent of Palestine Jews', and suggested that a beginning be made with the training of officer cadres, a proposal warmly supported by Wingate[34] who envisaged himself as commander of the future Jewish division. General Ironside, CIGS, agreed 'in principle' with this suggestion, but added, bodingly for the future, that 'there are other implications which will have to be taken into consideration'.[35] The British stuck to their principle of parity, much to the chagrin of the Zionists. Namier summarized this stage of the negotiations:

the most ardent desire of the Jews was, and is, to serve *as Jews* under their own national flag, like every other nation. But the policy of H.M.G., so long as MacDonald was Colonial Secretary, was to transform the Jews into an anonymous minority in Palestine. The formation of units of a Jewish national character was opposed. Therefore, when the Palestine administration declined to enlist 1,200 Jews and Arabs in two mixed 'Palestinian' units for service in France, the Jewish Agency did not co-operate in the raising of bodies thus composed. It did, however, co-operate in raising Jewish recruits for British regiments.[36]

Complementing the efforts to establish a JFF was the Agency's proposal to transform Palestine into a vast supply-base to furnish the British war machine in the Middle East. In many ways the *Yishuv* was uniquely qualified to fulfil this task. As a result of the spread of anti-Semitism in Europe, a considerable reservoir of highly trained scientists, engineers, and technicians, augmented by a relatively large and skilled labour force, stood waiting to be utilized in Palestine. Moreover, three first-rate centres of research and study, at Haifa, Jerusalem, and Rehovoth, constituted a sound academic base for such a development. These ideas were first presented to the Government in 1937, at the height of the Arab disturbances, though without any success.[37] The offer was renewed almost immediately after the outbreak of war.

On the face of it, the Zionist programme was an extremely attractive

[34] Orde Charles Wingate (1903–44): served in army in Palestine, 1936–9; organized Jewish special night squads; commanded liberation forces, Abyssinia, 1940–1; led 'long range penetration groups', Burma campaign, 1943–4; Major-General, 1943; killed in air crash.
[35] Ibid.; and *Dugdale Diaries*, 17 Jan. 1940.
[36] 'War Effort . . .'.   [37] See *The Gentile Zionists*, 110.

one. If acted upon it would have released tens of thousands of British soldiers for duty elsewhere, and would also have established, in a particularly sensitive area and one of vital strategic importance, an industrial-arms complex of inestimable value to the British war effort. Yet, despite the gravity of the situation, the Agency's proposals were turned down. In early September, Hore-Belisha[38] vetoed the formation of independent Jewish units. Pownell[39] later explained to Weizmann that the chief problem was lack of equipment not men. Although Weizmann was disposed to accept this clarification, most Zionists, including Namier, dismissed it, seeing in it only another manifestation of British ill-will.[40] Yet the general's argument should not be rejected out of hand. Fully equipped, mass armies are not created overnight. Britain was now paying dearly for those long years of lack of preparation. Total conscription had just been introduced and the shortage of supplies was a real, even if at times an exaggerated, issue. Moreover, this proved to be a problem without an immediate solution, at least not for the first years of the war. Dunkirk and other British setbacks, and in particular the need to prop up the Soviet Union after June 1941, only magnified the shortage.

Nevertheless, there were other, in the long run more telling, considerations. Namier had no doubt that the British were moved solely by political motives. Any obligations incurred to the Jews resulting from the establishment of a JFF would destroy the White Paper policy and would unquestionably provoke the hostility of the Arab, perhaps Moslem, world. The political implications, within the context of the Arab–Jewish conflict, of maintaining such a force, commanded by its own officer corps and allowing it to fight under its own flag, were too radical for the Government to sanction. It was General Barker, GOC British forces in Palestine, who voiced the most violent expression of this attitude. He told Ben Gurion that the *Haganah* 'were preparing for rebellion against Great Britain', and that 'he felt it his duty to smash that organization'.[41] Barker's views were but a reflection of much

---

[38] Leslie Hore-Belisha (1893–1957): Liberal MP, 1923–42; Independent MP 1942–5; Minister of Transport, 1934–7; Secretary of State for War, 1937–40; Minister of National Insurance, 1945. Created Baron, 1954.

[39] Henry Royds Pownell (1887–1961): Vice-Chief of Imperial General Staff, 1941; held C-in C. posts, Far East, and Persia and Iraq, 1941–3; Chief of Staff to Supreme Allied Commander, South-East Asia, 1943–4; Kn. 1940.

[40] See 'War Effort . . .'; *Dugdale Diaries*, 7 Sept. 1939; Weizmann to Hore-Belisha, 11 Sept. 1939, WA.

[41] From minutes of an interview, 1 Nov. 1939, WA.

deeper currents prevailing throughout much of the Palestine administration and some elements in the Government.[42] Not all the generals,
however, felt as Barker did; and this fact gave the Zionists some hope for
the future. Many high-ranking officers, particularly those based in
London, supported the Zionists' proposals, perceiving in them a
practical and rational way of combating their difficulties.

Namier held MacDonald chiefly responsible for the deplorable state
of relations between the Jewish Agency and the Government. He felt a
deep sense of personal betrayal, for he had established the most friendly
relationship with MacDonald during the 1930 crisis, to the immense
benefit of the Zionists, and they continued to be on close terms until the
volte-face in British policy in the late 1930s. The incident over the Land
Regulations was the final straw. Clearly MacDonald had to go before
there could be any substantial improvement in Anglo-Zionist relations.
Namier pursued him relentlessly and with a vindictiveness out of all
proportion to the extent of his actual influence. The long-awaited
change occurred in May 1940 when Churchill was elevated to the
premiership as a result of the Norwegian fiasco. MacDonald, eventually
'banished' to Canada as High Commissioner,[43] was removed from the
Colonial Office and Lord Lloyd[44] appointed in his place. Weizmann
immediately renewed his offer to mobilize Jewish resources for the war
effort.[45] Some days later the Zionists were informed by two new
members of the Government, Arthur Greenwood[46] and Herbert
Morrison,[47] that 'things are quite different in the War Cabinet now,

---

[42] Ben Gurion, when asked how the Jews were getting on with the army, replied: ' "We
have two armies, the Australian and the British. With the Australians we get on very
well." It appears that one British battalion had 100 Palestinians in a Pioneer unit, of
whom seven were Arabs. The British objected to eating with these "natives", whereupon
the CO decreed that the "Palestinians" should have their meals apart!' "God what
fools!" ', Mrs Dugdale commented. See *Dugdale Diaries*, 1 May 1940.

[43] *Dugdale Diaries*, 10 Feb. 1941.

[44] George Ambrose Lloyd (1879–1941): Conservative MP, 1910–18, 1924–5; Governor
of Bombay, 1918–23; High Commisioner for Egypt and Sudan, 1925–9: Chairman of the
British Council, 1937–40; Secretary of State for Colonies, 1940–1. Kn. 1918. Created
Baron, 1925.

[45] Weizmann to Churchill, 29 May 1940, WA, copy in CZA A312/33.

[46] Arthur Greenwood (1880–1954): Labour MP, 1922–31, 1932–54; Minister of
Health, 1929–31; Minister without Portfolio, 1940–2; Lord Privy Seal, 1945–7;
Paymaster-General, 1949.

[47] Herbert Stanley Morrison (1888–1965): Labour MP, 1923–4, 1929–31, 1935–59;
Minister of Transport, 1929–31; Minister of Supply and Home Secretary, 1940–5;
Member of War Cabinet, 1942–5; Lord President of Council, 1945–51; Foreign
Secretary, 1951. Created Baron, 1959.

they are "three to two" and the P.M. on our side in Jewish matters.'[48]
On 29 May, Weizmann wrote to Churchill a four-point programme
outlining the manner in which the Jews could now contribute to the
British war effort:

We can mobilise at once the economic, military, political and technical
resources of the Jewish people in Palestine and elsewhere for the British cause.
1. *Supply*: Agriculture and industry in Palestine should be adapted and
developed in accordance with war needs. We have a large number of highly
skilled chemists, engineers, etc. who could undertake to manufacture ex-
plosives, motor vehicles, arms, etc. We have equipment for making shoes and
clothing for the troops.
2. *Economic Warfare*: We can mobilise Jews all over the world —the Near East
(Palestine, Turkey, Iran, the Balkans), North and South America, etc. to help
Britain in her economic warfare. Among the refugees from Germany, Austria,
Czechoslovakia, there are numbers of men who were owners or managers of
factories, and could supply information of economic and military importance.
Their co-operation would also be valuable under (1) and (3).
3. *Military Help*: (a) We can raise several divisions in Palestine and elsewhere
for service with the British Army. We have in Palestine about 30,000 men who
have had some training either as auxiliaries to the British Force there, or in
European armies. (b) We can organise an Air Force unit (squadron). We have
in Palestine a school of aviation which, with Government help, could be readily
enlarged. (c) We can help with Military Intelligence.
4. *Propaganda*: We can intensify pro-Ally propaganda in neutral countries,
especially in the Americas.[49]

During the coming months, as Britain's international position
deteriorated, relations with the Government improved. At a meeting
with Lloyd in June it was agreed that 'larger numbers of Jewish
Palestinian recruits' should be enlisted and formed 'into distinctive
Jewish units', while in cabinet circles the idea was mooted of a JFF
composed of Palestinians and non-Palestinians to be trained outside
Palestine.[50] Weizmann and Namier pursued this matter further in
September at another meeting with Lloyd; and more importantly when
Weizmann lunched with Churchill himself. The Prime Minister, wrote
Mrs Dugdale, had given 'his blessing for the Jewish Army on the first
anniversary of the war . . . Also there will probably be a "Desert

---

[48] *Dugdale Diaries*, 22 May 1940. The balance of forces in the war cabinet was as follows:
Churchill, Chamberlain, and Halifax, Conservatives; Attlee and Greenwood, Labour.
[49] Weizmann to Churchill, 29 May 1940, with enclosure, WA. In 'War Effort . . .'.
[50] 'War Effort . . .'.

Force" (Jewish) destined to strike up at Libya from the South. This is Orde Wingate's idea and it is hoped that he will train them.'[51] A week later Weizmann met Eden and Lord Lloyd and heard from them details of the Government's proposals. The results of these consultations were submitted to the War Cabinet and later summarized in a letter from Lloyd to Weizmann:

I write to confirm to you what I told you at our conversation on the 14th October. It has been decided in principle that proposals on the following lines should be generally approved. You will be authorised to recruit 10,000 Jews for incorporation in Jewish units in the British Army. Not more than 3,000 of these will be drawn from Palestine. The remainder will be drawn from America or wherever else you can recruit them. Each recruit will have to produce a guarantee that he will be accepted by his country of origin after the war. These Jewish units, including their officers, will be trained in the United Kingdom, the officers being selected by yourself or your representative with the approval of the War Office. No guarantee can be given as to the theatre of war in which the force, when trained and equipped, will be employed. Equipment will be provided by His Majesty's Government as and when their resources allow. The cost of the equipment and maintenance of the force and its pay and allowances will be borne by His Majesty's Government, though it is understood that you are in hopes of obtaining gifts from the United States as a contribution towards the cost.

The measures necessary to give effect to the above decision will have to be considered further after the Presidential election in the United States. Meanwhile, no action should be taken in the matter and no announcement on the subject made.

The above information is communicated to you for your strictly personal and confidential information and I shall be grateful if you will ensure that nothing is done or said about this, even after the election, without prior consultation with me.[52]

In early January Namier met Brigadier Leonard Arthur Hawes, the newly appointed commander of the Force, for the first of several talks. He impressed Namier: 'a man with a neat and determined mind, very keen, who would do his best to make a good job of the Division'.[53] On the whole his contacts with Hawes were fruitful and must have left

[51] *Dugdale Diaries*, 6 Sept. 1940.

[52] Lord Lloyd to Weizmann, 17 Oct. 1940, 16 WA. For details of proposals see 'Recruitment of Jewish Units', 8 Oct. 1940, WP (40) 404, CAB 66/12; for details of cabinet decisions, 10 Oct. 1940, see CAB 65/9. See also *Dugdale Diaries*, 13, 14 Sept. and 11 Oct. 1940.

[53] Namier to Mrs Dugdale, 8 Jan. 1941, CZA A312/44.

Namier full of expectancy for the future. Having successfully disposed of the great principles concerning the JFF, they began to discuss the minutiae of its operation: flags and badges, national anthems and regimental music, even the status of rabbis.[54] Hawes also told him, on the authority of the CIGS, General Dill, that it was 'the intention' to foster 'a national spirit in the Jewish Division'.[55] This was an 'intention' with incalculable political connotations, and it must be asked whether or not the soldiers fully realized the implication of their words. Certainly the politicians displayed more caution. And this was apparent even after the cabinet decision in October. On one occasion Lloyd, by now 'ill, and very irritable', bluntly informed Weizmann that 'no Force had been intended, only units in British Army'.[56] This was confirmed when Namier interviewed Lloyd early in the new year. Although the discussion was 'very friendly', at one point Lloyd remarked, 'No, no-one ever talked of a Division; it is units.'[57] Namier did not press him 'so that he should not harden in his opposition on that point or commit himself too deeply before we could bring a certain amount of influence to bear on him from other quarters.' The discussion broadened to include more general, though related, topics:

At one point he [Lloyd] started his usual song about all the Cabinet being Zionists. Winston always from time to time says to him—here he imitated Winston's voice—'What are you doing to my Jews?' The Prime Minister was a Zionist, his own private secretary was a Zionist: here I interrupted 'and poor you are sandwiched in between them; but you know it is the stuff in the middle which determines the flavour and taste of the sandwich.' I told him that I would prefer Winston to feel as he does and him like Winston, because Winston intervenes once in a blue moon in our affairs, while we have him every day. He said that he was not anti-Jew—he had too many Jewish friends for that—but anti-Zionist. I replied that I would prefer him to be anti-Jew and pro-Zionist.

Despite Lloyd's candour, Namier retained a soft spot for him. After all, as he pointed out to Lloyd, they shared joint imperialist ideals, and Namier was convinced that sooner or later he would come to see the role

[54] Namier replied to this query: 'I told him that I could not give him a very authoritative answer about this side, but that certainly the position of Rabbis was not comparable with that of a Roman Catholic priest as among us there was to a high degree the priesthood of every man.'

[55] Summary of the meetings, 27 Jan. 1941, CZA A312/34.

[56] *Dugdale Diaries*, 6–7 Nov. 1940.

[57] From minutes of the meeting, 7 Jan. 1941, WA. Also Namier to Mrs Dugdale, 8 Jan. 1941, CZA A312/44.

which Zionism ought to be assigned in imperial affairs.[58] Lloyd died on 4 February. Namier wrote handsomely of him:

In the last talk I had with him, less than a month ago, I said to him, 'After sterile years of an empire-weary generation, when the time came for new work and sacrifices for the Empire, the three of you, the Prime Minister, Amery, and yourself, were called in to bring back to us the creed of an older generation. Those who sneer at you would call you Kipling imperialists.' He replied, 'I am not ashamed of being one.'

With regard to Palestine he took over from his predecessor a grievous burden, a policy not of imperialist thinking on great and general lines, but the miserable compromises of appeasers who tried to placate those whom they feared at the expense of the weak. Lord Lloyd was a pro Arab and not a pro Zionist. But had it fallen to him to write his own text on a new page he would not have tried by subterfuges to evade commitments and obligations, but would by an act and effort of true statesmanship have endeavoured to realise the national aspirations both of Jews and Arabs.[59]

* * *

The difficulties hinted at by Lloyd came to a head almost immediately after his successor, Lord Moyne,[60] took office. He informed Weizmann that 'the Prime Minister had decided that owing to lack of equipment the project must for the present be put off for six months but may be reconsidered again in four months.'[61] Moyne's phrasing, if interpreted literally, left the issue open for the future. It also set off a controversy over tactics within the Zionist camp. Some, including Weizmann and Mrs Dugdale, believed that the Government should be informed that the Jewish Agency intended to publicize in restricted circles in the United States and Britain the contents of Moyne's letter. This would have the effect of nailing down the political pledge of a JFF while emphasizing the non-political nature for its current postponement, thereby, it was optimistically believed, manœuvring the Government into a position from which it would be unable to retreat.

[58] Namier held quite specific ideas about the character of British imperialism: 'Again, he found that he was an imperialist because he thought the Romans had discovered the principle and had worked out a very good system of consorting together; they had preserved peace as a result of it. Like the Romans, the English had mastered the principle, and—individually, at least—were kind enough, humane enough, to teach it to their subjects' (Mehte, 220–1).

[59] *Manchester Guardian*, 6 Feb. 1941.

[60] Walter Edward Guinness (1880–1944): Conservative MP, 1907–31; Minister of Agriculture, 1925–9; Secretary of State for Colonies, 1941–2; Minister Resident in Cairo, 1944; murdered by Stern gang, 1944. Created Baron Moyne, 1932.

[61] Moyne to Weizmann, 4 Mar. 1941, WA. For Churchill's instructions, see Churchill to Lord Moyne, 1 Mar. 1941, PREM 4/51/9.

Namier vigorously rejected this line. He considered it both rash and utopian. 'Bitter beyond bearing'[62] at the Government's pusillanimity, he made little effort to conceal his rancour, and his intemperate behaviour brought him into conflict with those he could least afford to alienate. 'The irritation between me [and Weizmann] and Lewis continues, owing to his *defaitiste* attitude.'[63] Namier explained his attitude:

The difference between us goes back primarily to our different estimate of the motives behind the postponement. You consider that the reason given by the Government—lack of equipment—is the main reason, and you merely admit that political motives may have entered into it . . . I consider that 'lack of equipment' is a mere excuse, and that it counted for very little in the postponement. I strongly protest against my view being labelled as accusing the Government of 'treachery' or anything of that description. Giving an excuse instead of giving one's reason is not treachery and in this case, as I have not ceased repeating again and again in the course of the last few days, this excuse is convenient even to us because it puts the matter on a much lower level, and does not unroll big political problems.

. . . I briefly summed up the position yesterday by saying that if lack of equipment had been the real or main reason of the postponement, no postponement would have been necessary: the announcement could have been made, whatever could be done technically without certain equipment would be done, and for the rest we would have to wait, as many a British regiment has waited during the last year, as the Poles have waited, as the Home Guard is still waiting, etc. In fact, if I believed the reason given by Moyne to be the true one, I would have said to him: 'Publish the announcement and say, if you like, that for technical reasons full action will be taken on it only four or six months hence.'[64]

. . . I am afraid that should semi-publication of Moyne's letter result in newspaper publicity, this will give a handle to the propaganda and attacks of the Arabs and pro-Arabs, may interfere with the ultimate implementing of the promise, and even at an earlier date result in HMG being blackmailed by the Arabs and its own official 'underworld' [i.e. the permanent officials] into concessions painful and harmful to us.[65] In other words we shall be made to pay

[62] *Dugdale Diaries*, 5 Mar. 1941.   [63] Ibid., 12 Mar. 1941.

[64] Namier's analysis came very close to the mark. Mounting hostile opinion in the Foreign Office and in military and propaganda circles, on mainly political, not technical grounds, finally convinced Churchill of the veracity of their case. See Churchill to Moyne, 1 Mar. 1941, and Churchill, *The Second World War* (London, 1950), iii, 658.

[65] Namier had specifically in mind the implementation of the constitutional clauses of the White Paper, together with unfavourable declarations about the post-war settlement in Palestine. Once again, Namier's reasoning came remarkably close to the truth. The idea of a *quid pro quo*, of linking the Jewish army question with the implementation of the constitutional clauses of the White Paper had already entered the minds of some British decision makers. See Zweig, 135–6.

for a mere promise a price, perhaps not quite as high, but still of a similar character as I feared that we might have to pay for the reality of a Jewish Division.

This being so, while acknowledging that some explanation has to be given to the Jewish leaders, I consider that this matter has to be handled in the most careful and gingerly manner, that no permission given by the Government will safeguard us against possible bad consequences, and that, so far from playing on a good wicket, we are in a tight corner. We have to move with supreme caution and not in a spirit of exuberant optimism.[66]

Having unburdened his conscience, Namier again took up the offensive. In Weizmann's absence—he was in the United States and did not return to London until July—Namier's role in these affairs was enlarged. Letters and memoranda were dispatched to the relevant Government bodies, even the question of a Jewish air squadron was raised again.[67] These efforts bore some fruit, though not as much as had been anticipated, mainly because the British position in the eastern Mediterranean was now desperate owing to the Greek débâcle and Rommel's advance into Egypt. Namier was informed that the rule of parity for enlisting Jews and Arabs for army service was to be dropped; that the military role of the Jewish supernumerary police was to be expanded; and that Jewish settlements were to be developed into defensive, strong points.[68] These concessions, generous in relation to previous Government decisions, fell far short of Zionist expectations. They elated Namier however, who arrived at the Zionist office 'quite over the moon' at what he had heard.[69] This was the kind of work at which he excelled. Interminable discussions, raising the same points time and time again, slowly extracting concessions from his adversaries; or, if unsuccessful, returning to square one and starting patiently all over again. This was the bread-and-butter aspect of diplomacy without which nothing could be achieved; and if it dismayed those of his colleagues self-endowed with greater vision, Namier apparently re-velled in it:

Chaim talked to me, alone, about all this dreary quarrelling with the Colonial Office, which takes so much of our time, and (as *he* thinks) absorbs all Lewis's

---

[66] Namier to Mrs Dugdale, 12 Mar. 1941, CZA A312/44.
[67] See, for example, Namier's notes on 'Jewish Self-Defence in Palestine', 14 Apr. 1941; Namier to Moyne, 22 Apr. 1941; and minutes of an interview with Sir Archibald Sinclair [Secretary of State for Air], 26 May 1941, CZA A312/35, 55.
[68] Minutes of meeting, 6 May 1941, WA.   [69] *Dugdale Diaries*, 6 May 1941.

attention, is 'not Zionism'. I most warmly agreed, and said we are *not* enough in touch with the Jewish masses at 77.[70]

By the autumn this stage of the negotiations had run into the ground. Pleading difficulties in shipping and transport, Moyne put 'the matter of a Jewish contingent into cold storage for the present'.[71] This was only partially true. The cabinet had discussed the matter on 13 October. Moyne himself had then emphasized that the raising of Jewish contingents should be decided on military grounds alone. And it was for this reason that the scheme was opposed by Margesson,[72] the Secretary of State for War, who argued that given the prevalent supply situation 'we could not spare equipment for troops of doubtful value'. This dubious assumption was reinforced by a genuine and widespread fear that any Jewish armed force would be used to solve the Palestinian question along Zionist lines once the war had come to an end. Why, the ministers rationalized,[73] should they train and equip a Jewish military force only for it ultimately to be turned against British interests? Hence, the idea of a JFF as an autonomous unit was again rejected. As an alternative it was proposed to expand the conscription of Jewish 'technical personnel (doctors, engineers, etc.)'; and, as a further sop, to encourage the enrolment of additional Palestinian Jews, though only for local military and police duties.[74] Weizmann appealed in vain to Churchill. He angrily rebuked Moyne: 'the floor is littered with broken promises',[75] and announced his intention of making public the reasons for the Government's reneging on its previous pledges. Small wonder that Weizmann complained about the 'Buffs and Rebuffs'[76] he had received from the Government.[77]

---

[70] *Dugdale Diaries*, 18 Jan. 1941.   [71] Moyne to Weizmann, 28 Aug. 1941, WA.

[72] Henry David Reginald Margesson (1890–1965): Conservative MP, 1922–42; Chief Government Whip, 1931–40; Secretary of State for War, 1940–2. Created Viscount, 1942.

[73] The chief opponents of the scheme were, apart from Margesson, the Foreign Secretary, Anthony Eden; the Minister of State at Cairo, Richard Casey; and the Colonial Secretary, Lord Moyne.

[74] See Cabinet conclusions, 13 Oct. 1941, CAB 65/19; and a memorandum by Moyne, composed after consultations with Eden, Oliver Lyttleton, Minister of State in the Middle East, and Margesson, on 'Recruitment of Jewish Units for General Service in the British Army', 9 Oct. 1941, WP (G) (41) 105, CAB 67/9.

[75] *Dugdale Diaries*, 23 Oct. 1941.

[76] The Palestinian units were attached to the East Kent Regiment, 'The Buffs'.

[77] *Dugdale Diaries*, 5 Oct. 1941. For these events, see Weizmann to Moyne, 19 Aug. 28 Oct., and 1 Dec. 1941; to Churchill, 10 Sept. 1941; Moyne to Weizmann, 28 Aug., 15 and 29 Oct., and 5 Dec. 1941. The correspondence is in WA, also, 'War Effort . . .'

The situation did not materially alter until the summer of 1942. Prompted by Rommel's renewed advance into Egypt, the Government eventually decided to abandon its principle of strict numerical parity and to form a Palestine Regiment with separate Jewish and Arab battalions.[78] Namier, bypassing the permanent officials, approached Churchill through his principal private secretary, John Miller Martin, requesting that Wingate be brought back from the Far East to command the proposed force.[79] Wingate, owing to his violent Zionist views, remained where he was. And, although Grigg's statement was considered 'a real step in the right direction',[80] it was not until the autumn of 1944 that the disparate Jewish units were welded together into a truly Jewish fighting force, one which met in some measure the original demands first raised by the Jewish Agency in September 1939.[81]

* * *

The war situation contributed to Namier's temperamental unpredictability. Anxiety about the fate of his family and friends, those still trapped in eastern Europe, left him emotionally drained. The state of his general health was also affected. Frequent attacks of indisposition—all indiscriminately termed by him as 'The Flu'—often left him bedridden,[82] and on at least three occasions he was hospitalized for far more serious complaints.[83] But his emotions were the chief casualty of the war. He was prone to swift changes in mood. At times he would be consumed by an intense gloom, at others by an unshakeable optimism that the war, in spite of its horrors, would prove to be the catalyst for the creation of a Jewish sovereign state, the realization of his most cherished dreams.

He was not alone in these rapidly alternating humours. The Zionist leadership as a whole was affected; and their behaviour was but a reflection of the intractable nature of the problems they faced but were

---

[78] See statement by Sir James Grigg, Secretary of State for War, on 6 Aug. 1942, PD, C, v. 382, c. 1271–72, and cabinet conclusions, 5 Aug. 1942, CAB. 65/27.
[79] Namier to J. M. Martin, 27 Aug. 1942, CZA A312/44.
[80] *Dugdale Diaries*, 6 Aug. 1942.
[81] See Namier to Mrs Dugdale, 24 Aug. and 8 Sept. 1944, CZA A312/44; and *Dugdale Diaries*, 8 Aug. 1944.
[82] Lady Namier's Notes.
[83] See *Dugdale Diaries*, 24 Feb. 1941 and 31 July 1942; and CZA A312/30.

unable to solve. Even Weizmann's relations with Mrs Dugdale, usually conducted on an absolutely even keel, did not emerge unscathed. Shortly before Christmas 1940 they quarrelled over a trivial matter, a piece of gossip that Weizmann had overheard and which appeared to impugn his capacity for leadership. Namier dismissed the incident 'as a petty rumpus over a piece of tattle',[84] as it undoubtedly was. The following day Mrs Dugdale visited Weizmann at the Dorchester Hotel where he now lived.

He talked from 3.30 to 5.00 p.m. without drawing breath, the most extraordinary jumble of thoughts, accusations (of Gestetner[85] and others), of descriptions of his lonely position in Jewry, the faults and findings of his colleagues (e.g. Lewis), in fact of everything under the sun, some of it showing his greatness, some showing his smallness, all of it showing that he is under an almost intolerable strain. When at last he had done, I did my best to disentangle the parts that bear on our personal relationship and explained to him the point at which I thought they had gone wrong, in October and November, when he began to neglect the office for the laboratory,[86] and Vera had let out to me that he thought we were 'bothering' him. I also told him that I must reserve my right to speak of him as I chose behind his back . . . We parted friends of course. But the whole episode has been an experience which I shall not forget.[87]

Namier's 'faults' were exposed to public attack at a Zionist meeting held early in the New Year. Speaking of his wish to see Palestine evolve into an international force, in the humanities no less than the sciences, Weizmann turned on Namier declaring that he should be writing his books in Jerusalem not in London: like others he should 'reverse his system' and visit England but live in Palestine. Weizmann's outburst conjured up memories of similar scenes enacted many years ago.[88] Namier declined to be drawn into yet another heated exchange on the same topic. He was prepared to visit Palestine yearly for a matter of weeks, though a longer stay was out of the question since 'the sources of

---

[84] Lady Naimer's Notes.

[85] Sigmund Gestetner (1897–1956): Chairman and Man. Dir. of Gestetner business; active in refugee work; Treasurer of Jewish National Fund, 1949, President, 1950.

[86] From the outbreak of war Weizmann was heavily involved in scientific work, both in Rehovoth and in London. He was working in particular on a cheap process to manufacture tuolene, an essential constituent for the production of TNT and, because of its anti-knock properties, of high octane aviation gasoline, and also on a synthetic rubber process. In June 1940 his appointment as chemical adviser to the Prime Minister was under consideration (see *Dugdale Diaries*, 5 June 1940).

[87] *Dugdale Diaries*, 21 Dec. 1940.

[88] See p. 69.

his work were in England'.[89] As has been noted, this was a long disputed point of friction between them and one which touched upon Namier's psychological, hence unquantifiable, need to attach himself to a traditional, stable society. It was a condition which Weizmann was curiously unaware of, even though he must have sensed that Namier could never agree to his demands. In all probability Weizmann was exploiting this by now threadbare argument in order to score off Namier for his demonstrative intolerance and monumental lack of tact, for which there is abundant evidence, towards his co-workers, including even Weizmann himself.

For his part, Namier scarcely reacted to this slight. This stemmed in large measure from his deep feeling of veneration towards Weizmann which was often indistinguishable from hero-worship. He was not, however, blind to the ageing leader's faults. Quite the contrary, he was painfully aware of them and made little attempt to stifle his opinions,[90] a fact which clearly provoked Weizmann's attack upon him. There was another, more profound reason why Weizmann's verbal assault fell flat. By this time Namier had come to regard Weizmann in a revised light. Firstly, he was bound to the past. For almost a whole generation, certainly since the Balfour declaration, Weizmann had dominated Zionist, indeed Jewish, political life. For Namier, the astonishing achievements of the Zionist movement were but a consequence of Weizmann's superb political skill and diplomatic finesse. But Namier also simultaneously perceived that however outstanding an asset to Jewry he had once been, now, because of his inability to cope with the cruder realities of the politics of the 1940s, he showed signs of becoming

[89] Lady Namier's Notes. In a letter written after the war, Namier turned once again to this point which clearly allowed his conscience no rest. 'I frankly admit that I myself have not made, and shall not make, one [an application to emigrate to Palestine]. The reason is very simple though I would not care to discuss it in public, where I think personal explanations or excuses are out of place—attaching too much importance to one's own person. I am nearly sixty; I was not brought up as a Jew by religion, and know no Hebrew; I could not pull my weight in Palestine; and I can do the historical work which is my profession—on British Eighteenth Century Parliamentary History, and Nineteenth and Twentieth Century International Politics—only in this country, where, in these circumstances, I feel I can best serve the cause. Moreover, I have no children—if I had, I might wish to settle them in Palestine. It is for the young, or for those who have a family, to make a fresh start there. What I have said about myself above is for your information only—I say it because you ask me the question point-blank.' See Namier to Jose Mirelman, 23 Sept. 1946, CZA A312/55.
[90] See pp. 86–9. Also Namier to Mrs Dugdale, 6 Aug. 1940: 'And in my opinion even Chaim is not sufficiently concentrating on these issues and not speaking out sufficiently sharply about them.' CZA A312/44.

its liability. There was some truth in this analysis, though, as events moved to their bloody climax in the immediate post-war era, Weizmann again proved his indispensability to his movement. But for Namier, even though his idol had become somewhat tarnished, the Zionist movement without Weizmann, even a Weizmann in decline, was inconceivable. Whatever his faults, Namier was convinced that no other leader of Weizmann's stature and distinction had so far emerged to replace him.[91]

*   *   *

Namier was not concerned exclusively with Zionist politics. The extinction of Poland rekindled his interest in Polish affairs. Early on in the war he met Sikorski[92] and other leaders of the Polish Government-in-Exile. He fostered close relations with them and regularly reported his impressions to the Foreign Office.[93] Of course, he was acutely aware of the intrigues and personality clashes inherent in Polish *émigré* politics.[94] Of all the Polish leaders, Sikorski appealed to him most—'Sikorski and Zaleski[95] are essentially non-party men with a liberal West European outlook . . . I found Sikorski a really charming fellow, curiously outspoken and I might say almost indiscreet . . . he has a certain pleasant military directness'[96]—and in general supported his faction.

Namier reported to the Foreign Office that the Polish Government-in-Exile included 'certain ill-assorted and not altogether reliable elements . . . nationalists of a Fascist or semi-Fascist mentality who opposed the late dictatorship only because it was not their own, and would have run a much worse one if they had had the chance'.[97] He feared that these unreliable elements would eventually pull Sikorski down. He dreaded a resurgence of Polish chauvinism, the same madness

[91] From Lady Namier's Notes. Mrs Dugdale shared Namier's views, though to a lesser degree. Noting Namier's complaint about 'Chaim's unbusinesslike way', she concluded: 'I fear it is true that he is *not* the leader he was' [*Dugdale Diaries*, 12 Aug. 1941].

[92] Wladyslaw Sikorski (1881–1943): Polish General and Statesman; Prime Minister of Poland, 1922–3; Minister of Military Affairs, 1924–5; Prime Minister of Polish Government-in-Exile and Commander in Chief of Polish forces, 1939–43; killed in air crash at Gibraltar, 1943.

[93] See, for example, his memorandum to R. A. Butler, 28 Nov. 1939, FO 371/23153, C19384/8526/55.

[94] See *Dugdale Diaries*, 22 July 1940 [unpublished].

[95] August Zaleski (1883–   ): Foreign Minister of Poland, 1926–32; of Polish Government-in-Exile, 1939–41.

[96] Namier's memorandum, 28 Nov. 1939.   [97] Ibid.

which had brought Poland to ruin and which he had opposed, unsuccessfully, in 1918–20. 'The Allied Governments should do nothing', he warned, 'which would give even the remotest appearance of countenancing such intrigues.' The first priority therefore was to ensure that the 'indiscreet' but 'charming' Sikorski remained in control.[98]

He was also cognizant of another, in the long run far graver, problem: the need to maintain continuous contact with those who had remained behind in Poland to continue the struggle, and to co-ordinate policy with them. For 'however well the emigrées may work or fight, those who have been left behind or who have stuck to their land or posts, will entertain a feeling of superiority over the emigrés or even a grudge against them. This is a matter of human psychology.'[99]

He foresaw the rise of a new leadership, politically independent, rooted in the Polish resistance, and unwilling or unprepared to surrender their authority to those based in London. He did not view this development with any great enthusiasm, but saw it as an unavoidable consequence of the German occupation, one that should be tolerated and not opposed:

It is all to the good . . . provided the emigré government keeps in touch with them. This, of course, is not an easy matter in present circumstances. But in a way it is also a question of mental attitude: it is important that the emigrés in their minds should subordinate themselves to those who have stayed behind. The problem of finding proper contacts and equation with 'the country' (the name which has arisen for Poland in earlier emigrations and has remained current to this day) is perhaps the greatest problem facing the Polish emigré government.[100]

The cardinal issue of course was how to sustain Polish independence in the face of German–Soviet collusion to crush it. Namier reconciled himself to the realities of the situation. If forced to choose between the Soviet or German conquests, he would unhesitatingly opt for the former. After all, he rationalized, in September 1939 the Red Army had

---

[98] Anti-Semitism was rife among the Polish 'nationalists of a Fascist or semi-Fascist mentality' against whom Namier warned. This matter proved to be of some concern also to the British Government. Sikorski, to his credit, repudiated in public on a number of occasions the anti-Semitic outbursts of his followers (see Wasserstein, 120–30), an act which must have increased Namier's admiration for him.

[99] Namier's memorandum, 28 Nov. 1939.

[100] Ibid.

advanced approximately up to the old Curzon line,[101] Poland's eastern border as ratified by the Allies after the First World War. In this way he could claim that the Soviet Union was upholding the Versailles settlement; or, put differently, was reversing the conquests of the Polish imperialists some twenty years ago. The expurgation of non-ethnic Polish territories would revive the true spirit of Polish nationalism and thereby stabilize European relations. His views were succintly recorded after a conversation held in July 1940 with Sikorski and a liaison officer from the War Office:

General Sikorski and Professor Namier are anxious to work for a *rapprochement* with the USSR with a view to a new Polish State being reconstituted with the USSR's help, and entirely at the expense of Germany; this, they believe, is the only hope for Poland's future. They are anxious that Germany and the USSR shall not collaborate in forming the new Polish State, and further they are most anxious that the United Kingdom should avoid any talk of reconstituting Poland along lines which might tend to force Germany and the USSR into collaboration with each other. They are definitely against any proposals to revive Polish interests in the Ukraine, which they regard as being essentially a Russian sphere of influence.[102]

Namier maintained contact with the Poles throughout the war. In 1947, he summarized his feelings towards the post-war settlement in a book of collected essays:

A 're-setting' of Poland had to be achieved through a withdrawal of scattered Polish minorities in the east, and a consolidation of Poland's territory, cleared of Germans, in the west. An end had to be put to a situation bound to recreate, again and again, a Russian–German alliance. To live, Poland had to be made 'fair and square,' with the Curzon line for her eastern border, a similar straight

---

[101] The original proposal regarding the Russian–Polish frontier dispute was first made by Lloyd George in July 1920; subsequent negotiations were conducted by Lord Curzon, the Foreign Secretary. The proposed line ran from the East Prussian border through Grodno and Brest Litovsk, between Przemyls and Lvov, and terminated at the Czech frontier. This scheme closely approximated to the border attained by Russia after the third partition of Poland in 1795, and would have excluded from Poland territories mainly inhabited by White Russians, Ukrainians, and Lithuanians. It was upheld by Namier on these grounds. The Poles however rejected the plan and, as a result of the border war of 1920–1, succeeded in pushing the frontier some 150 miles east of Brest, thereby conquering almost twice the area first proposed by Lloyd George.

[102] See FO 371/24482, C8027/7177/55. Also minutes of a discussion between Frank Roberts [of the Central Dept.] and Namier, 24 July 1940, FO 371/24474, C7639/252/55; and Namier to H. Wilson Harris [ed. of the *Spectator*], 30 July 1940, A312/44.

line in the west, and a broad frontage on the Baltic; and with no Polish enclaves outside, or alien enclaves inside, Poland.[103]

The political perversity of the Poles, however, never failed to exasperate him, and he quoted with evident relish Briand's quip to Austin Chamberlain: 'Que voulez-vous, mon ami, la Pologne c'est le rhumatisme de l'Europe.'[104]

*   *   *

On 29 May 1941, at the Mansion House in London, the Foreign Secretary, Anthony Eden, reviewed, in the words of *The Times*, 'some fundamental aspects of British policy'.[105] He referred briefly but significantly to the affairs of the Middle East. The brevity of his statement stood in marked contrast to the controversy it later aroused. Opening with a reference to British sympathy with Syrian desires for independence, he continued:

This country has a long tradition of friendship with the Arabs, a friendship that has been proved by deeds, not words alone. We have countless well-wishers among them, as they have many friends here. Some days ago I said in the House of Commons that His Majesty's Government had great sympathy with Syrian aspirations for independence. I should like to repeat that now. But I would go further. The Arabs world has made great strides since the settlement reached at the end of the last war, and many Arab thinkers desire for the Arab peoples a greater degree of unity than they now enjoy. In reaching out towards this unity they hope for our support. No such appeal from our friends should go unanswered. It seems to me both natural and right that the cultural and economic ties between the Arab countries and the political ties too, should be strengthened. His Majesty's Government for their part will give their full support to any scheme that commands general approval.[106]

The speech was generally interpreted as a plea in favour of pan-Arabism, foreshadowing an extension of Arab independence and unity. It conspicuously failed to mention the future of the Jewish National Home within this context. One commentator drew the conclusion that the Arabs had interpreted Eden's reference to Syrian independence to include both Northern and Southern Syria, a clear hint as to the fate which awaited Palestine.[107] This was a challenge the Zionists could not

[103] See *Facing East*, 97. See also *Dugdale Diaries* for the war period for his relations with the Poles.
[104] Ibid., 84.
[105] *The Times*, 30 May 1941.   [106] From report in *The Times*, 30 May 1941.
[107] See *Manchester Guardian*'s correspondent's report from Cairo, 2 June 1941.

allow to go by default. Ben Gurion reacted in characteristic fashion, describing the speech as 'the worst that had happened to them since war broke out', while in Jerusalem the executive of the Jewish Agency decided to launch a propaganda offensive in the United States to counter Eden's supposed machinations.[108]

On 3 June Namier, accompanied by Berl Locker, met Moyne at the Colonial Office. Moyne immediately assured them that the phrase postulating a scheme commanding general approval was intended to cover Jewish rights also.[109] This explanation was accepted without much conviction.[110] Moyne then invited Namier to put the Zionist case:

> We replied that we need a sufficient area to receive great numbers of Jewish immigrants after the war, and to form the basis for a sound Jewish Commonwealth; that we should then not be averse to some kind of connexion with the neighbouring Arab States, but that our full sovereignty would have to be safeguarded; that we desire to maintain a connexion with the British Empire; that this would give the Empire naval bases, aerodromes and a strategic base for the Suez Canal; but that the degree of this connexion should be regulated by mutual convenience. You asked about the absorptive capacity of Palestine. We replied that throughout the last twenty years it had proved its remarkable elasticity; the absorptive capacity of any country depends on the economic system adopted, which develops with the density of the population.
>
> While our rights and aims in Palestine cannot be made dependent on new advantages to be acquired by the Arabs, we hope that when the Arabs, as a result of this war, obtain independence over wide additional territories, and are given opportunities of achieving whatever degree of unity they desire and are capable of, they will be required, as a counterpart, to accept such a thorough settlement in Palestine as would go far to solve one of the most disturbing world-wide problems, the Jewish Question.[111]

Namier rejected outright Moyne's suggestion that 'the Jewish Question' be solved, in part, in territories other than Palestine:

[108] See Zweig, 68.

[109] There was perhaps some truth in this. Only two days before his Mansion House speech, on 27 May, Eden had circulated a paper to the cabinet which envisaged 'a Jewish State' as one of 'the component units' in a 'Federation of Middle Eastern States'. (See Cohen, 142.) Of course, this was not a decision in favour of a Jewish state; it only indicated that certain members of the Government had not entirely excluded this option. In fact, the cabinet had had no time to discuss Eden's views before his speech, and only approved its contents on 2 June, four days after it was delivered. (Ibid.) This was a rather casual approach to what was generally considered to be a major foreign policy statement.

[110] See Zweig, 68.

[111] Namier to Moyne, 10 June 1941, CZA A312/16; a copy also in FO 371/27044, E 3201/53/65. See also his remarks to Oliver Harvey, Eden's private secretary, J. Harvey, ed., *The War Diaries of Oliver Harvey, 1941–1945* (London, 1978), 19.

We do not hesitate to warn you and all those who mean honestly by the Jewish people against such manœuvres; some vague vision of a bright future in an unnamed, undiscovered country will be painted to defeat our claim to the land of our fathers, fully acknowledged under the Mandate, and to a Return which for more than two thousand years has formed the essence of our national existence; and after it has been used in this way to lull the honest doubts and scruples of well-wishers, it will be regretfully declared a failure, and the Jewish people will once more be left in the lurch.

The Jewish people, he had once noted, in a different context, wished to redeem themselves in 'Eretz Israel', not in an 'Ersatz Israel'.[112]

The British record of this conversation, although couched in a manner unflattering to the Zionists, does not materially differ from Namier's account.[113] But a more accurate indication of Foreign Office feelings towards Namier and his opinions can be gauged from the officials' minutes. 'Dr. Namier is utterly uncompromising', wrote one, while another commented:

I hope that if the Zionists air these views to us, they will be told quite firmly that their realisation is out of the question, and that they had better abandon such fantastic dreams at once. The only result of patiently listening to this sort of thing is to arouse unrealisable hopes, as we have so often done in the past, and to create more difficulties for the future, and charges of breaches of faith, when we eventually have to come down to realities.

These remarks were not aimed in particular at Namier, despite the fact that his belligerent style invariably antagonized his listeners. Even the diplomatic and sagacious Weizmann generally encountered a hostile audience. 'Among the officials concerned the only one who was friendly to Zionism was Oliver Harvey,[114] Caccia[115] [also] had made a very good impression on Weizmann.'[116]

[112] From notes of 13 Nov. 1939, A312/27.

[113] See FO 371/27044; E3101/53/65, and PREM 4/52/3.

[114] Oliver Charles Harvey (1893–1968): Private Secretary to Eden and Halifax, 1936–9, 1941–3; Minister at British Embassy, Paris, 1940; Assistant and Deputy Under-Secretary of State at the Foreign Office, 1943–7; Ambassador to France, 1948–54. Kn. 1946. Created Baron, 1954. Harvey was certainly among the more sympathetic of the officials. He consistently advocated the establishment of a Jewish state in Palestine within the framework of a federation of Middle East states, an over-all settlement to be guaranteed by Anglo-American co-operation in the area (see *Harvey Diaries*, 41–2), and he may well have provided the inspiration for Eden's paper of 27 May 1941 (see p. 120, n. 109).

[115] Harold Anthony Caccia (1905–   ): entered Foreign Office, 1929; Ambassador to Washington, 1956–61; Permanent Under-Secretary, 1962–5; Provost of Eton since 1965. Kn. 1950. Created Baron, 1965.

[116] From the record of an interview between Namier and Prof. R. Coupland, 30 June 1942, WA.

Both Namier and Weizmann pinned their hopes for a favourable settlement on the basic sympathy and goodwill of the Western leaders, Churchill and Roosevelt, hoping in this way to evade the ingrained prejudice of the officials. Churchill had once told Weizmann:

I want you to know that I have a plan, which of course can only be carried into effect when the war is over. I would like to see Ibn Saud made lord of the Middle East —the boss of bosses —provided he settles with you. It will be up to you to get the best possible conditions. Of course we shall help you. Keep this confidential, but you might talk it over with Roosevelt when you get to America. There's nothing he and I cannot do if we set our minds on it.[117]

There was, however, a marked degree of superficiality and wishful thinking about this approach. Personalities, however charismatic and dominant, would not decide the central issues. Although Churchill fought valiantly for Zionism throughout the war, he fought largely in vain. His interventions, powerful and persuasive, reinforced by the authority of his office, came to nought against the combined weight of his chief political and military advisers. Time and again they turned his arguments, guiding him back to the same incontrovertible point: any far-reaching concessions to the Zionists would severely, perhaps fatally, damage Britain's imperial interests in the Middle East and probably throughout the Muslim world. Their reasoning was sufficiently cogent to remind Churchill of where his true duty lay.

*   *   *

What kind of post-war settlement did the Zionists envisage? The prospect of a redrawing of the map of the Middle East at the conclusion of the war had rekindled the idea first mooted, and never since abandoned, in the Peel Report of a Jewish State, if not in the whole of western Palestine, as expressed in Philby's plan, then in a vastly improved Peel proposal. Perhaps it would eventually be linked with an Arab federation, or perhaps with the British Empire. The alternatives were deliberately left open. Only one goal was constant: that a Jewish State would emerge as a result of the post-war settlement. This goal, yet to be ratified formally at a Zionist gathering, was in practice an integral part of Zionist diplomacy from the beginning of the war; at least on the part of those functionaries who conducted Zionist diplomacy from

[117] C. Weizmann, *Trial and Error*, 525–6. This was perhaps the final fling of the so-called Philby plan (see pp. 94–96). Churchill had earlier displayed some support for the scheme (see minutes of 24 Sept. 1941, CAB 65/23).

London. Namier never deviated from this line. His papers are crammed with references relating to the future Jewish Commonwealth; and he never ceased informing the officials that this aim would be realized once hostilities had come to an end.

The Zionists first publicly staked their claim to a Jewish state in a well-known article by Weizmann in *Foreign Affairs* in January 1942 entitled 'Palestine's Role in the Solution of the Jewish Problem'. The article had been in preparation for some months, and both Namier and Mrs Dugdale had lent a hand in its drafting.[118] Namier's influence is clearly discernible in both its style and content—great play was made, for example, on the statistics of the post-war Jewish problem and its solution, always a favourite theme of his. The call for a Jewish state was unequivocal. But as to its eventual boundaries and constitution, the actual formulation of the article was sufficiently ambiguous to leave several options open. Weizmann wrote both of 'a Jewish Palestine' and 'a Jewish State in Palestine'; at times he envisaged a completely independent state, unencumbered by association with the mandatory power, at others he toyed with the idea of 'the inclusion of the Jewish State within the British Commonwealth of Nations'.[119] The crux of his demand was that:

the Arabs must, therefore, be clearly told that the Jews will be encouraged to settle in Palestine, and will control their own immigration; that here Jews who so desire will be able to achieve their freedom and self-government by establishing a State of their own, and ceasing to be a minority dependent on the will and pleasure of other nations.

As for Weizmann's own preference, he would surely have preferred a Jewish state in the whole of western Palestine in some form of close association with the British Empire. Whether he believed this goal to be attainable or not in the light of existing circumstances is another matter. This was a maximalist aim; he would settle for less if no other feasible alternative presented itself.

These ideas were further refined at a Zionist gathering at the

---

[118] *Dugdale Diaries*, 7 Oct. 1941 [unpublished].

[119] This undue emphasis on the semantics of the article may strike some readers as utterly trivial and unimportant. The author has a great deal of sympathy with such sentiments. But in fact semantics and rhetoric have always played a considerable role in the Palestine question, and on occasion have wreaked havoc with it. All parties to the dispute relied heavily on ambiguity as a hedge against future developments, studiously ignoring Harold Nicolson's wise injunction that 'The essential to good diplomacy is precision.'

Biltmore Hotel in New York in May 1942. It is now clear that the so-
called Biltmore programme drew its inspiration from Weizmann's
article.[120] Its pertinent sentences read:

The new world order that will follow victory cannot be established on
foundations of peace, justice and equality, unless the problem of Jewish
homelessness is finally solved. The Conference urges that the gates of Palestine
be opened; that the Jewish Agency be invested with control of immigration into
Palestine and with the necessary authority for upbuilding the country,
including the development of its unoccupied and uncultivated lands; and that
Palestine be established as a Jewish Commonwealth integrated in the structure
of the new democratic world.[121]

This platform was broad enough to encompass the mainstream of
Zionist thought. Before the year was out, the three major forces of world
Zionism, American and British Jewry, and the *Yishuv* in Palestine, were
committed to the Biltmore programme.

*   *   *

In April 1943 Churchill took the first step, perhaps inadvertently,
towards reintroducing partition as a practicable solution to the
Palestine problem. As an unwavering supporter of the Balfour Declaration, he had consistently opposed the White Paper policy. His own
views on the subject were clear. As early as October 1941 he had
committed himself on paper to the notion that:

if Britain and the United States emerge victorious from the war, the creation of a
great Jewish State in Palestine inhabited by millions of Jews will be one of the
leading features of the Peace Conference discussions. The Liberal and Labour
Parties will never agree to the pro-Arab solutions which are the commonplace of

---

[120] The genesis of the Biltmore programme can now hardly be disputed. The
controversy which later surrounded it stemmed from Ben Gurion's fierce and passionate
advocacy of the programme in Palestine in the autumn of 1942, almost browbeating the
Yishuv into agreement. In this way, he appeared as the inspirer, sole author, and only
champion of the programme. As Weizmann put it: '[he conveyed] the idea that it is the
triumph of his policy as against my moderate formulation of the same aims'. (Quoted by
Cohen, 135.) In fact, the policy differences between them were slight. Commentators with
a sense of the dramatic build much out of the nuances of meaning between Weizmann's
interpretation of Biltmore and Ben Gurion's. A clash between these two almost
diametrically opposite personalities there undoubtedly was. But it was a clash based more
on differences in temperament than on broad lines of actual policy. Here, after all, was the
classic confrontation in politics: that between a young, abrasive leader, anxious to get on,
and an older statesman, blocking his path and reluctant to relinquish his grip.

[121] Quoted by J. C. Hurewitz, *The Struggle for Palestine* (New York, 1950), 158.

British (Civil) Service circles; nor, so long as I remain in British public life, will I.[122]

The burdens of office had not eroded his position. He told General Spears[123] in the most unequivocal terms that 'he had formed an opinion which nothing could change. He intended to see to it that there was a Jewish State. He told me not to argue with him as this would merely make him angry and would change nothing.'[124] His administration, he now informed his colleagues, was therefore free to review, and if necessary revise, the entire question at the end of the war.[125]

During the weeks following Churchill's initiative, the cabinet was inundated with papers relating to Palestine.[126] None of them disputed Churchill's basic contention, but equally none of them displayed the slightest sympathy for the aims of Zionism as expressed in the Biltmore programme. Quite the contrary, the general tone of these memoranda was overtly hostile. In the spring and summer of 1943 there appeared to have been a widespread conviction in Government circles that the *Yishuv*, the Jewish Agency, the entire Zionist leadership, was dominated by a band of fanatics and extremists who were bent on political, and if necessary military, confrontation with the British and the Arabs. The Middle Eastern War Council summarized these opinions, although perhaps in more vehement phrases than the Government would have liked.

[122] His minute of 1 Oct. 1941, PREM 4/52/5, pt. 2.

[123] Edward Louis Spears (1886–1974): Brigadier-General, 1918; National Liberal MP, 1922–4, Conservative MP, 1931–45; Head of British Mission to de Gaulle, 1940; Minister to Syria and the Lebanon, 1942–4. Kn. 1942. Created Baronet, 1953.

[124] See Zweig, 490, quoting from a conversation which took place in May–June 1943.

[125] See his paper, 27 Apr. 1943, WP (43) 178, CAB 66/36; also *Harvey Diaries*, entry for 21 Apr. 1943. Of course, neither he nor his Government were ignorant of the Zionists' aim to establish a Jewish state at the end of the war. A great deal of evidence had accumulated to this effect. To take one example, in Nov. 1941 documents had been purloined from Ben Gurion's luggage by British censorship authorities which quoted Weizmann as asserting that 'there would be 2½–3 million Jewish refugees who could not be re-settled in Europe after the war, and that that would require the creation of a Jewish state in Palestine' (Zweig, 435; and 483–5). These sentiments could only have strengthened Churchill's own convictions.

[126] See a memorandum by Lord Cranborne, Lord Privy Seal, 4 May 1943, WP (43) 187, CAB 66/36; by Oliver Stanley, Colonial Secretary, 4 May 1943, WP (43) 192, CAB 66/36; by Eden, Foreign Secretary, 10 May 1943, WP (43), CAB 66/36; by Richard Casey, Minister Resident in Middle East, 21 Apr. 1943, WP (43) 246, CAB 66/37; by Oliver Lyttelton, Minister of Production, written on 3 Apr. 1942 but circulated on 23 June 1943, WP (43) 265, CAB 66/38; by Attlee, Deputy Prime Minister, 23 June 1943, WP (43) 266, CAB 66/38; by Sir Stafford Cripps, Minister of Aircraft Production, 1 July 1943, WP (43) 288, CAB 66/38. See also minutes of Middle East War Council meeting, 19 May 1943, WP (43) 247, CAB 66/37.

The principal danger lies in an endeavour on the part of the Jews, who are rapidly producing a highly organised military machine on Nazi lines, to seize the moment which is most favourable for themselves for the prosecution by force of their policy of establishing an exclusively Jewish State in Palestine.[127]

These evaluations were highly colourful. There was in fact very little chance of a Zionist *coup de main* in Palestine. As one commentator has put it:

The fear that the Zionists would attempt a coup against the Mandate and the British Army in the Middle East and impose its own solution was a more accurate reflection of the sense of Britain's vulnerability to pressure on Palestine policy . . . then it was a measure of the real strength of the *Yishuv*.[128]

As a consequence of these soundings a cabinet committee on Palestine was set up in July 1943. Its composition, owing to its supposed pro-Zionist bias,[129] provoked murmurs of discontent from the Foreign Office.[130] Before long, news that partition was again in the air had reached the Zionists.[131] Their London-based political committee now spared no effort to reawaken an interest in partition to as wide an audience as possible. Namier was particularly active. He propounded the case for a Jewish state to his friends and acquaintances, to his contacts in Government, and in the columns of the press:

The feeling grows that the Jewish problem must be grappled with at its core rather than treated with palliatives on the surface . . . Theoretically there are two ways in which the situation can be ended: either by the Jews being absorbed into the Gentile peoples or by reintegrating them as a nation in a State and country of their own . . . and thought turns more and more in this direction.[132]

He dismissed the arguments of the territorialists, those who fought to

[127] Minutes of meeting, Ibid.   [128] Zweig, 488–9.

[129] The committee members were: Herbert Morrison, Home Secretary, chairman; L.S. Amery, Secretary of State for India; Oliver Stanley, Colonial Secretary; Sir Archibald Sinclair, Secretary of State for Air; and Richard Kidston Law, Parliamentary Under-Secretary of State at the Foreign Office. Amery and Sinclair were well-known Zionist sympathizers, while Morrison had also on occasion ventured his approval. Stanley, untainted by Zionist ardour, was no match for this combination; nor, apparently, for any other. Churchill was reported to have told him that 'he had not enough drive or initiative to carry anything through, but he was a Stanley and might do for the Dominions' (*Dugdale Diaries*, 14 May 1940).

[130] See Churchill's note to Eden, 11 July 1943, PREM 4/51/1; also Cohen, 165.

[131] See *Dugdale Diaries*, 21 July, 20 Oct., 14 and 23 Nov. 1943; and 4 Dec. 1943 [unpublished].

[132] From his article, 'The Jewish Problem Re-argued. A Palestine State the Only Solution', *Manchester Guardian*, 16 Nov. 1943.

solve the Jewish problem of homelessness in San Domingo, or Madagascar, or Alaska: 'The rebirth of the Jewish nation is bound up with Palestine', he affirmed. He quickly turned to the crucial issue: the Jewish–Arab problem:

The time cannot be long delayed before His Majesty's Government must decide whether to stand by the policy of the Balfour Declaration and the Mandate, or to pursue the line of the MacDonald White Paper of 1939. If the Jews are condemned to remain for ever a minority in Palestine under Arab rule there will be for them, in the words of Mr. Churchill, 'the end of the vision, of the hope, of the dream.'[133] They will never submit to such a renunciation nor accept in Palestine the minority status from which they have suffered so much in the Dispersion, least of all at the hands of a people notoriously intolerant of minorities. To the Jew, Palestine is all in all, for which he could not be compensated; to the Arab, Palestine is 'only a small notch'[134] in his vast territories which have been liberated for him by Allied arms in two World Wars.

The Jew, if deprived his State in Palestine, is deprived of all independent natural existence; the Arab enjoys it in a number of States.

But what of the Palestinian Arabs?

If it be accepted that the age-long tragedy of Jewry can be solved, and solved in Palestine alone, it would not seem unreasonable to demand from the Arabs the necessary renunciation, which, in fact, is not as great as it might seem. Palestine can never be simply an Arab country; the rights and achievements of the Jews and the Jewish community already rooted in the country, the rights of the Christian Churches, and British strategic necessities, all forbid this solution of its future.

The basic Arab aims are complete independence, national unity, and the elimination of European political influence and interference; these can never be attained with Palestine included. Anglo-American public opinion would not allow the Jews of Palestine to be reduced to the status of the Baghdad ghetto. But if they had to be protected from outside, this would defeat the British hope of being rid of a difficult duty and the Arab claim to full independence. If, on the contrary, at the price of Palestine the Arabs obtained complete independence everywhere else, plus ample financial compensation, they would strike a not unfavourable bargain. Palestinian Arabs might object, but nowhere can the

[133] From Churchill's speech in the House of Commons on 23 May 1939, PD, C.v. 347, c.2129–90.
[134] Namier has here borrowed Balfour's phrase. In a speech to a Jewish audience at the Albert Hall in July 1920 he said: 'I hope . . . they [the Arabs] will not grudge that small notch, for it is not more geographically, whatever it may be historically – that small notch in what are now Arab territories being given to the people who for all these hundreds of years have been separated from it' [See B. E. C. Dugdale, *Arthur James Balfour* (London, 1939), ii, 163].

fate of empires be made to depend on the willing consent of a 'Tyrone and Fermanagh'.

There can be no way of accurately estimating the extent this public campaign had on the deliberations of the cabinet committee. It is to be hoped it was not counter-productive. At any rate, it provided a new point of departure for Zionist tactics. When partition had first been aired in 1937–8 the Zionists had veered in the opposite direction, overstating in public their opposition to the scheme thereby encouraging the anti-partitionist camp. Now they faced the same acute dilemma. Weizmann and his entourage would undoubtedly accept the right kind of partition;[135] but it had to be forced upon them. They had cast themselves to play the role of the unwilling bride being dragged reluctantly to the altar. As in the Peel debate, they had to tread a very delicate line indeed: 'he [Weizmann] asked us whether, if partition is suggested, we would back him in considering it. Lewis and Brodetsky said *yes, on condition only* (said Lewis) that no one knows at this stage that Chaim would even consider it.'[136]

There were other factors which also had to be taken into account. There can be no room for doubt that the substance of Namier's argument would have cut no ice whatsoever with the Palestinian Arabs, nor with their supporters in London. All previous experience had taught that such a solution could only be imposed by force. How would Churchill, the key to a Zionist-orientated policy, react to such a situation? In 1937 he had adopted an anti-partitionist line, not out of lack of sympathy for the Zionists, but because he was unable to countenance a great imperial power abdicating its pledges in the face of violence.[137] Would he not, upon victory, be encouraged in this attitude when Britain's imperial role was likely to be enlarged and his own personal prestige and authority immensely strengthened?

These were imponderables to which the Zionists had no definite

---

[135] In 1943 the Zionist leadership underwent a severe crisis. Relations between Weizmann and Ben Gurion had steadily deteriorated throughout the year. In October Ben Gurion resigned from the executive, perhaps more as an act of defiance against Weizmann than as an indication that he intended to abdicate his power. Of course, he had never considered himself a member of Weizmann's group, but his defection during these crucial months seriously weakened the Zionist ranks and adversely affected their ability to negotiate from a position of strength. There can be little doubt, however, judging from Ben Gurion's behaviour in 1937, that he would have lent his support, eventually, to Weizmann's policy.

[136] *Dugdale Diaries*, 20 Oct. 1943.

[137] See *The Gentile Zionists*, 132–3, 139.

answer. In any case, it was too early yet to make any binding decisions. In December 1943 the cabinet committee recommended partition on a modified Peel line.[138] The scheme deprived the Jewish state of most of Galilee, though it made some minor territorial gains elsewhere and, of greater importance, held out hope of eventually including the Negev area. The committee, clearly unwilling to relive the 1937–8 experience, further recommended that if it was decided to accept the plan, it must be implemented. A month later, on 25th January, the cabinet agreed in principle to the partition proposal.[139] Only Eden voiced dissent from the general view.[140] The Foreign Secretary deferred judgement on the scheme until he had canvassed opinions from his ambassadors in Cairo and Baghdad. This afforded the Foreign Office sufficient breathing space to orchestrate an anti-partition campaign, repeating their performance of 1937. During the coming months the officials, backed by the chiefs-of-staff, mounted a concerted attack against the concept of partition, an idea they considered ruinous to British interests.[141]

These preliminary skirmishes were inconclusive; but clearly the seeds of doubt had been extensively sown. It would need a massive effort on the part of the Government, and in particular from Churchill, to overcome the combined wisdom of the officials and their political backers. Weizmann and his supporters, Namier among them, scarcely concealed their predilection in favour of partition, provided it conformed with Zionist requirements. Leakages from the committee's deliberations, although at times contradictory, left them with sufficient hope that such indeed would be the case.[142]

In the autumn of 1944, Churchill replaced the issue on the Cabinet's agenda,[143] an act which provoked a renewed outburst of hostility from

---

[138] For the committee's report of 20 Dec. 1943, see WP (43) 563, CAB 63/44.

[139] For cabinet conclusions of 25 Jan. 1944, see CAB 65/45.

[140] Eden's private secretary, usually an unabashed admirer, wrote of his chief and his colleagues 'Jewish policy': [It] is largely due to the blind pro-Arabism of the F.O. which A.E. has never resisted. Indeed he is a blind pro-Arab himself . . . he is hopelessly prejudiced. The Arab myth clouds his mind . . . Unfortunately A.E. is immovable on the subject of Palestine. He loves Arabs and hates Jews.' See *Harvey Diaries*, 30 Nov. 1942, and 21 Apr. 1943.

[141] See in particular a memorandum by Eden, 15 May 1944, WP (44) 253, CAB 66/50, containing reports from Sir Miles Lampson [Lord Killearn] in Cairo, and Sir Kinahan Cornwallis in Baghdad, opposing the scheme; and WP (44) 46, CAB 66/45, a report by the chiefs of staff on British strategic needs in the Levant states, 22 Jan. 1944.

[142] See *Dugdale Diaries* for this period.

[143] See a memorandum dated 16 May 1945 by Oliver Stanley (Colonial Secretary) WP (45) 306, CAB 66/65. This file also contains a summary of the fortunes of the cabinet committee and its proposals.

the Foreign Office.[144] He now favoured partition. Over lunch at Chequers he told Weizmann that he supported the scheme and even spoke of the inclusion 'of the Negev in the Jewish territory', although he made it clear that 'no active steps would be taken until the war with Germany was over.' Weizmann believed 'they could get the whole of Western Palestine if America would sponsor it.'[145] These encouraging developments were eclipsed by the assassination in Cairo of Lord Moyne, now Minister Resident in the Middle East, by two members of the Stern gang. Churchill reacted with anger at this senseless murder, warning the Zionists in public that friends like himself would have 'to reconsider the position we maintained so consistently in the past' if Zionism continued to tolerate such outrages.[146]

The Moyne killing effectively removed the partition proposal from the centre of the stage and put it into cold storage until the spring of 1945. This was sufficient time to enable the anti-partitionists to seize the initiative.[147] By April 1945, with the end of the European war in sight, the Government's policy was as vague as ever. With the break-up of the wartime coalition, the interim administration had no option but to adopt a policy of wait-and-see. Churchill informed Weizmann that the 'Jewish Question could not be touched till the Peace Conference.'[148] This 'terrible blow' left the Zionist leaders understandably bitter. At first, Namier inclined to the view that the officials were chiefly responsible for this decision, still clinging to the illusion that Churchill would carry them through. Labour's victory at the polls in July finally put paid to any hope of an immediate, positive decision. The Zionist leadership, whose aim—the creation of a Jewish state—remained constant, had now to adapt itself to a new and totally unexpected political scenario. Their main prop in Government, Churchill, had gone. Admittedly, the Labour leadership had recently declared in

---

[144] See Cohen, 175.

[145] Record of meeting, 4 Nov. 1944, WA; copy in CZA A312/39; see also *Dugdale Diaries*, 5 Nov. 1944.

[146] See his statement to the House of Commons, 17 Nov. 1944. The Jewish Agency, fully aware of the incalculable political and moral damage precipitated by such terrorist deeds, also reacted angrily to Moyne's murder, even to the extent of co-operating with the mandatory authorities in a campaign directed against the extremist organizations, the *Irgun Zvei Leumi* and the Stern gang. More than 250 terrorists were rounded up during the coming six months and deported from Palestine.

[147] See, for example, a memorandum by Eden, 19 Apr. 1945, WP (45) 229, CAB 66/64, opposing partition, and another by Sir E. Grigg, Minister Resident in Middle East, 4 Apr. 1945, WP (45) 214, CAB 66/64.

[148] *Dugdale Diaries*, 11 June 1945.

favour of their cause.[149] But their Government was confronted by almost insuperable problems. At home, the immensely complicated tasks of post-war reconstruction. Further afield, there existed an enormous chasm between Britain's European commitments and imperial responsibilities and the resources at her disposal to fulfil them. While in the background lurked the menace of Soviet global ambitions. The tragic history of the last three years of British rule in Palestine demonstrates beyond peradventure the incapacity of the Government to reconcile these contradictory forces.

*   *   *

Inseparable from the problem of partition was the fate which awaited the so-called illegal immigrants. Namier's correspondence and notes leave no doubt that for him this was an issue of terrifying dimensions, in some ways far outweighing the rather academic debate about partition. For whereas all were of the opinion that partition, even if agreed upon, could only be implemented in the future, the immeasurable human tragedy of the immigrants would brook no such delay. This was the 'umbilical cord' which bound Namier to every Jew and which became 'tautened agonizingly when one, or a group, fell into dire adversity'.[150] He never ceased petitioning the Government on their behalf, pleading for more lenient treatment and for a more humane attitude towards these wretched people. He did so in a manner unlikely to win him many friends but which reflected accurately his overwrought emotions. In March 1942, in an article entitled 'Refugee Boats', he summarized his feelings on this issue. Even today, almost forty years after it was first published, it can hardly be faulted as a reasoned attack on the Government's immigration policy. It is worth quoting in full.[151]

Very few boats with uncertificated immigrants[152] reached Palestine in the last eighteen months, but the way in which these were handled has attached the name of each to a tragedy.

---

[149] It had done so in a manner likely to cause embarrassment to moderate Zionists. At its annual conference in December 1944, the Labour party had adopted an extreme pro-Zionist resolution. It called for mass Jewish immigration, for the transfer of populations— 'Let the Arabs be encouraged to move out as the Jews move in'—and even for the extension of 'the present Palestinian boundaries, by agreement with Egypt, Syria and Transjordan'.

[150] See Introduction, p. 6.   [151] From *Time and Tide*, 14 Mar. 1942.

[152] Namier explained: 'Officially these people are described as "illegal immigrants", but as this so-called illegality arises under the White Paper of May 1939, which the Permanent Mandates Commission of the League of Nations and the leading British Statesmen, including Mr Churchill, have declared to be contrary to the Mandate, I use the objective term which, while witholding judgement, expresses the undeniable fact that they have no certificates'.

In November, 1940, two boats, the *Pacific* and the *Milos*, reached Haifa with 1,771 uncertificated immigrants. Hitherto such immigrants were interned and released, after careful examination, their number being deducted from the certificates in the next schedule. Now a new procedure was adopted: they were re-embarked on the S.S. *Patria*, and were to be deported to Mauritius; and Sir Harold MacMichael[153] announced in a broadcast that even after the war they would not be allowed to enter Palestine. These were not wanton breakers of the law, but wretched victims of the Nazis fleeing for their lives—it is not clear by what authority or for what reasons this ban was pronounced, prejudging even their distant future and heightening their anguish. While still in harbour the boat blew up, and some 250 lives were lost; the credit for the death roll not being even larger is due to simple British soldiers and policemen who did their utmost to save lives. It is generally believed that the explosion was not an accident, but an act of despair of some of the people on board.[154] Even after this tragedy, it was still the intention to deport the survivors—but finally they were interned, and from the first batch of 100 young men released, 82 enlisted in the British Army. These were the 'illegals' condemned to deportation, banned for all time, and when rescued, once more threatened with forcible removal from their National Home.

Meantime, another boat, the *Atlantic*, reached Haifa with about 1,700 uncertificated immigrants, and these were made to suffer what had been spared to the survivers from the *Patria*. When police entered the Athlit internment camp forcibly to remove them, the men offered resistance, lying down naked on the ground. It is alleged that scenes of brutal violence ensued. The case seemed to call for an impartial inquiry and a preliminary investigation was suggested by the Jewish Agency in London to ascertain whether there was ground for ordering it in Palestine. It was proposed that a certain Englishman, enjoying the confidence of all concerned, should be sent to Mauritius and gather from the deportees what had happened; further, that the officers of the ships in which these people were deported should be examined concerning the state in which they were brought on board. But the Colonial Office preferred to make those whose actions were impugned, sole witnesses and judges in their own case.[155]

[153] High Commissioner for Palestine, 1938–44.

[154] It now seems clear that the explosion, far from being an 'act of despair', was the result of an unforeseen error. An attempt had been made by the Haganah to immobilize the ship's engines with the intention of keeping the refugees in Haifa, thereby exerting political pressure on the authorities to allow them entry into Palestine. This plan miscarried with the most tragic consequences.

[155] For further details of this incident see Moyne to Namier, 31 Mar. 1941, WA; record of an interview between Namier and Moyne, 21 Mar. 1941, WA; and minutes of a Zionist meeting, 8 Jan. 1941, CZA A312/34. See also Wasserstein, 73–6. Moyne strenuously denied Namier's charges of brutality, claiming that the 'screams' were part of 'a campaign of obstruction', and the stories of 'blood' and the 'hurling of bodies into lorries' were entirely fictitious. For these reasons, among others, he did not consider that 'there is even a *prima facie* case for the independent enquiry which you seek'. The Zionists had proposed that Sir Wyndham Deedes, a well-known Gentile Zionist, should conduct the enquiry.

On March 19, 1941, the *Darien* arrived in Haifa with 793 Jewish refugees, mainly from Rumania and Bulgaria. More than half were trained agriculturists or skilled artisans, and all were keen to help in the war effort. Now they have spent a year in an internment camp in enforced idleness, under constant threat of forcible removal, in an atmosphere of growing tension and exasperation. Five have lost their reason, and two of these have been removed to a Mental Hospital; the only ones allowed to leave the camp.

And now the *Struma*. There were 769 passengers on board, including a considerable number of young men fit for work or army service; 15 doctors, 10 qualified engineers; several persons with expired visas for Palestine, and students registered in Palestine schools; people who had property in Palestine; 250 women and 60–70 children. As certificates covering about 3,000 persons had been issued to the Agency for the next six months, the *Struma* passengers could have been admitted without adding to the number allowed. But every request or suggestion from the Agency was met by the Palestine Administration with the customary negative; and even permission of entry for children under 16 was not given till it was too late.[156]

Various reasons are alleged for such treatment of Jewish refugees from Nazi persecution by the Mandatory trustees of the Jewish National Home, and at times they receive most peculiar accessions, the fruit of embarrassed improvisation. The 'security argument' is placed in the forefront—the most impressive argument in wartime. But Frenchmen, Dutchmen, Belgians, Norwegians, etc. are admitted to this country in spite of the Quislings and Vichy; Polish, Czech, Yugoslav, and Greek non-Jews are admitted to Palestine. Only Jews who have experienced the sweets of Jewish life under the Nazis, are now hopelessly 'contaminated' if their goal is Palestine, although several thousand Jews who had been under the Nazis were admitted to Palestine before the new practice was adopted in November, 1940, besides the Patria refugees, and not a single case is known of a Nazi agent having entered among them.

The way in which the 'security argument' is handled is seen in the case of Hungarian and Rumanian Jews who received certificates but had been unable to convert them into visas before the the British Consuls were withdrawn—their certificates were invalidated because of alleged danger of 'impersonation'. The Jewish Agency pleaded in vain that they should be placed in an internment camp in Palestine, from which no one should be released unless his identity was established to the satisfaction of the Palestine administration.[157] Certificates for Palestine are to such Jews the door of salvation, and the few doled out by the

[156] The *Struma*, a dilapidated vessel of some 250 tons lay at anchor off Istanbul; she was eventually towed out to sea by the Turkish authorities and sank in the Black Sea on 25 February 1942 following an explosion which, according to most accounts, was caused either by a torpedo or a mine, leaving one survivor from her 769 passengers.

[157] See Namier to Sir Cosmo Parkinson [Permanent Under-Secretary at the Colonial Office] 25 Nov. 1941, CZA A312/16, where he makes a number of detailed proposals for solving the security question.

Palestine Administration are allocated to people well-known to the Agency. Would the Nazis risk a valuable agent in such an easily traceable fraud? And would they be keen to let any Jew into their spy system and risk its exposure? If they require agents and spies in Palestine, they will know where to find them. The Mufti of Jerusalem works for the Nazis, and in the recent disturbances many thousands of his followers have proved their readiness to face perils and death at his behest. Here is material for a Fifth Column—but the Palestine Administration saw no danger in re-admitting to Palestine men who had been with the Mufti in Baghdad and Iran. Only Jews whom Hitler despoils, degrades, tortures, and kills, appear suspect to the Palestine Administration.

It is argued that were lenient treatment accorded to uncertificated refugees in Palestine, ever growing numbers would be knocking at the gates. Seeing what the Jews suffer under the Axis, those who can, will escape, be it on the merest off-chance of of reaching Palestine. Even a Palestine internment camp or Mauritius are infinitely preferable to any place under the Nazis—and of the painful incidents which mar the story of the refugee boats none need have occurred. But seeing how the Palestine Authorities have dealt with those boats, making each into a tragedy or running sore, it would indeed pay the Nazis to arrange for a procession of such boats, if they thought it worth the trouble and if they could spare the shipping.

The meanest of all the arguments employed against admitting the *Struma* passengers was that they would enlarge the 'consuming' population. But the majority among them were people able to work, and only 200 were elderly persons. These would not have made much difference in a country of $1\frac{1}{2}$ million inhabitants, where few commodities are rationed. Moreover, the admission of a number of 'mere consumers' had been sanctioned in the current schedule.

Lastly there is the argument about arousing disquiet among the Palestine Arabs (though this argument was never used in the case of the *Struma* by the Administration). In no year since the outbreak of the war has the maximum immigration set out for each year by the White Paper been reached, and the *Struma* passengers could have been deducted from the existing schedule.

How easy it would have been to avoid these tragedies, and the ensuing bitterness! When the Colonial Secretary, in November, 1940, expressed the fear that the Nazis were about to arrange a procession of boats carrying uncertificated immigrants (but besides the three known at that time, only two have materialised in fifteen months!) Dr Weizmann offered him the help of the Jewish Agency in coping with the problem, suggesting that immigrants landed in Palestine should be admitted in the manner hitherto practised; that the passengers on boats intercepted en route, and diverted to some British colony, should be joined by Agency representatives who would look after them and re-assure them; and such refugees should be eligible for immigration permits for

Palestine, to be given of course only to such as were found suitable, and for whom certificates were available. The offer was ignored.[158]

As he wrote, 'The offer was ignored.' This was the most disquieting feature of Britain's Palestine policy. It was not possible, except by force, to sustain a policy which coldly elevated political calculation above humanitarian principles. The agony of European Jewry at once compounded and simplified the problem. Some officials, particularly in the Colonial Office, appeared incapable of grasping the true dimensions of the tragedy, seeing the root of the problem in the perfidy of the Zionists. The 'illegals', in their estimation, did not constitute 'a genuine refugee movement' but 'a political conspiracy' designed 'to fill Palestine with Jews and secure domination over the country'.[159] This was sheer fantasy, impossible to rationalize except by the most convoluted mental gymnastics. If the Zionists on occasion exploited the situation to their own advantage, as they undoubtedly did, those responsible in the British Government had only themselves to blame. They could expect no respite from so resolute and passionate a campaigner as Namier. And the judgement of his inveterate adversary at the Colonial Office, Stephen Luke, that he 'has a twisted and embittered personality'[160] would have been interpreted by him as a tribute to his pertinacity on behalf of a noble cause.

*   *   *

The war sharpened Namier's appetite for political controversy and made of him a more awkward colleague than ever before. Mrs Dugdale, his most loyal friend, recorded, almost on a daily basis, his constant waywardness. 'Talked [to Berl Locker] . . . of difficulties arising from Lewis' intolerance', she noted. The following month, she remarked: 'Lewis back, but still very ill and rather grumpy'. A few days later she 'went to the Zionist Office in the morning, found everyone much upset, and Lewis determined to make the worst of everything'.[161]

---

[158] See Weizmann to Lloyd, 22 Nov. 1940, WA; also Namier to Butler, 21 Dec. 1940, CZA A312/30.

[159] From a memorandum by H. F. Downie (then Head of Middle East Department of Colonial Office) quoted by Zweig, 175.

[160] See his memorandum of 2 Dec. 1941, CO 733/444 (1)/75872/26A. Namier's article, 'The Jews' (*Nineteenth Century and After*, Nov. 1941) provided the occasion for Luke's outburst. I am grateful to my colleague, Dr R. W. Zweig, for bringing this reference to my attention.

[161] *Dugdale Diaries*, 7 Jan., 24 Feb., and 6 Mar. 1941. [unpublished].

These were internal altercations, squabbles with associates who acknowledged his idiosyncrasies even if they found it difficult to reconcile themselves to them. He was not quite as patient with those outside his inner circle, particularly when he detected signs of anti-Semitism everywhere around him. Colonel S. F. Newcombe, a noted Arabist who had served with Lawrence, was accused of using methods 'reminiscent of continental anti-Semites, who often try in argument with Jews to exert pressure on them by questioning their loyalty as citizens.'[162] Namier promptly cut off all further relations with him. Another victim, Wilson Harris, editor of the *Spectator* and an erstwhile friend and valuable contact of Namier's, discovered, to his astonishment, that he possessed 'deeper anti-Semitic inclinations'.[163]

He was involved in a controversy of a quite different order with Kingsley Martin, editor of the *New Statesman and Nation*. Martin had asked him to review G. P. Gooch's *Studies in Diplomacy* (London, 1942), but had then rejected Namier's article on the grounds 'that we cannot use reviews which express a point of view categorically opposite to that of the paper. I might add that in this particular case I was really shocked that you should have expressed some of the opinions you did. They seem to me bad morals, bad history, and bad politics.'[164]

To what precisely was Martin objecting? Namier had strongly criticized Gooch's main thesis: that the *entente* of April 1904 with France had prohibited better relations with Germany. 'Grey', Gooch wrote, 'could not be friends with France and Germany at the same time. The choice had been made before he took office.' 'The European system was the main cause of war,' he continued. 'Germany was dragged in by Austria, England by France and Russia. It was an East European quarrel.' Great Britain need not have become involved in the war had she sincerely sought 'reconciliation with Berlin' and not become entangled 'in the traditional quarrels of our new friends'. Namier was

---

[162] Namier to Newcombe, 4 Dec. 1940, CZA A312/55. The correspondence concerned Newcombe's plan to secure Arab co-operation by implementing the White Paper, a notion which was bound to fan Namier's anger.

[163] Namier to Harris, 23 Mar. 1941, CZA A312/55. There was, however, some justification for Namier's reaction. Harris, in an article on the art of reviewing, had written: 'The procedure is simple. Mr Abrahams, the well-known publisher, sends Mr Isaacs the well-known authority on this or that or nothing in particular, a pre-publication copy of the well-known Mr Jacobs' latest book, asking, or at any rate, expecting, to be favoured with a eulogistic sentence or two regarding it.' Namier, rightly, took vigorous exception to this clumsy choice of names.

[164] Martin to Namier, 27 Aug. 1942, CZA A312/55. This file contains the entire correspondence, including the censored review.

unable to accept this 'lenient' and 'hopeful' view of pre-war European diplomacy, so typical of 'Liberal-pacifist critics of his [Gooch's] type' who 'favoured appeasement at any price before 1914, and seem to regret there having been an *entente* even now':

Time after time, before the *entente* was formed, Germany refused to come to a working understanding with this country, but tried to form a Continental bloc against it; both before and after, she refused a naval agreement. Great Britain was threatened, and appeasement at any price would have been no less dangerous in the years before 1914 than it proved 25 years later. From that we were saved by the statesmen who made the Triple Entente —apparantly to Dr Gooch's lasting regret.

From these arguments Martin concluded, and this was his reason for vetoing the review, that

the whole philosophy in your article, which is purely nationalistic and which would rule out any possibility of peace in Europe (since somehow or other we and some lot of Germans have to live together in the same continent) is what I personally mean to spend the rest of my life combatting. And I do not believe that if it were not for the emotions of the moment·that Namier, the sober historian, would differ from me.

In more than thirty years of reviewing Namier had never had a review rejected by an editor; and he was horrified at 'the totalitarian action of scrapping it altogether'. But more to the point,

I take exception to the personal remark that 'if it were not for the emotions of the moment' I would not have differed from you. It did not require either 1914, or 1933, or 1939 to teach me the truth about the Germans. Long before the last war I considered them a deadly menace to Europe and to civilisation. Anyone who knew me in those years will confirm it—ask, for instance, Kenneth Bell.[165] When I went in for the All Souls Fellowship in 1911, one of the reasons why I was turned down was that I took what might now be described as the Eyre Crowe-Vansittart view of Germany.[166]

The correspondence, extending throughout August–September 1942, petered out harmlessly enough. But Namier had no intention of allowing the controversy to terminate with an indeterminate, un-published note to the editor of a weekly journal, however influential. He

---

[165] Kenneth Bell (1884–1951): Fellow and Tutor in Modern History, Balliol College, 1919–41. He was a good friend of Namier's. At the end of Sir Isaiah Berlin's first encounter with Namier, a monologue which lasted for two hours, 'he marched out of my room to tea with Kenneth Bell . . . "whose family is very fond of me"'. (Op. cit.)

[166] Eyre Crowe (1864–1925) and Robert Gilbert Vansittart (1881–1957). Two distinguished diplomats, noted for their extreme anti-German views, both of whom served as permanent under secretary at the Foreign Office.

wished to deprive Gooch, and all others of his ilk, of the opportunity of propagating similar legends regarding the diplomacy of the 1930s. One method of achieving this was by publishing the true record of pre-war diplomacy. He was an early advocate in favour of publishing the official British records of the origins of the 1939 War:

> But, Sir, [he wrote to *The Times*], a version of pre war events is already taking shape, without the best intentioned student being able to do justice to our side; and it is almost impossible to eradicate even a patently erroneous version once it has struck roots and covered the field. After the last war we suffered by allowing the Germans to put out their story long before ours was published; book after book appeared based on the *Grosse Politik*, written by historians, many of whom sincerely believed that its presentation of diplomatic transactions could be accepted as full and reliable . . . Is it not high time that this utterly abnormal situation, not justified by any national interest and indeed highly prejudicial to it, was rectified?[167]

For once, the Foreign Office officials, at least those at the junior level, were in full agreement with his demands.[168] However, in 1946, when Namier was working on his diplomatic histories of the 1930s, the officials evinced rather less patience when responding to his persistent and detailed enquiries about the intricacies of British diplomacy in 1938–9.[169]

*   *   *

With the war drawing to a close Namier prepared to leave his Zionist work and return to his university duties. On the whole he had overcome the physical dangers of the war without undue concern. Although he was 'blitzed' on at least one occasion, German bombs held no fear for him, and he periodically took his place among the fire-watchers of London:

> The air raid warnings do not interfere with any of my habits, nor even with my sleep: except that the All Clear usually wakes me up. I had only one bad night and that was largely due to a discussion about what I should do for my family[170] . . . and Chaim had one bad night having eaten too many salt

---

[167] *The Times*, 25 Sept. 1943.   [168] See FO 371/34478A, C11145/1558/18.

[169] See FO 371/1252, L3937, 4958, 5026, 5325, 5446/3937/405.

[170] His mother, sister, and two nieces had been trapped in Lvov since the Nazi conquest in September 1939. Throughout the occupation he had received no indication as to their fate. After the Red Army reconquered Lvov he contacted friends in the Foreign Office requesting their help in tracing his family. [See Namier to Alan Walker, 18 Apr. 1944, FO 371/42743, W6154/22/48.] It is not clear what happened to the surviving members of his family. There is no mention of them, after his request to the Foreign Office, in his papers. Lady Namier wrote [op. cit., 182] that 'He never saw Ann or Theodora again', though his sister, Theodora, certainly survived the war.

cucumbers. Otherwise we two wise men slept in our beds and did not bother about the Nazi planes.[171]

As has been noted, it was his mental state which gave cause for the greatest concern. Lady Namier remarked:

During what remained of the summer of 1942 L[ewis] continued in so bad a shape that, when I first saw him, in the autumn, he gave me the impression of a great ship trapped in some fabulous polar solitude, creaking slightly as it moved—or let itself be pushed—further into the ice.[172]

Towards the end of the war, as the result of an overpowering combination of personal and political pressures, he seriously contemplated suicide.[173]

Certainly one political issue which profoundly depressed him was the upsurge in Jewish terrorism in Palestine from the beginning of 1944. Weizmann had once remarked to Smuts that 'Hitler has won this war as far as the Jews are concerned.'[174] He was referring specifically to British adherence, and Great Power indifference, to the White Paper policy in the face of the mass liquidation of European Jewry. But he might equally have had in mind the revival of terrorism in Palestine which, to his mind, was tearing apart the moral and political fabric of Zionism. The depth of his revulsion can be gauged from a speech he made in Palestine during his first visit there since the outbreak of war. He confided to his audience:

You all know my personal tragedy in losing my son.[175] You can imagine how great was the shock to me. But the shock when I heard of the murder of Lord Moyne was not less. When my son was killed it was my personal tragedy— *Hashem natan, Hashem lakach* (God gives, God takes)—but here it is the tragedy of the entire nation.[176]

Most responsible Zionists shared his feelings. But, as always, Namier's attitude resembled that of others only marginally. Never a pacifist, he was certain that a nation must, if necessary, fight for its survival. It was the nation's viability—its skill to exist as an inde-

[171] Namier to Mrs Dugdale, 30 Aug. 1940, CZA A312/44.
[172] Julia Namier, 247.   [173] Ibid., 259.
[174] *Dugdale Diaries*, 14 Oct. 1943.
[175] His youngest son, Michael, a flight-lieutenant in the RAF, was reported missing in action over the Channel in February 1942. His eldest son, Benjamin, was also a casualty of war. He was invalided out of the army in September 1940, after being hospitalized for several months in a state of shell-shock.
[176] See *Jewish Chronicle*, 24 Nov. 1944; and on the same subject his letter to Churchill, *Trial and Error* (London, 1950), 537–8.

pendent political entity—that was being put to the test. But he despised terrorism, an insidious, corrupting manifestation of the nationalism he upheld. He saw it ultimately as the crazed acts of desperate, irresponsible men; the work of a lunatic fringe who, by their insane provocations, brought the entire movement into disrepute. Above all, he regarded it as morally corrupting and politically counter-productive. His abhorrence of terrorism, reinforced by his sense of national responsibility, and his concomitant feeling that healthy societies should produce statesmen able to foster in the young a sense of national responsibility no less potent than their own, was absolute.[177] As he ironically noted: 'The spiritual affinities between them (the *Irgun* and the *Haganah*) are about as close as between the I.R.A. and the late Mr Lansbury.'[178]

He was undergoing a phase of disappointment with the two communities most dear to him. In the case of the British the disillusionment was far less intense because less personal; any disappointment in a Jew, however, was echoed by a gnawing despair in himself. His vision about a great river of political Zionism,[179] guided by Weizmann's humane and civilized teachings, flowing out of Judaism's melting glacier appeared to be dying an unnatural death. The future was uncertain, even foreboding. What would be his place in the emerging scheme of affairs? Again, there could be no categorical answer to this question. Despite these formidable quandaries there was a happy sequel to his wartime career as a Zionist politician:

Chaim gave a wonderful supper at the Dorchester for the 'Polar Expedition' i.e. our dear old Yeshiva[180], with the Palestinian inner circle, and Vera, Mr Ben Gurion, Malkah Locker, Mr Brodetsky and Miss May. It was really a sort of farewell to Lewis, who is returning to his history work. Chaim made a beautiful speech, mostly about him, and several of us spoke also. Brodetsky made a really wonderfully generous tribute, especially as they have not always got on, and Ben Gurion spoke of Berel Katzenelson and what *he* had felt about Lewis. I am sure dear Lewis was pleased. He made a very moving little speech. I spoke about him too, and also about what it means to me to have been made so one with

[177] Lady Namier's Notes.

[178] Letter to *The Times*, 11 May 1940. George Lansbury (1859–1940), leader of the Labour Party, 1931–5, was a well-known pacifist. See also Namier's letter to *The Times*, 13 Apr. 1944, pointing out the manner in which moderate Jews were co-operating with the authorities in containing terrorist activity.

[179] See pp. 30–31.

[180] Hebrew: literally a 'sitting'; colloquial usage for a 'meeting', but also, and perhaps on occasion more appropriately, used to describe a religious seminar.

them all. It was one of the most utterly harmonious gatherings of friends it has ever been my lot to take part in.[181]

It must have been with very mixed feelings that he returned to Manchester in the autumn of 1945.

[181] *Dugdale Diaries*, 8 Aug. 1945.

Chapter 5

Mellowing with Age

None of those present at his farewell party believed he was withdrawing from Zionist work for good. The scale of the tragedy of European Jewry was too great, the details of the holocaust too horrendous to allow his troubled mind any respite. Moreover, the new Labour Government proved to be a grievous disappointment. Instead of embarking on a new and more positive policy, as had confidently been expected, Attlee's administration refused to abrogate the White Paper. Hoping to involve the United States in the post-war settlement in the Middle East, it was decided that Palestine's future be assessed by an Anglo-American Commission of Inquiry. Once again the Zionists were faced with the prospect of presenting their case and explaining it in public. Canvassing support, lobbying supporters, drafting statements, writing letters— these were activities which eminently suited Namier's talents; and he did not stint his services. His views about organizing the debates in the House of Commons were received with interest.[1] More to the point, he re-established himself as Weizmann's 'ideas man'. The Commission began its investigations in London. Mrs Dugdale reported its deliberations in great detail to Namier. As a result, he produced for Weizmann a summary of 'The Jewish Question' over the last sixty-five years.[2] Weizmann read it just as he was leaving London to attend the Commission's sessions in Jerusalem. He wrote: 'I have just finished reading your excellent (most excellent) statement. There is a good deal which I could use with effect and shall do so with your permission. A hearty *shalom* to you and all the best.' In the tradition of their last twenty years Namier answered: 'I'm glad you liked my sketch and found it useful.[3]

The article was an eloquent reappraisal of Namier's thoughts on the Jewish question in the light of recent events. Recognizing that European Jewry had been decimated or was incarcerated in the Soviet Union, he shifted the burden of responsibility on to the English-

[1] See Namier to Weizmann, 4 Feb. 1946, WA or CZA A312/47.
[2] First published in *Manchester Guardian*, 8 Mar. 1946; later in *Facing East*.
[3] Weizmann to Namier, 19 Feb. 1946, and Namier to Weizmann, 20 Feb. 1946, CZA A312/47.

speaking Jews. Upon their response would hang the fate of the Jewish people:

For the core of the Jewish problem is now the 55 per cent of world Jewry resident in English-speaking countries, and the question is whether on that stage too the recurrent Jewish tragedy is to be re-enacted. A Jewish Commonwealth in Palestine within the framework of the British Empire, or possibly of an even wider 'Atlantic Union', would differentiate the future of the Jews from their past; and now is the time for the Anglo-Saxons to make their decision. But it is incumbent on the Jews of the English-speaking countries to pose the problem unmistakably: if a hundred thousand young Jews, of American or British birth, came forward and demanded admission to Palestine, national redemption and not individual salvation would be fixed as the goal. But if they and the English-speaking nations shirk the issue, and wait until an acute Jewish Question has arisen in their own countries, they will have waited too long.

It was perfectly understandable that after the Second World War Namier should have viewed the Jewish question in such limited and apocalyptic terms. Eventually the response he sought came not from the Anglo-Saxon world but from the Arabic-speaking countries, not by immigration of one hundred thousand but of one million, and not voluntarily but as a result of lack of choice. Still, the result was the same: national redemption and not individual salvation. Israel still awaits its one 'hundred thousand young Jews of American or British birth'.

Throughout 1946 Palestine slipped steadily into chaos. The British were losing their grip, in effect abdicating power and responsibility. In Jerusalem Weizmann had pleaded for immediate admission into Palestine of 100,000 'displaced persons', a proposal supported by President Truman but rejected by the British Government who responded with the derisory figure of 1,500 a month. The leaders of the *Yishuv*, although opposed to terrorism, now encouraged a policy of 'activism': running the British blockade; landing refugees in ever-increasing numbers; establishing new settlements. The Administration recognized no such fine distinction between 'terrorists' and 'activists'. In a letter written immediately after the Moyne killing, General Paget, C.-i.-C. Middle East Command, voiced sentiments representative of most British officials in the area:

I hope it will be a warning to the P.M. and others as to what we are up against in Palestine. The Jewish Agency cannot escape responsibility. They could if they wished provide us with information which would enable us to arrest the leaders of the Stern Gang. I am afraid these acts of terrorism will continue unless we take very strong action against them . . .[4]

On 29 June 1946, the so-called Black Sabbath, over 2,000 leaders of the *Yishuv* were arrested, the most important of whom were interned in Latrun.[5] Although not a member of the Zionist Executive, Namier, when in London, frequently attended its meetings. Another participant recalls his presence:

The meeting was tense and perplexed. Namier was, so far as I can recollect, taciturn at these meetings, but when he did speak was always very much to the point. On that occasion he broke one of his silences to say, in effect: 'You needn't worry, ladies and gentlemen. George III did the same thing to the Americans in 1776 but look what happened at the end. So it will be with us.' The tension was released.[6]

His views regarding the settlement of the Palestine question had not altered substantially since the late 1930s. He wrote to his old friend, Walter Elliot:[7]

Remember that the most essential thing now is that we should be offered decent frontiers based on the need and prospect of immigration, and should not be limited to what we hold already—in other words, that we should go back to the Peel Report and not to the terms of reference of the Woodhead Commission.[8]

What had altered, however, was the calibre of the men now responsible for upholding the mandate, or relinquishing its burden in the most cowardly manner. Gone were the leaders of genuine distinction: Balfour, Lloyd George, Amery, and Churchill. They had been replaced

---

[4] General Paget to Sir J. Grigg, 12 Nov. 1944, Grigg Papers, PJGG 9/7/19 (Churchill College, Cambridge). On the same topic, see notes of an interview between Ben Gurion, George Hall, and Arthur Creech-Jones, CZA A312/41.

[5] The arrests resulted, ostensibly, from the intensification of Jewish underground activity—mainly blockade-running and the establishment of new settlements—since the end of the war. Just two weeks before the arrests, the *Haganah*, in a spectacular demonstration of the techniques of guerrilla warfare, had totally disrupted the road and rail communications system, cutting off Palestine from its neighbours, an action known as the 'Night of the Bridges'. The intention of the arrests was, no doubt, to curb such provocations to British authority. The effect, inevitably, was to escalate the violence to an even more horrifying dimension. On 22 July the *Irgun* blew up a wing of the King David Hotel, which housed the British army headquarters, killing 91 persons and wounding 45 others; the casualties included British, Arabs, and Jews.

[6] Mr S. Rosenne to the author, 24 Apr. 1977.

[7] Walter Elliot (1888–1958): Conservative MP, 1918–23, 1924–45, 1946–58; Minister of Agriculture, 1932–6; Secretary of State for Scotland, 1936–8; Minister of Health, 1938–40. Elliot was a great friend of both Mrs Dugdale and Namier.

[8] Namier to Walter Elliot, 17 July 1946, WA, CZA A312/41.

by men of dubious quality, faithful to the tradition of Ramsey MacDonald's Government of 1929. Everywhere, from India to Palestine, the Empire was disintegrating in a vicious circle of violence, surrender, and humiliation. Namier expressed nothing but contempt for Attlee and his fatuous attempts at firm Government; his Foreign Secretary, once a helpful sympathizer, was now always referred to as 'the calamitious Bevin'.[9] 'Sir George Gater [Permanent Under Secretary at the Colonial Office] and the Permanent Officials will just make rings round both these little men.[10] It takes a long, long time to make a Governing Class', confided Mrs Dugdale to her diary,[11] a sentiment which Namier would have heartily endorsed.

*   *   *

Namier's relationship with Weizmann was also about to undergo a violent upheaval. They were still in broad agreement on policy, though Namier was inclined to adopt a more activist approach. In May 1946 he wrote an adulatory article on Weizmann, commemorating his seventieth birthday:

Weizmann is the first leader in the Dispersion acknowledged as such by the vast majority of Jews throughout the world and officially recognized by the Powers; and for the first time since the destruction of the Temple has a chance of national resurrection and reintegration come to the Jewish people. Weizmann was instrumental in securing it, and has guided the effort to convert it into a reality.[12]

But Weizmann's leadership was now under the most heavy pressure. Isolated from developments in Palestine, he found it impossible to impose his authority any longer on the movement. Events moved to a climax at the twenty-second Zionist Congress in Basle in December 1946. Weizmann was inclined, reluctantly, to accept the Government's proposal to convene yet another tripartite conference, not because he believed that such a gathering would prove successful but because the alternatives, for him, were too horrible to contemplate. It would be a last-ditch attempt, however forlorn, to avoid unnecessary bloodshed. Despite a valiant speech,[13] Congress rejected his policy and he felt he

[9] Lady Namier's Notes.

[10] The reference is to George Hall, Colonial Secretary, and Arthur Creech-Jones, his Under-Secretary.

[11] *Dugdale Diaries*, 3 Aug. 1945.

[12] See Namier, 'Leadership in Israel: Chaim Weizmann', *Time and Tide*, 31 May 1946. Reprinted in *Facing East*.

[13] See *Dugdale Diaries*, 16 Dec. 1946.

had no alternative but to resign as president of the movement, though in fact the elected leadership followed closely his line if not his lead.[14] 'It is an age of pygmies', Mrs Dugdale complained, 'and so much squalor, spite, folly and party hatreds seem to be devouring Zionist politics. I think the day is done for Zionists of the old school.'[15] To some of his closest associates, Mrs Dugdale and Namier, he spoke of forming an opposition group. 'Lewis suggests it be called "The Last Attempt Group".'[16] This was a wild idea from which nothing materialized.

In any case, Namier's days of close co-operation with Weizmann were almost at an end. He was about to marry Julia de Beausobre, a Russian *émigrée* who had arrived in England in the late 1930s after spending many years in Stalin's labour camps in Central Asia.[17] They were married on 4 June 1947 at the Russian Orthodox Church of All Saints, London. It was a small, private affair. Passionately religious, she insisted on a religious ceremony and Namier's baptism into her church.[18] That his marriage brought him great happiness and emotional tranquillity is beyond dispute. 'His marriage is imminent and he looks radiant,' remarked Mrs Dugdale.[19] Weizmann, however, reacted in a style reminiscent of an ancient Jewish patriarch:

As regards Namier, we, of course, heard the facts here; for some time it was the talk of the town [Weizmann wrote the letter in Rehovoth]—and no wonder. It is difficult to imagine a greater breach than Namier's apostasy. Here is a man who was an extremist in his Zionist views and suddenly decides to sever his connections with his people, because however he may try to gloss it over it is a severance, and there is no formula with which you can cover it up. Change of the Jewish religion into Christianity, whether one is an orthodox Jew or not, means abandoning the weaker and joining the stronger—in simple words—a betrayal. What he tells you about the integration of Christianity and Judaism are meaningless phrases which do not make this act any better or more beautiful. It is a bad thing at all time, and particularly in the state of the Jewish people in which it finds itself now, it is unpardonable. He did say to me, when I

[14] In fact, the composition of the Executive, with the notable exception of Weizmann, differed little from its predecessor. It included: Ben Gurion, Weizmann's leading contender; Shertok and Locker, among Weizmann's most loyal supporters; rabbi Silver, an articulate opponent of Weizmann's; and rabbi Wise, Silver's greatest rival in American Zionism. Its policy was also without substantial change. Early in the New Year it was involved yet again in official talks with the British Government.

[15] *Dugdale Diaries*, 18 Dec. 1946.
[16] *Dugdale Diaries*, 9 Jan. 1947 [unpublished].
[17] She wrote a book about her experiences, *The Woman Who Could Not Die* (London, 1938).
[18] Julia Namier, 269–70.   [19] *Dugdale Diaries*, 23 May 1947 [unpublished].

visited him at the Hospital after his operation, that I might find that he got married during my stay in Palestine. He also spoke to Vera and myself about the insistence on the part of his wife that they should marry in Church. But marrying in Church, bad enough as it is, is one thing, and joining the Church of England [*sic*] on the top of it, is something quite different. Well, he has gone; he has left the fold and there is nothing more I have to say about it. I trust that they will make no attempt to see me when I return to England.[20]

How did Namier equate his entry into the Orthodox Church with his Zionism? Or, to put the question in a wider dimension, how did he reconcile his Zionism and his new-found Christianity with his utter contempt for anything connected with what he described as *Ideengeschichte*? 'The less, therefore,' he once elucidated, 'man clogs the free play of his mind with political doctrine and dogma, the better for his thinking.'[21] As with most acts of human behaviour, there can be no wholly rational explanation for his conduct. In his own mind, his return to religion and his commitment to Zionism were intimately connected, one complemented the other. In 1941 he wrote:

Nineteen centuries ago our people divided: one branch, the Hebrew Nazarenes, carried into the world our national faith coupled with their new tidings, the other, as a closed community, preserved the old tradition. Yet both were part of one nation, and both are part of our national history. Only by seeing them as one whole shall we recover the full sense and greatness of our history . . . How much of the hatred which turned against the Jewish remnant was hostility to Christianity, diverted against those among whom it had originated?[22]

Clearly, his childhood memories haunted him. He had never completely abandoned his intellectual interest in Christianity. At Balliol, he had read widely on the subject. It appeared as though he was in constant search for a symbiosis between the two branches of his people divided nineteen centuries ago. It was not entirely by coincidence that he first met Lady Namier during the war at a meeting convened to find common ground between 'enthusiastic Christians and persecuted Jews'.[23] After the war, with the experience of the holocaust deeply embedded in his consciousness, Lady Namier recollected the painful discussions she had conducted with him about his attitude to religion. At one point, he even declared his readiness to abandon his current historical research in favour of a study in depth of 'the

[20] Weizmann to Mrs Dugdale, 8 June 1947, WA.
[21] *Personalities and Powers* (London, 1955), 5.
[22] See his essay 'The Jews', *Nineteenth Century and After* (Nov. 1941), reprinted in *Conflicts*.
[23] Julia Namier, 248.

most significant theme in man's development—the emergence of Christianity on the shores of the Mediterranean' in order to reveal 'the message of the real church, lost when the Christian Synagogue was crushed between conservative Jews and converted barbarians.'[24] His intention was clear: 'baptism into Christ was the proper development for a Jew aware of his people's history in its worldwide significance.'[25]

He had never concealed the fact that his Judaism had nothing to do with adherence to a particular form of religious ritual. For Namier it was determined by its national content. 'Except for the Return', he once wrote, 'Jewish survival would be a tragic absurdity.'[26] He continued:

The ultimate answer to the Jewish Question, that mysterious age-long and world-wide problem, can only be given in the crystal-clear terms of the creed which has created and continued it, in terms of the Jewish nation: survival was the behest and the Return is the purpose.

From this it was but a short intellectual step to the belief that a baptized Jew could work as effectively for the realization of the Zionist programme, 'the Return', as a Jew who adhered to the traditional values. He developed the argument a stage further: the creation of a Jewish state would enable the Jew, if he so desired, to merge into Gentile society. Once rejected as a humiliating and illusory solution, the fulfilment of 'the Return' transformed it into an honourable alternative. In an arresting passage, he elucidates these points:

There have been Jews who, though deeply attracted by Christianity, refused baptism in order not to separate from their people—Bergson and Werfel are examples; others who, though baptised remained outspokenly conscious Jews— for instance, Disraeli and Heine. The charge of 'irreligion' is sometimes levelled against the Zionists by Gentile opponents. But the Jew who works for the Return, and still more the one who effects it, bears the truest testimony to his faith, and it is a spiritual indiscretion in unfriendly strangers to set up as interpreters of the Jewish religion.

. . . The ghetto must disappear, the Galuth (Exile) must end. This can be achieved in two ways: through national reintegration in Palestine, and through deliberate dissolution, or ultimate dissolubility, in the Diaspora. The two methods are mutually complimentary; both achieve normality and put an end to the Jew of 'the Jewish Question.' The rebuilding of Zion is the fulfillment of God's promise and bidding, or, in terms of unbelief, of the most peculiar and most persistent obsession in history. When this is accomplished day will break

[24] Julia Namier, 262.   [25] Ibid.
[26] From his article, 'The Jewish Question', *Manchester Guardian*, 8 Mar. 1946.

and the guard will be relieved. We shall be a nation, like unto all nations, a nation and not a problem. Then those who have struck roots in other soil will be able to separate with dignity . . .[27]

Did Namier see himself as a latter-day Disraeli or Heine? An outspokenly conscious Jew, unashamed of his past, proud of the contemporary achievements of Jewish nationalism, confident of his future among his Gentile neighbours. To Mrs Dugdale, on the eve of his marriage, he confided his innermost thoughts, reconciling his Zionism and acceptance into the church. 'He spoke with great dignity and simplicity. He is more Zionist than ever, convinced that Judaism and Christianity must in the end be reconciled, and this can only happen in Palestine.'[28]

Thus, by virtue of peculiarly tragic circumstances, he remained remote, physically at least, from the affairs of Palestine at precisely the most critical months before the establishment of the state of Israel. His interest, however, never flagged.[29] On 29 November 1947, the United Nations, on the recommendation of its own investigating body, UNSCOP, voted in favour of partition. In Palestine, the Jewish Agency, in the absence of any effective British authority, and in a situation bordering on anarchy, began, in effect, to act as a Provisional Government. The Jews and the Arabs were already at war in everything but name. Arab irregulars infiltrated the proposed Jewish area, while on its borders the surrounding Arab countries made open preparations for war to destroy the Jewish state at its birth. In February the Security Council was perturbed enough to discuss a reversal of policy. The following month it was thought expedient that the partition proposal should be suspended, a temporary truce enforced, and a trusteeship formed to take over the running of the country. Lady

[27] Ibid.

[28] *Dugdale Diaries*, 16 Mar. 1947. Some of the material for the above interpretation is culled from Lady Namier's recollections (op. cit., 247–8, 261–4, 269–70). Lady Namier, herself an extremely devout Christian, clearly had a vested interest in presenting Namier in such a light. She conditioned their marriage upon his baptism; and Namier may well have agreed to her demand for purely personal reasons, an understandably human reaction. On the other hand, there is no convincing reason to discount her evidence, subjective as it is. Quite the contrary, whatever independent source materials are available, his article 'The Jews', for example, written well before he met Lady Namier, and chance remarks noted by Mrs Dugdale, all tend to substantiate Lady Namier's version.

[29] See, for example, his letter to his one surviving aunt, Mrs Henry Landau, settled in New York, 12 Mar. 1947, CZA A312/57.

Namier has recorded Namier's reactions, somewhat ambivalent regarding Weizmann's role, to these events:

Namier followed with excitement all accounts of the *Yishuv's* ingenious ways of immediately, despite incredible odds, building the rudiments of a state on the ruins which the Mandatory Power was deliberately leaving as it withdrew. The local Jews administrative abilities delighted him. But he followed with mounting anguish Weizmann's statements to the American press, as well as accounts of his activities in Washington and Sharett's at Lake Success. Not that either placed a foot wrong. Their statements were firm enough on Palestinian Jews having outgrown all forms of tutelage, and on their only true choice being between statehood and extermination. But the leader of a nation in peril can hardly ever be its envoy overseas—neither Washington or New York seemed the right place for Weizmann to be that spring.[30]

The mandate was scheduled to terminate on 14 May 1948. The days immediately before and after witnessed Namier's return to active Zionism. For a brief, intense period, with Weizmann far removed in the United States, he resumed those duties so familiar to him. He did not act in any official capacity, but on his own initiative. His lobbying, which had lost none of its incisiveness, was concerted with his former colleagues who, in turn, kept him in touch with the latest developments in Palestine, sending him secret envelopes marked for his 'information only'.[31]

*   *   *

After the state of Israel was established, something of Namier's inner turbulence subsided. No doubt the happiness of his marriage contributed to his state of mind. But he was also less inclined to view political, particularly Zionist, matters in apocalyptic terms. Despite the innumerable dangers that confronted it, he was confident that Israel would survive and prosper. The truly historic act of its creation could not be reversed. He would not share a part in its future, save as a committed spectator from the outside. But he had participated in great events. He had known intimately the architects of Israel's renaissance; he had shared their vision, and had aided them to the best of his ability. He hoped that they would put aside their petty quarrels and personal rivalries to meet the formidable challenges that lay ahead. The two outstanding leaders of the movement, Weizmann, for whom nothing could erode his hero-worship, and Ben Gurion, had both now found

[30] Lady Namier's Notes.   [31] See CZA A312/57.

their proper place, and they could combine their unique talents for the common good. Lady Namier recalled his spontaneous aside made shortly after the state was proclaimed. Striding along a ridge in the Peak District, he paused to exclaim, 'Thank God for Ben Gurion! Thank God for Chaim in Israel's pre-history.'[32]

Despite a general toning-down of Namier's political style, one topic never failed to revive his passion for political controversy. After the war he rejected in the most vehement terms an invitation to address a Foreign Office Seminar on Russian–German relations to which a number of Germans had been invited.[33] Two years later he was involved in a similar debate about Basil Liddell Hart's[34] latest book, *On The Other Side of the Hill* (London, 1948), an account of his interviews with German generals then in preparation. Replying to Namier's criticism, Liddell Hart had written that he 'found that their [the generals] behaviour was much better than I had expected from the effect of Nazi influence . . . The evidence of the extent to which their troops were impregnated with Nazism makes it all the more remarkable that they were able to exert so much restraint on their troops as they, clearly, did.'[35] In a further note he made crystal-clear his views regarding in particular the treatment of Jews by the German army and the need for objectivity on the part of Jews when assessing the evidence for and against:

The Nazi treatment of the Jews was appalling, but it is a bad omen for the future that so many Jews allow their judgement to be so biased by it that they cannot weigh facts dispassionately. I am more pro-Jew than most people in this country, or anywhere else, but I have come to realise sadly the fatal tendency of Jews to bring their troubles on themselves, by vindictiveness. Gollancz[36] is a happy exception, and also a wiser example . . . But all too few Jews have been

---

[32] Ben Gurion was elected Israel's first prime minister and defence minister, Weizmann her first president. Unfortunately, Namier's hopes never materialized. Ben Gurion, not without a touch of vindictiveness, deliberately excluded Weizmann from the machinery of effective decision-making, and turned him into a ceremonial, figure-head president, the very position Weizmann had always dreaded. In his own telling phrase, he had become 'the prisoner of Rehovoth'.

[33] See pp. 61–62

[34] Basil Henry Liddell Hart (1895–1970): military historian; military correspondent, *Daily Telegraph*, 1925–35, *The Times*, 1935–9; personal adviser to Hore-Belisha (Secretary of State for War), 1937–8. Kn. 1966.

[35] The correspondence is in CZA A312/55. In the same connection, see Namier's letter to *Manchester Guardian*, 6 Dec. 1943.

[36] Victor Gollancz (1893–1967): publisher and writer; organized 'Save Europe Now' for relief of starvation in Germany and elsewhere, 1945. Kn. 1965.

ready to follow his example. Instead they seem determined to prove once again that they are their own worst enemies. That is bound to lead to more trouble for them—it is like a ball rebounding from wall to wall. Because of your profound historical sense no-one is better fitted than you to give a lead.

Liddell Hart then clarified his evaluation of the professionalism of the German General Staff. While recognizing that it contained 'a few men of high talent', 'For the most part it is composed of the equivalent of competent branch managers . . . In military education I should rate most German generals on the undergraduate level, British ones on the secondary school level, and American ones on the primary school level.'

Having disposed of this contentious point, Liddell Hart swept on to pontificate on an even more controversial subject:

I do not follow your reasoning for refusing to recognise that 'unconditional surrender' was a mistake. That has come to be recognised now by almost everyone who was not directly responsible for the policy. It is the reverse of good strategy to help your chief opponent to strengthen his hold on his subordinates, satellites and troops—and stiffen their resistance. While policy should control strategy, bad strategy stultifies policy.

As I have remarked before, you seem to me the greatest living example on how real historianship can triumph over extraordinarily violent prejudices! But if you could free yourself from such prejudices you would be a still greater historian. I know no other with the mental equipment to equal yours.

Namier's reply was soon forthcoming. He defended the concept of unconditional surrender in the most emphatic terms:

In the first place, the experience of 1918 and of the years that followed, seemed to point to the absolute need of indisputable victory and surrender; so that the Germans should not be able to argue a second time that they had never been squarely beaten but cheated. Had we gone to Berlin in 1918–19, we might have been spared the need of fighting a second time. I expect you will agree that the legend which the Germans have spun about the Armistice of 1918, has done a great deal of harm. Peace negotiations with the Germans would have undoubtedly been disastrous. Had we attempted any negotiations with the Germans, with the present Russia for ally, it would have given the Germans a chance, and a first-class chance, of driving a wedge between the Western and the Eastern allies. The result could hardly have been in doubt; it would have led to a new Ribbentrop–Molotov treaty in reverse . . . In short, negotiations in 1944 would have produced a Russian–German Alliance under Russian leadership.

He next proceeded to deal with the disputatious question of the

German army and the Jews. He quoted chapter-and-verse from German army orders:

The soldier must appreciate the necessity for harsh punishment of Jewry, the spiritual bearer of the Bolshevik terror. This is also necessary in order to nip in the bud all uprisings which are mostly attributable to Jews[37]

'The German army undertook to play the hangmates to the Gestapo and the SD', he concluded, 'and I don't see why I should blink the facts.'

It was a matter of complete indifference to him how Gentiles, whether German or British or American, regarded the Jews:

Altogether I have never belonged to the O.T.I. (Organisation of Trembling Israelites), deeply concerned about what anti-Semites, or in general non-Jews, might think of us . . . Here is a perfectly authentic story.

A Scotsman with whom I had only a very superficial acquaintance, on my telling him that I was a Jew, said: 'I do not know how you will like what I am going to say, but you are the first Jew I ever liked.' I replied: 'Would it interest you to know whether I like Scotsmen?' He admitted that it would not. 'Then why do you expect me to be interested in what you feel about Jews?' He saw the point, as will any sane non-Jew to whom it is put.

He terminated this correspondence with a reaffirmation of his Zionist creed:

And this is the reason why I worked so hard for Zionism and Israel: that we should be 'like unto all nations', neither outcasts nor the 'chosen race' of our own imagination. But, if I may say so, I think you have still to revise your attitude in that matter; I hardly think you would have written a letter like yours of 22 March to a member of any other nation which had lost one third of its people, murdered, and most of them tortured to death, by an enemy nation.

*   *   *

During the period after 1948 Namier's links with Zionism became more tenuous, certainly less political. It could be argued that he was older, tired more easily, had less time on his hands. All this was unquestionably true. He was in the twilight of his career. His *History of Parliament*, a massive undertaking by any reckoning, consumed all his

---

[37] This quotation is taken from Field Marshal von Manstein's order to his army of 20 Nov. 1941. There was of course no shortage of similar statements from other German generals. Namier no doubt chose von Manstein's because he had acquired a reputation as a strictly professional soldier indifferent to National Socialist ideology. See G. Reitlinger, *The Final Solution* (London, 1953), 197–8.

time and demanded his full attention. During his last decade, professional honours were showered upon him from all directions. The recognition he had so eagerly sought was his. He had climbed out of the wilderness on to a new and higher plateau of personal and professional fulfilment. Perhaps, in consequence, he lost the urge to prove himself in politics.

But also, of course, the very act of the creation of the Jewish state diminished any role he might have played in active Zionist politics. By a curious paradox, the attainment of the goal he had fought for a generation to attain signalled his demise as a Zionist politician. The traditional, political framework of the Zionist movement had been transformed. Many of the functions of the Jewish Agency had been taken over by the Government of Israel. Most of his old comrades were occupying important positions in the Government and Administration from which he had deliberately excluded himself. Namier had long ago reconciled himself to the fact that he had no place in a Jewish state. He was nothing if not honest with himself. He wrote to Ben Gurion: 'I would like to add how much I agree with you about Israel and Diaspora Zionism.'[38] He would spend the remainder of his days as an armchair Zionist, occasionally participating in public debates, tendering advice when requested, but realizing, as he never had done in the past, the strict limitations of his current position.

One of his most profitable contacts with contemporary Israel was an old friend, Eliyahu Eilat,[39] who had arrived in London as his country's first diplomatic envoy. He opened wide for Namier a window into Israel: her conditions of life, her aspirations, the policies she intended to pursue. He listened to everything, but expressed particular concern that Israel's international standing should be enhanced by a body of skilled, professional diplomats. It was a subject on which he could claim some expertise, at least in the academic sense, having published several works on diplomatic history. Naturally, he also possessed strong views on this topic. He had once remarked to Sir Isaiah Berlin, in a different context, that 'four years in an embassy tends to desiccate one's style and petrify

---

[38] Namier to Ben Gurion, 29 July 1957, CZA A312/43. Ben Gurion's definition of 'who is a Zionist' had aroused fierce controversy in the Zionist, and Jewish, world. He attacked those Zionists, particularly from the Anglo-Saxon countries, who refused to recognize that the logical conclusion of Zionist belief and activity was to emigrate to Israel.

[39] Eliyahu Eilat (1903–   ): Israel diplomat and Arabist; director of Middle East section of Political Department of Jewish Agency, 1934–45; ambassador to United States, 1949–50; to Great Britain, 1950–9.

one's feelings'.[40] He wished to save future Israeli diplomats from such doubtful pleasures.

He discussed the matter extensively with Moshe Sharett, now Israel's Foreign Minister. And although he was most anxious to create a diplomatic service in keeping with the demands of a modern state, the methods he envisaged were purely traditional and betrayed his own prejudices:

Provincial universities I would rule out. He (the potential candidate) would be rather isolated and would not get in touch with men likely to enter the British Diplomatic Service. I should also like best to place him in one of the Oxford Colleges from which British diplomats are most frequently recruited—I have good friends in all of them, (Balliol, Magdalen, and Christ Church at Oxford, or Trinity College, Cambridge) who would look after the boy. I myself would be able to help in it: in the summer of 1953 I reach retiring age, and shall therefore leave Manchester and be in London all the year with easy access and frequent visits to Oxford and Cambridge in connexion with my History of Parliament.[41]

His professional interests intervened in Israeli politics in another matter on which he had entrenched views. The Government of Israel had decided to build a new *Knesset* (House of Parliament). He urged Ben Gurion to 'adopt the British and not the Continental arrangements of benches in the house. The point may seem of very secondary importance, but in reality the arrangement has far-reaching psychological effects.'[42]

In an essay written in 1941 he had analyzed this question deeply. After extolling the virtues of the British system:

The arrangement of benches in the House of Commons reproduces the lay-out of a playing field and fosters a team spirit. No one must intervene in a game from the flank and there is no place for a Centre party. The 'political pendulum' swings from side to side, and has only two points of arrest,

he extrapolated the negative aspects of the Continental method:

The Ministers sit in the centre facing both their supporters and their opponents; they are extraneous to the House, which reproduces the psychology of the theatre rather than that of a playing field—the Ministers are like actors performing under the eyes of the Members, the public. Even Members when wishing to address the House have to mount a tribune, and thus join the actors.

[40] See Sir I. Berlin, *Zionist Politics in Wartime Washington: A Fragment of Personal Reminiscence* (The Ya'akov Harzog memorial lecture, Jerusalem, Oct. 1972), 48.
[41] Namier to Sharett, 5 Mar. 1952, CZA A312/42.
[42] Namier to Ben Gurion, 29 July 1957, CZA A312/43.

Moreover, juxtaposition and continuity in the seating arrangements encourage groups and parties imperceptibly to shade into each other, expressing more truly gradations in views than does the clear-cut division in our House of Commons—this is one of those clever, logical Continental 'improvements' which make Parliaments 'representative' and unworkable.[43]

Needless to say Ben Gurion had little sympathy with Namier's rather romanticized conception of the workings of the House of Commons. Perhaps his experience did not qualify him to regard the British parliamentary system through such rose-tinted spectacles. Still, the adoption of the Continental system brought with it much of the theatricality and histrionics which Namier detested and which, when out of control, as it often is, diminishes the dignity of the *Knesset* and reduces the authority of its members.

*   *   *

Namier's expertise was called for in another field. The process of gathering in and cataloguing Weizmann's papers had already begun in the late 1940s. The intention was eventually to publish them at a later date. By the early 1950s the task had advanced far enough for Namier to be drawn in. It would be the last great service he would perform for Weizmann. Vera Weizmann remembered him speaking to her of the influence that the cross-currents in a man's life could have on each other. Would Chaim's letters to her be of historical interest? Affirming it, Namier explained that the first aim should be 'the fullest possible publication of papers based on strict chronology'.[44] A lifetime of experience had taught him that a 'chronological arrangement' was 'the most suitable even for impersonal diplomatic documents':

Between some affair in China and another in upper Silesia, which develop contemporaneously, there may be hidden connections and reactions which no one will trace if the documents appear in different volumes, each fitted into its framework; and indeed a document may be omitted altogether as unimportant when the fine threads leading over to something quite different are not perceived. This applies *a fortiori* to the papers of one man. If a man writes a dozen letters to different correspondents on the same day, even on quite different subjects, the subjects and letters will inter-act, and turns and expressions, attitudes and moods, lead across from one to the other producing otherwise inexplicable patterns. It is in the psyche of the writer that these things

---

[43] See 'The Two Party System', *Manchester Guardian*, 17 Feb. 1941, reprinted in *Conflicts*.
[44] Lady Namier's Notes; and Proceedings of Editorial Board of Weizmann Archives, 31 Mar. 1958, WA.

are focused and from which they radiate. A good index will enable the reader to pick out what he wants, subjects or persons, from the mass of chronologically arranged correspondence. But no one will ever be able to piece together the writer's days and thoughts from a disrupted collection; and the fuller the collection, the more contemporaneity there is in it, the more important it is to preserve that fine texture.[45]

He went on to explain the true task of an editor:

[It] is to elucidate documents or letters by the minimum of necessary annotation. This should be concise and factual, clear and anonymous; not erudite and never witty. Do not superimpose any ideology of your own, even if you think you are reproducing the ideology of the writer. His ideas must be allowed to emerge from his writings without any editorial midwifery. I would even deprecate dividing the material by 'periods', because these are artificial. Life is an unbroken stream. Divide by year 1 January to 1 January of the next year; this at least is an obviously meaningless division adopted for convenience sake, and without any ideological suggestion.

The ideal way of producing a correspondence was, of course, by allowing both sides to state their case: 'The writer cannot be fully seen unless also the person to whom he writes is seen; nor can his argument be properly appreciated. Moreover in fairness to the other side, it should be heard.' Next, Namier warned against pushing ahead too rashly with plans for an Institute of Historical Research at Rehovoth. In a country remote from where the events occurred, a premature launching could well prove ruinously expensive, while lack of properly trained personnel would constitute another crippling disadvantage.

In March 1958 Namier visited Israel to attend the inaugural meeting of the Editorial Board of the Weizmann Letters project. Lady Namier has left her impressions of the experience:

For the first ten days Namier and I were Vera's guests at Weizmann House. Though much sight-seeing had been planned for us, and she gave several parties to introduce us to the new men or help us resume relations with old friends, Namier spent every possible moment with Guriel[46] down in the cellars where the documents, some sorted, others not, were then kept. With the day's exciting social obligations over, Namier could not sleep; and in our rooms volubly communicated to me fresh details of his Zionist experiences between 1925–1945. As they echoed through his mind, he enacted many impersonations which

---

[45] From a letter by Namier, 28 Jan. 1957, in Report presented to Meeting of Editorial Board of Weizmann Archives, 31 Mar. 1958, WA.

[46] Boris Guriel had been appointed Curator of the Weizmann Archives early in 1950.

led to new flashes of insight into characters and their incompatabilities. Next morning he would rise early and hurry down to tell Guriel before breakfast some tricky point he wanted to get exactly right.[47]

Namier returned to London satisfied but not free of concern for the project whose course proved rougher than he anticipated. It was easier to write about the technique of editing the letters than actually to carry it out. The enterprise stumbled from crisis to crisis. This is neither the time nor the place to recount the whole unhappy episode, suffice it to say that the project is only just approaching fruition, more than twenty years after the initial decision was taken to publish the letters. Clashes of temperament and of principle hindered the day-to-day work. Namier was greatly upset by these developments, reminding him as they did of the intrigues and internecine strife he had encountered when active on behalf of Zionism, and which had proved so destructive to the cause he served. He strove his utmost to repair the damage caused by harsh words or rash action. Very often he dined with Leonard Stein, another old friend involved in the venture, to determine the situation, conniving together to ensure that the still unstable undertaking survived. Only a fortnight before he died, Namier remarked to his wife, 'Aren't we a troublesome lot!' 'The amusement in his eyes', Lady Namier observed, 'belying his weary tones, stressed the remark's wider, all-human implications.'[48]

Namier's trip to Israel in the spring of 1958 was his first visit to the country for twenty years. The state of Israel, then celebrating its tenth anniversary, was, for him, a completely new phenomenon. He had known and admired the old *Yishuv*, a community dominated by its willingness for self-sacrifice, its pioneering spirit, its ethos personified by its collective settlements. He spent three weeks in Israel, traversing it 'from end to end, from Kfar Giladi in sight of "the glistening shoulders" of Mount Hermon, to Elath in the deep south'. On his return to London, he wrote two articles for the *Sunday Times* describing his visit.[49] For the most part they were undistinguished, at least when compared to the normal standards by which Namier's political essays are judged. Through the laudatory prose one theme dominated, a theme he had first enunciated in a different context in 1919: the need for the Jews to ensure their own survival. Ultimately, they could depend on no one but themselves. The events of the mid-1950s, in particular the Suez

---

[47] Lady Namier's Notes.   [48] Ibid.
[49] See the *Sunday Times*, 27 Apr. and 4 May, 1958.

campaign and its aftermath, revived his memories of the 1930s. Once again the Great Powers were prepared to sacrifice smaller ones in the name of greater interests. 'Czechoslovakia', he reminisced, 'was treated as a liability and a nuisance, as Israel is at present.' 'Better', he warned, 'for the Israelis to die fighting with whatever arms they possess—a beacon light for their people,'[50] than allow themselves to be dragged down by untrustworthy and self-centred Powers. He later concluded that 'The Arab attitude has not changed.' Adopting a curious analogy, he expanded:

Byzantium, with savagery at its gates, long continued to develop a civilization of its own. In Israel a new civilization is being built under the constant threat of immediate obliteration. The number of men of high distinction is great, but they are not brittle 'intellectuals'; for there is a tension in each of them due to the daily infusion into their lives of a toughness, or even roughness, ensuing from the position in which their nation is placed . . . The extent of this danger depends not on the strength of Israel's neighbours but on what is planned and done by their distant backers. So much, however, is certain: whatever the threat, the Israelis will not allow themselves to be led up the Munich path of territorial concessions complete with guarantees, and followed by complete extinction. If they have to die, they will go down fighting, with their morale unbroken.[51]

*   *   *

Namier's last sojourn in Israel was in one memorable way the culmination of his life's dedication to Zionism. This strange, truly eccentric man, deeply troubled, often cruelly isolated, whose extra-ordinary contradictions baffled and bewildered both his admirers and detractors, found some form of spiritual and emotional release as a consequence of his first-hand experiences in Israel. An academic platform provided him with his opportunity. Invited to address a seminar in modern history at the Hebrew University, he made his way to the rostrum:

The reception hall of the Sherman Building was packed with teachers and students. Lewis Namier rose to his feet. His voice trembled and tears rolled down his cheeks as he began with the Hebrew: 'If I forget thee, O Jerusalem, let my right hand forget her cunning. If I do not remember thee, let my tongue cleave to the roof of my mouth; if I prefer not Jerusalem above my chief joy'.[52]

There could be no more fitting epitaph for this turbulent Zionist.

[50] Letter to *The Times*, 25–8 Nov. 1955, copy in CZA A312/58.
[51] *Sunday Times*, 4 May 1958.   [52] J. L. Talmon, op. cit.

Appendix 1

An Appraisal of Weizmann

Namier wrote the following sketch some time in the mid-thirties. It relies, as is evident from its contents, mainly on Namier's impressions of how Weizmann handled the 1929–31 crisis.

I doubt whether in the course of these memoirs I shall be able to do Weizmann full justice. Naturally his weakness will come out more than his virtues and strength; for his weaknesses are all in every day action. He is unsystematic, indiscreet, self-indulgent and whimsical; the accusations raised against him about giving in too easily and improvising on the spur of the moment are fully justified; and when I deal with the day to day work which we had to do together, these things naturally move to the foreground, while the greatness of the man disappears; and it is anyhow much easier to specify mistakes and shortcomings than to convey the real greatness of spirit and charm of a man. Baffy, who has marvellous verbal memory and can reproduce conversation almost as well as Boswell or Nassau Senior, told me once that Weizmann is the one man whose conversations she is unable to reproduce. One has to hear him and somehow get under the magnetic spell which he has when he is at his best to understand the power which he has exercised on so many crucial occasions, and the devotion which people, great and small, have felt for him.

To start with minor matters: in every day work he has the great advantage of being brief and knowing his mind. Whenever I had a mass of problems to discuss with him and had to get decisions from him, he almost invariably got through the whole business in 20 minutes or half an hour (provided I could get him to the point and to talk business at all). He is a good listener, takes in points quickly, and completely concentrates on the subject under discussion. Further, if he trusts his collaborator, he will leave him very wide latitude. He knew that I had a greater grasp of detail than he had and that while, on the surface, I managed to preserve appearances of courtesy and compromise, I was a hard bargainer. He therefore left that part to me to such an extent that when across the Conference Table, at the Cabinet Conference, we had to go through certain points, the Lord Advocate (Craigie Aitchison) would always look at me when he asked 'is this agreed to?', although I was not even formally a delegate but merely secretary to the delegation. Altogether for those whom Weizmann likes he is the easiest and most pleasant man to work with.

He is endowed with an almost uncanny flair and (like Lloyd George with whom he has many points in common) has a way of knowing things much earlier than others do. When the Government decided to send Luke to Geneva to the Spring Session of 1930, Weizmann, with whom Baffy and I were staying at Merano, at once felt the significance of the move; and linked it to a favourite Jewish story of his: In White Russia, he said, there were Jews who used to live out in the forests far away from the bigger communities and were known as *Yishubniks*. For the High Holidays the *Yishubniks* would come to the nearest town to take part in the religious services. One such *Yishubnik* left a half-imbecile son in charge of the farm. One day that son arrived in a state of extreme excitement and explained that a knife had gone *trife* (unclean).

'Well, what of it?', said the father. 'How did it happen?'

'We had to use it to kill the cow.'

'The cow, why did you kill the cow?'

'Because it was half-burnt.'

'Burnt! How burnt?'

'Well the farm was burnt to the ground.'

'The farm!'

'Grandmother in bed upset the lamp; she was burnt alive; the farm was burnt down.'

The story has bearing on Chaim's ability to see a string of events at a flash. When a knife goes trife, he knows all that led to it; and it was so in Merano. When we returned to London, he would ask me in the morning, coming in to the office, 'Any more cutlery?'

The outstanding quality of Chaim is probably his almost quixotic generosity. He is a warm hearted man with uncalculating generous impulses. The story told about him by Lloyd George, in his memoirs, concerning the discovery of Acetone and the way in which he made a present of it to the Government without asking anything at all in return for himself, either in the way of money or honours, is only one typical example.[1] Winston once told me that if Weizmann had asked £250,000 for his discovery, the Government would have given it him. Anyone who comes into contact with Chaim must be aware of that streak in him. I have seldom known a man with so many warm and disinterested friends, just because he is so disinterested himself.

Now this I want to put on record here and the whole of these memoirs should be read in the light of this statement: Baffy and I have to our credit most of the tangible achievements of 1930 and the opening month of 1931. Without us the things could never have happened; but we were only, in a sense, the pace-

---

[1] See David Lloyd George, *War Memoirs* (London, 1938), i. 349. This question was slightly more complicated than Namier imagined. In March 1916 Weizmann had writtern to C. P. Scott that he would like an over-all sum (approximately £50,000) yielding an annual income of £2,000 as recompense for his war work, a request that Scott thought reasonable. In September 1917 he wrote to Scott that the Admiralty had decided to pay him a royalty of £4 per ton of acetone. Government files reveal no evidence indicating the total amount paid to Weizmann but in his memoirs he refers to a 'token reward of royalties' amounting to £10,000 or about 10s. for every ton of acetone. (See *The Weizmann Letters August 1914–November 1917* (Jerusalem, 1975), vii. 313, 517; and *Trial and Error*, 222.)

makers for Weizmann. We would prepare the ground, but he was needed to clinch the matter. How we prepared the ground can be easily told. His clinching of the matters cannot be described.

I know from Archie Sinclair[2] about a dinner at the Travellers Club, of a Society (I forget its name) consisting mainly of crusted die-hards. Weizmann was invited as speaker to one of their dinners at which Howard Bury,[3] one of our most passionate opponents, was present. Archie told me that Chaim's success was simply phenomenal. He swept them of their feet and he did it in such a way that even H.B. could not personally resent it. Chaim's reports, though pointed, are never offensive, (unless intentionally so) and leave no bad feeling behind. I remember only one from that dinner. Speaking of Palestine H.B. said: 'The Arabs have been there 1500 years.' Chaim replied: 'Yes, the Arabs and the goats, and the country bears the mark of it.'

He is spontaneously generous in money matters and, if I ever had to take money from anyone, I would much rather accept it from him than from anyone else that I know. This has its bad sides of course. Not having an Anglo-Saxon's training in money matters, he is sometimes too easy in the management of public funds—he will over-pay useless officials, squander public money on purposes which would not pass the control of Treasury accountants, etc. But the man has to be taken whole, and one has to suffer the defects of his qualities. Had he the British Treasury mind, . . . we would never have got the Balfour declaration, or having got it would have made nothing of it.

Chaim's imagination amazes. A great scientist, he is also a visionary; and his visions can run away with him. The number of fantastic plans with which he has played during the time I have worked with him is astounding. But once when in 1933 I talked to him about employing certain German refugees in Palestine; having explained all the merits and good sides of the men, I added: 'But he is *meshugge* (dotty).' Chaim laughed and said, 'if we were not all *meshugge* would we ever have gone to Palestine?'

At Merano, after dinner, in his room, he would tell Baffy and me stories from his youth. Had either of us written them down they would have proved as good, or even better than Shmarya Levin's memoirs.[4] But although he has started writing his memoirs, I doubt if he will ever be able to get such things onto paper; and if he does, I am sure that a good deal of their unique essence will have evaporated. His best photos may possibly convey something about him to future generations. Nothing else will. His portraits and even his bust by Epstein are very poor pictures of the man. He is most impressive when he works himself up

[2] Archibald Henry MacDonald Sinclair (1890–1970): Liberal MP, 1922–45; Secretary of State for Air, 1940–5; Leader of parliamentary Liberal Party, 1935–45; a lifelong supporter of Zionism. Created 1st Viscount Thurso, 1952.

[3] Charles Kenneth Howard Bury (1883–1963): Conservative MP, 1922–4, 1926–31; a leader of the pro-Arab lobby in parliament.

[4] Shmarya Levin, *Youth in Revolt* (London, 1939); *Childhood in Exile* (London, 1939).

into an almost prophetic fervour. There were moments at the second meeting of the Cabinet Conference at which all those Labour men, some of them very dull, were impressed and pretty well carried away. Chaim knew that his speech had been highly successful, and from the verbatim transcripts of the Cabinet Conference he wanted me to work it up into a report which might someday be published (of course it could not have been done directly since proceedings of Cabinet Conferences are strictly secret). But when I came to read the speech in type I almost felt that it would be an outrage to publish it. The words alone could not convey its spirit.

Incidentally the story was told—possibly a pure invention—that Tom Shaw of the Weavers' Trade Union who was secretary and a member of the Conference, said after that meeting in his broad Lancashire dialect: 'It does a maan good to have been in Lancasheer.' He knew that Weizmann had been Reader at Manchester University.

But if Weizmann does not hit it off with someone, or still worse, somehow gets across them, there is no way of putting things right. He will carry no conviction and will achieve nothing; the situation will lead to bitter hostility. It was so with Justice Brandeis,[5] and as likely as not with Passfield; also I believe,—although I never saw them together—with [Sir John] Chancellor. On the other hand, Balfour, Lloyd George, Winston, McKenna, Mark Sykes, Ormsby Gore, and Amery of the older generation, were fast friends to Weizmann, and remained his friends throughout. I could see it happen—the mutual sympathy strike root— during my own time, in people like Archie Sinclair, Malcolm MacDonald, Craigie Aitchison; even Ramsey MacDonald professes warm friendship for Weizmann and told him at Chequers on July 13th, that he would always look upon him as a friend.[6]

His prophetic fervour at Conferences has some grave disadvantages. First, he must never be allowed to go into such a Conference alone; because when he returns he knows what he said, but has hardly any notion of what the other people said. Secondly, pursuing broad lines and fundamental ideas, he fails to drive the things to a point; he does not coin the bullion into hard cash. The impression is produced, but unless there is someone to translate it into positive terms it evaporates without leaving positive results. It was great luck that during the War of 1914–18 he came together with two such men as Lloyd George and Balfour who themselves were imaginative and followed broad lines of thought. Had he been shored up against Asquith and Stanley Baldwin we would never have got the Jewish National Home, because their minds would

---

[5] Louis Dembitz Brandeis (1856–1941): prominent American jurist; nominated Justice of Supreme Court, 1916; Chairman of Provisional Committee for General Zionist Affairs in America, 1914; resigned in 1921 after controversy with Weizmann's group about the economic and financial development of Palestine.

[6] For once Namier's memory failed him. Weizmann was not at the Chequers meeting that day, but in Basle preparing for the seventeenth Zionist Congress. See below, pp. 56–57.

not have followed his along those broad lines; and he would hardly have translated the gist of his thoughts into concrete terms.

As so many imaginative men, he can often be surprisingly inaccurate in detail, which is the more odd since he is a scientist, accustomed to accurate and minute work. But then he could answer, like Burke on one occasion, 'By gad, Ma'am, does anyone swear to the truth of a song?'

One more point. Chaim is by nature benevolent and extraordinarily patient; a faithful friend; and, barring a few people whom he detests, absolutely devoid of real vindictiveness. Even the people against whom he feels a deeper hatred he will forgive if they approach him in a nice and friendly manner, though I am not certain that in those few cases their conciliation would ever be lasting. Some people accuse him of being jealous, and trying to thwart anyone who might come up in competition against him. Personally I have seen no trace of it. Of course, it might easily be said that he never had any reason to suppose that I might compete with him, but then any number of people, of whom this has been alleged, are similarly (?) and obviously no competitors of his.

The worst of Chaim is his incredible lack of self-discipline. A most important matter may have to be dealt with but, if he is not in the mood, or if he wants to go home for tea, or if his sons are back from school, he will leave the office, and not do the thing; occasionally he is like an impish naughty child and likes to upset the apple-cart to then see others struggle as they straighten out the mess.

Appendix 2

Judaica

(*Zionist Review*, April 18, October 17, November 7, November 21, 1941)

In 1921, on my first visit to Vienna after the war, I happened to engage in a discussion about Jewish Nationalism and Zionism with one of those high-minded, broad-minded, open-minded, shallow-minded Jews who prefer to call themselves anything rather than Jews. 'First and foremost', he declared in a pompous manner, 'I am a human being'. I replied (and this was twenty years ago): 'I, too, once thought so; but I have since discovered that all are agreed that I am a Jew, and not all that I am a human being. I have therefore come to consider myself first a Jew, and only in the second place a human being.'

President Masaryk was one of the truest philo-Semites I ever knew; he did not believe the Jews to be cleverer than the non-Jews; he, for one, did not think us different from other human beings.

According to Aristotle, the 'Stateless' must be a god or a beast; nowadays he is usually a Jew.

Overheard anywhere on the European Continent between 1919 and 1939:
'Look at this Jew! What did he do in the war? Some racketeering?'
'He was in the Army.'
'Ye-e-s! Somewhere behind the lines.'
'He served four years in the trenches.'
'Well—even there he knew how to take care of himself. Why wasn't he wounded?'
'He was wounded several times.'
'But so many of our best men were killed. Why is he alive?'
Indeed, why not cut the cackle by starting with the last question?

A. J. Nock, in his articles on 'The Jewish Problem in America', published in the *Atlantic Monthly*, quotes a friend as saying about the Jews: 'They have got something which they don't need to tell one another, and they can't tell us'. What is it? Obviously a '*maase*' (a Jewish story); of which the definition is: 'something every Jew has heard before, and no Gentile can understand'.
Sometimes I think that Zionism itself answers this definition: every Jew knows it, and hardly any non-Jew truly understands it.

In June 1940 I dined alone at a restaurant, and at the neighbouring table sat a Colonel wearing several ribbons of the last war, a Captain just returned from

Dunkirk, and two ladies. The Colonel talked in so loud a voice that I could not help overhearing scraps of his conversation—possibly he wished it to be heard. 'They call themselves Czechs, but they are all Germans.' And next: 'Two hundred yards from me lives a German Jew. I can't understand why the fellow is not interned. When the first Hun lands in this island, I shall shoot that Jew out of hand.'

In the last war, a Jewish artist, with permission from the War Office, was making sketches at the front. He looked foreign. One day a Colonel found him at work.

'What are you doing here?' the Colonel asked sharply.

'Drawing your battery.'

'Have you a permit?'

The artist fumbled in his pockets—no, he had left the permit at home.

'What is your name?' thundered the Colonel.

'Goldberg.'

'Carry on, carry on,' replied the Colonel, fully satisfied. 'Had you said Smith, I should have put you under arrest.' This Colonel had sense.

'Assimilation', as the word indicates, is a halfway house. The true and clear alternatives are fusion or full and separate national existence. Both mean normalisation. The Irish in Great Britain, the United States, or Australia never feared lest an Irish State in Eire should render their position in these countries difficult or ambiguous. Only assimilated Jews entertain such fears.

The position of the Jews in the Diaspora will become easier once the Jews have attained full national existence in a Jewish State in Palestine. They will have attained equality with other nations. They will be able to live among these nations and preserve their nationality, as the Swiss usually do; or they may preserve merely a certain racial identity, as the Irish in Anglo-Saxon countries in which they are assimilated; or they may fuse completely, as the Huguenots have in this country.

But the real history of the Huguenots has never been written: how long they preserved their identity, intermarrying among themselves and maintaining in their Church a separate national character; how much they suffered, feeling uprooted and in a way *déclassé*; how the shadow of homelessness lay on them, sapping their vitality; how families, numerous at first, died out, or were reduced to very small numbers.

Shmarya Levin once said to President Masaryk: 'The only Czechoslovaks are the Jews: everyone else is either a Czech or a Slovak.' At the time of the last census I was staying in the house of a Scottish friend who, proudly but incorrectly, entered her nationality as 'Scottish'. She was followed likewise by a Scottish guest. A 'depressed' Englishman in protest entered himself as 'English'. I alone put myself down as 'British', and could not have done otherwise had I wished to.

In May 1919 I had in Paris a long talk with Paderewski, then Polish Premier. The Jewish problem naturally figured largely in it.

'The Jews in England speak English,' started off Paderewski, 'French in France, German in Germany. Why do they not speak Polish in Poland?'

'But do you want them to speak Polish?' I asked in reply.

'Of course I do.'

'Please consider,' I said. 'In Germany the Jews form about one per cent in a highly educated population; and yet this has sufficed for them powerfully to influence German literature, science, the Press, and the theatre. If you want the Polish Jews, who form 10 per cent of the population, to give up Yiddish and learn Polish, you will have to educate them. And then *you* will have to adopt a different language if you want to think your own thoughts.'

After a moment's reflection Paderewski said: 'You may be right. But let them at least speak Hebrew and not Yiddish, which jars on us.'

'As a Zionist I certainly should wish the Jews to adopt Hebrew,' I replied. 'But you must allow me to say that once you give up your demand that the Jews in Poland adopt Polish, what language they speak is an internal affair of ours.'

A few days later, I met one of the leaders of the Polish Left, a fine and fair-minded man. 'With us,' he said, 'one hardly ever mentions the Jews now without cursing.' Still, he and his friends were prepared to stand up for Jewish rights—'but,' he added, 'then you must go with us.' 'Do what your conscience bids you,' I replied, 'but don't, on that basis, claim to mortgage our existence.'

It is curious how often even upright men think that doing justice to the Jews entitles them to levy, at least political, tribute.

Years ago I heard the son of a millionaire of Jewish extraction, in the presence of non-Jews, deny being a Jew. I replied: 'As you aren't a Jew, let me explain to you something about my people. Like all nations, we have patricians and plebeians. The plebeians are ashamed of their origin.' The non-Jews laughed.

Sir Lionel Abrahams, of the India Office, was an assimilated Jew with a warm feeling for Palestine. He told me that after the war he wrote to one of the most prominent opponents of Zionism: 'I remember the feeling which my old grandfather had for Palestine. I also remember how in the 'eighties when Russian Jews were flying from pogroms, you and I, then young men, tried to establish some as pedlars in the City; they had no heart for the place, and they were not wanted there. On what grounds can we now refuse to help them when they wish to go to a country to which they feel deeply attached?' His friend replied: 'You are too clever for me.'

Shmarya Levin said to me: 'Before 1914, a couple of million Jews went to America, a mighty stream; but each of them thought only about himself or his family. A few thousand went to Palestine, a mere trickle; but everyone of them was thinking about the future of our nation.'

The Balfour Declaration marks the end of the period of the '*shtadlonim*' (the Jewish oligarchs who spoke for Jewry on the strength of their wealth and their position in the Gentile world), and the beginning of democratic leadership in Jewish politics. Still, the Declaration was addressed to a Lord Rothschild—at that time Dr. Weizmann was not yet sufficiently prominent to be its immediate recipient—but the then Lord Rothschild, and still more Baron Edmond de Rothschild, were more than '*shtadlonim*'. The protest issued after the Balfour Declaration had been published will probably count in Jewish history as the dying speech of the '*shtadlonim*'.

A most generous American-Jewish millionaire, who was bitterly opposed to Zionism, once talked to me about our settlers as a 'subsidised immigration'. I then showed him passages in James Truslow Adams' book, *The Founding of New England*, recounting how 'the English-American balance-sheet showed a colossal amount spent in exploration and attempted development' against a handful of people settled in Virginia and Bermuda; how the London merchants, who backed the *Mayflower*, 'received almost no interest upon their investment', and soon came to see 'that the principal itself was lost'; and how in spite of the enormous natural resources, the Colonies, short of capital, 'borrowed heavily from England' till 'the inherent unsoundness of the position', concealed by continued immigration, became evident when that immigration stopped.

Some years before I first visited Palestine, I spent a week-end with a well-known Colonial Governor. At dinner I talked enthusiastically about Palestine; next morning at breakfast, asked when I had been there last, I confessed that I had never been there.

'Then how can you be so enthusiastic about it?'

'And how could the Love of Zion have survived two thousand years of Dispersion,' I replied, 'if we were unable to feel it without having seen Palestine?'

In the Spring of 1929 I met a certain Palestine official who, in an aggressive manner—only too well known to us—began to enquire about Jewish colonisation in the Crimea (he was one of the well-wishers to Jews *in absentia*).

'There you get land free, whereas in Palestine you have to pay for it through the nose.'

'Yes,' I replied, 'we have to pay for permission to drain marshes.'

'And you spoil our duck-shooting.'

I wonder what an Englishman would think if, say, an American made such a remark about England. But he was not the only one from whom I have heard it. I did not leave it unanswered.

'Anyhow,' he said, 'we have saved your throats from being cut.'

'Leave our throats to ourselves; but when trouble comes, don't try to disarm us.'

This was a few months before the disarming parade in Jerusalem.

One of the better Palestine officials thus explained to me his preference for the Arabs: 'When I go to an Arab village and give an order, they obey; in a Jewish village, they argue.'

A very common attitude towards our work in Palestine is to pay it compliments, and then raise barriers against it; and tell us that we are so clever and persistent that we shall overcome them. The well-known maxim of the British Administration about 'holding the scales even' in practice means 'to make the obstacles to our work proportionate to our effort'.

Some Christians choose to lecture us for not being sufficiently pious in Palestine. Our ancestors placed their religion above all worldly considerations—but was the treatment meted out to them for it such as to entitle non-Jews to prescribe to us now what form our religion should take, and to pin us down to the traditional form for which these critics have developed so deep a respect? A story is told about the late Rabbi Kook which they had anyhow better ponder on before talking about this matter.

Some ultra-orthodox Jews came to Rabbi Kook, and accused the chalutzim of being '*epicorsim*' ('Epicureans', *i.e.* irreligious). Rabbi Kook replied:

'When we had the Temple, no one was allowed to enter the Holy of Holies, except the High Priest; and even he only on the Day of Atonement, after prayers and ablutions. But when they were building the Temple, any workman could enter it, dusty and dirty, at all times of the day and night. Keep silent—they are building the Temple.'

During the exceptionally hot summer of 1911, a railway strike broke out in this country, and during the railway strike a small pogrom occurred in South Wales. It started at Tredegar, spread to Rhymney, Bargoed, etc. As soon as the train service was resumed I went down to see what had happened, and went the round of these mining villages. In one small place I went to the house of an ultra-orthodox rabbi; he kept me for a meal, but before we sat down I realized that I was in for some elaborate prayers. I had to explain to my host that, not having been brought up in the Jewish religion, I did not know our religious customs. He looked at me with real feeling, and said: 'You have come to see what has happened to us. You have a good Jewish heart. That's all that matters.'

I hope that man has lived to see the Jewish revival in Palestine, and that his honest Jewish heart and understanding will yet rejoice in the re-birth of a Jewish State.

When I was a boy, there was an old Jew on our estate in Eastern Europe who used to tell me stories about my ancestor, Eliyahu ben-Solomon, the Gaon of Vilna. The one which made the greatest impression on me was this:

About the middle of the eighteenth century a distinguished French Jew came all the way from Paris to Vilna to discuss the Law with the Gaon. On the third day of their discussions the Gaon said: 'When we go back to Jerusalem . . .' The French Jew interrupted: 'And if we do not?' The Gaon did not reply. He called his servants and told them to put his honoured guest into the pillory for twenty-four hours.

Appendix 3

The MacDonald Letter

House of Commons | Friday, 13 February, 1931.

LIEUT.-COMMANDER KENWORTHY asked the Prime Minister if he is now able to communicate to the House the text of the letter to Dr. Weizmann on the policy of His Majesty's Government in Palestine.

THE PRIME MINISTER: Yes, Sir. The following is the text of the letter which I have addressed to Dr. Weizmann to-day:

'10, Downing Street, Whitehall | 13 February, 1931.

Dear Dr. Weizmann,

In order to remove certain misconceptions and misunderstandings which have arisen as to the policy of His Majesty's Government with regard to Palestine, as set forth in the White Paper of October, 1930, and which were the subject of a Debate in the House of Commons on the 17th November, and also to meet certain criticisms put forward by the Jewish Agency, I have pleasure in forwarding you the following statement of our position, which will fall to be read as the authoritative interpretation of the White Paper on the matters with which this letter deals.

2. It has been said that the policy of His Majesty's Government involves a serious departure from the obligations of the Mandate as hitherto understood, that it misconceives the Mandatory obligations, and that it foreshadows a policy which is inconsistent with the obligations of the Mandatory to the Jewish people.

3. His Majesty's Government did not regard it as necessary to quote *in extenso* the declarations of policy which have been previously made, but attention is drawn to the fact that, not only does the White Paper of 1930 refer to and endorse the White Paper of 1922, which has been accepted by the Jewish Agency, but it recognises that the undertaking of the Mandate is an undertaking to the Jewish people and not only to the Jewish population of Palestine. The White Paper placed in the foreground of its statement my speech in the House of Commons on the 3rd April, 1930, in which I announced in words which could not have been made more plain, that it was the intention of His Majesty's Government to continue to administer Palestine in accordance with the terms of the Mandate as approved by the Council of the League of Nations. That position has been reaffirmed and again made plain by my speech in the House of Commons on the 17th November. In my speech on the 3rd April

I used the following language:—

> "His Majesty's Government will continue to administer Palestine in accordance with the terms of the Mandate as approved by the Council of the League of Nations. This is an international obligation from which there can be no question of receding.
>
> Under the terms of the Mandate His Majesty's Government are responsible for promoting "the establishment in Palestine of a National Home for the Jewish people, it being clearly understood that nothing shall be done which might prejudice the civil and religious rights of existing non-Jewish communities in Palestine or the rights and political status enjoyed by Jews in any other country."
>
> A double undertaking is involved, to the Jewish people on the one hand, and to the non-Jewish population of Palestine on the other; and it is the firm resolve of His Majesty's Government to give effect, in equal measure, to both parts of the Declaration, and to do equal justice to all sections of the population of Palestine. That is a duty from which they will not shrink, and to the discharge of which they will apply all the resources at their command."

That declaration is in conformity not only with the articles, but also with the preamble of the Mandate, which is hereby explicitly reaffirmed.

4. In carrying out the policy of the Mandate the Mandatory cannot ignore the existence of differing interests and viewpoints. These, indeed, are not in themselves irreconcilable, but they can only be reconciled if there is a proper realisation that the full solution of the problem depends on an understanding between the Jews and the Arabs. Until that is reached, considerations of balance must inevitably enter into the definition of policy.

5. A good deal of criticism has been directed to the White Paper upon the assertion that it contains injurious allegations against the Jewish people and Jewish Labour organisation. Any such intention on the part of His Majesty's Government is expressly disavowed. It is recognised that the Jewish Agency have all along given willing co-operation in carrying out the policy of the Mandate, and that the constructive work done by the Jewish people in Palestine has had beneficial effects on the development and well-being of the country as a whole. His Majesty's Government also recognise the value of the services of labour and trades union organisation in Palestine, to which they desire to give every encouragement.

6. A question has arisen as to the meaning to be attached to the words 'safeguarding the civil and religious rights of all inhabitants of Palestine, irrespective of race and religion,' occurring in article 2, and the words 'ensuring that the rights and position of other sections of the population are not prejudiced,' occurring in article 6 of the Mandate. The words 'safeguarding the civil and religious rights,' occurring in article 2, cannot be read as meaning that the civil and religious rights of individual citizens are to be unalterable. In the

case of Suleiman Murra, to which reference has been made, the Privy Council, in construing these words of article 2, said: 'It does not mean . . . that all the civil rights of every inhabitant of Palestine which existed at the date of the Mandate are to remain unaltered throughout its duration; for if this were to be a condition of the Mandatory jurisdiction, no effective legislation would be possible.' The words, accordingly, must be read in another sense, and the key to the true purpose and meaning of the sentence is to be found in the concluding words of the article: 'irrespective of race and religion.' These words indicate that, in respect of civil and religious rights, the Mandatory is not to discriminate between persons on the ground of religion or race, and this protective provision applies equally to Jews, Arabs, and all sections of the population.

7. The words 'rights and position of other sections of the population,' occurring in article 6, plainly refer to the non-Jewish community. These rights and position are not to be prejudiced, that is, are not to be impaired or made worse. The effect of the policy of immigration and settlement on the economic position of the non-Jewish community cannot be excluded from consideration. But the words are not to be read as implying that existing economic conditions in Palestine should be crystallised. On the contrary, the obligation to facilitate Jewish immigration and to encourage close settlement by Jews on the land, remains a positive obligation of the Mandate, and it can be fulfilled without prejudice to the rights and position of other sections of the population of Palestine.

8. We may proceed to the contention that the Mandate has been reinterpreted in a manner highly prejudicial to Jewish interests in the vital matters of land settlement and immigration. It has been said that the policy of the White Paper would place an embargo upon immigration, and would suspend, if not, indeed, terminate, the close settlement of the Jews on the land, which is a primary purpose of the Mandate. In support of this contention particular stress has been laid upon the passage referring to State lands in the White Paper, which says that 'it would not be possible to make these areas available for Jewish settlement in view of their actual occupation by Arab cultivators, and of the importance of making available additional land on which to place the Arab cultivators who are now landless.'

9. The language of this passage needs to be read in the light of the policy as a whole. It is desirable to make it clear that the landless Arabs to whom it was intended to refer in the passage quoted, were such Arabs as can be shown to have been displaced from the lands which they occupied in consequence of the lands passing into Jewish hands, and who have not obtained other holdings on which they can establish themselves, or other equally satisfactory occupation. The number of such displaced Arabs must be a matter for careful inquiry. It is to landless Arabs within this category that His Majesty's Government feel themselves under an obligation to facilitate their settlement upon the land. The recognition of this obligation in no way detracts from the larger purposes of

development, which His Majesty's Government regards as the most effectual means of furthering the establishment of a National Home for the Jews.

10. In framing a policy of land settlement, it is essential that His Majesty's Government should take into consideration every circumstance that is relevant to the main purposes of the Mandate. The area of cultivable land, the possibilities of irrigation, the absorptive capacity of the country in relation to immigration are all elements pertinent to the issues to be elucidated, and the neglect of any one of them would be prejudicial to the formulation of a just and stable policy.

It is the intention of His Majesty's Government to institute an inquiry as soon as possible to ascertain, *inter alia*, what State and other lands are, or properly can be made, available for close settlement by Jews under reference to the obligation imposed upon the Mandatory by article 6 of the Mandate. This inquiry will be comprehensive in its scope, and will include the whole land resources of Palestine. In the conduct of the inquiry provision will be made for all interests, whether Jewish or Arab, making such representations as it may be desired to put forward.

11. The question of the congestion amongst the fellahin in the hill districts of Palestine is receiving the careful consideration of His Majesty's Government. It is contemplated that measures will be devised for the improvement and intensive development of the land, and for bringing into cultivation areas which hitherto may have remained uncultivated, and thereby securing to the fellahin a better standard of living, without, save in exceptional cases, having recourse to transfer.

12. In giving effect to the policy of land settlement, as contemplated in article 11 of the Mandate, it is necessary, if disorganisation is to be avoided, and if the policy is to have a chance to succeed, that there should exist some centralised control of transactions relating to the acquisition and transfer of land during such interim period as may reasonably be necessary to place the development scheme upon a sure foundation. The power contemplated is regulative and not prohibitory, although it does involve a power to prevent transactions which are inconsistent with the tenor of the scheme. But the exercise of the power will be limited and in no respect arbitrary. In every case it will be conditioned by considerations as to how best to give effect to the purposes of the Mandate. Any control contemplated will be fenced with due safeguards to secure as little interference as possible with the free transfer of land. The centralised control will take effect as from such date only as the authority charged with the duty of carrying out the policy of land development shall begin to operate. The High Commissioner will, pending the establishment of such centralised control, have full powers to take all steps necessary to protect the tenancy and occupancy rights, including the rights of squatters, throughout Palestine.

13. Further, the statement of policy of His Majesty's Government did not

imply a prohibition of acquisition of additional land by Jews. It contains no such prohibition, nor is any such intended. What it does contemplate is such temporary control of land disposition and transfers as may be necessary not to impair the harmony and effectiveness of the scheme of land settlement to be undertaken. His Majesty's Government feel bound to point out that they alone of the Governments which have been responsible for the administration of Palestine since the acceptance of the Mandate have declared their definite intention to initiate an active policy of development which it is believed will result in substantial and lasting benefit to both Jews and Arabs.

14. Cognate to this question is the control of immigration. It must, first of all, be pointed out that such control is not in any sense a departure from previous policy. From 1920 onwards, when the original Immigration Ordinance came into force, regulations for the control of immigration have been issued from time to time, directed to prevent illicit entry and to define and facilitate authorised entry. This right of regulation has at no time been challenged.

15. But the intention of His Majesty's Government appears to have been represented as being that 'no further immigration of Jews is to be permitted so long as it might prevent any Arab from obtaining employment.' His Majesty's Government never proposed to pursue such a policy. They were concerned to state that, in the regulation of Jewish immigration, the following principles should apply, namely, that 'it is essential to ensure that the immigrants should not be a burden upon the people of Palestine as a whole, and that they should not deprive any section of the present population of their employment' (White Paper, 1922). In the one aspect His Majesty's Government have to be mindful of their obligations to facilitate Jewish Immigration under suitable conditions, and to encourage close settlement of Jews on the land: in the other aspect they have to be equally mindful of their duty to ensure that no prejudice results to the rights and position of the non-Jewish community. It is because of this apparent conflict of obligations that His Majesty's Government have felt bound to emphasise the necessity of the proper application of the absorptive capacity principle. That principle is vital to any scheme of development, the primary purpose of which must be the settlement both of Jews and of displaced Arabs upon the land. It is for that reason that His Majesty's Government have insisted, and are compelled to insist, that Government control of immigration must be maintained and that immigration regulations must be properly applied. The considerations relevant to the limits of absorptive capacity are purely economic considerations.

16. His Majesty's Government did not prescribe and do not contemplate any stoppage or prohibition of Jewish immigration in any of its categories. The practice of sanctioning a 'Labour Schedule' of wage-earning immigrants will continue. In each case consideration will be given to anticipated labour requirements for works which, being dependent on Jewish or mainly Jewish capital, would not be or would not have been undertaken unless Jewish labour

was made available. With regard to public and municipal works falling to be financed out of public funds, the claim of Jewish labour to a due share of the employment available, taking into account Jewish contributions to public revenue, shall be taken into consideration. As regards other kinds of employment, it will be necessary in each case to take into account the factors bearing upon the demand for labour, including the factor of unemployment amongst both the Jews and the Arabs. Immigrants with prospects of employment other than employment of a purely ephemeral character will not be excluded on the sole ground that the employment cannot be guaranteed to be of unlimited duration.

17. In determining the extent to which immigration at any time may be permitted, it is necessary also to have regard to the declared policy of the Jewish Agency to the effect that in 'all the works or undertakings carried out or furthered by the Agency it shall be deemed to be a matter of principle that Jewish labour shall be employed.' His Majesty's Government do not in any way challenge the right of the Agency to formulate or approve and endorse such a policy. The principle of preferential and, indeed, exclusive employment of Jewish labour by Jewish organisations is a principle which the Jewish Agency are entitled to affirm. But it must be pointed out that if in consequence of this policy Arab labour is displaced or existing unemployment becomes aggravated, that is a factor in the situation to which the Mandatory is bound to have regard.

18. His Majesty's Government desire to say finally, as they have repeatedly and unequivocally affirmed, that the obligations imposed upon the Mandatory, by its acceptance of the Mandate, are solemn international obligations, from which there is not now, nor has there been at any time, an intention to depart. To the tasks imposed by the Mandate His Majesty's Government have set their hand, and they will not withdraw it. But if their efforts are to be successful there is need for co-operation, confidence, readiness on all sides to appreciate the difficulties and complexities of the problem, and, above all, there must be a full and unqualified recognition that no solution can be satisfactory or permanent which is not based upon justice, both to the Jewish people and to the non-Jewish communities of Palestine.

I am, my dear Dr. Weizmann,
Yours very sincerely,
(Signed) J. Ramsay MacDonald.

The President
of the Jewish Agency'

A Bibliographical Note

The Namier papers are deposited at the Central Zionist Archives (A312 series). Together with Lady Namier's Notes (see Acknowledgements) they constituted the main archival material upon which this study was drawn. Papers from the Public Record Office (FO 371, CAB, PREM, and WP(G) series), the Weizmann Archives, and interviews and private correspondence (already acknowledged), augmented the primary sources. I also drew extensively from the original Dugdale Diaries; these references are marked 'unpublished'. Many of Namier's essays have been reprinted elsewhere. I have here noted the main collections; the original place and date of publication of these essays may be found in the Notes. The following list contains only those articles and books which have been used directly in the writing of this book. It makes no pretence at being a comprehensive bibliography of the topics which interested Namier, an almost impossible task by any reckoning. The place of publication, unless stated otherwise, is London.

Sir I. Berlin, *Zionist Politics in Wartime Washington: A Fragment of Personal Reminiscence* (Jerusalem, 1972).

Sir I. Berlin, 'Lewis Namier. A Personal Impression', in *A Century of Conflict, 1850–1950. Essays for A. J. P. Taylor* (1966), ed. M. Gilbert.

J. Brooke, 'Namier and Namierism', *History and Theory*, 3 (1964).

H. Butterfield, *George III and the Historians* (1957).

H. Butterfield, 'Sir Lewis Namier as Historian', *The Listener* (May 1961).

M. Cohen, *Palestine. Retreat from the Mandate* (1978).

C. Coote, *Companion of Honour. The Story of Walter Elliot* (1965).

Julia de Beausobre [Namier], *The Woman Who Could Not Die* (1938).

ESCO Foundation: A Study of Jewish, Arab, and British Policies (Yale University Press, 1947).

P. Goodman, ed., *Chaim Weizmann. A Tribute on his Seventieth Birthday* (1945).

J. Harvey, ed. *The War Diaries of Oliver Harvey, 1941–1945* (1978).

J. C. Hurewitz, *The Struggle for Palestine* (New York, 1950).

Ved Mehte, *Fly and the Fly-Bottle. Encounters with British Intellectuals* (Pelican ed., 1965).

K. Middlemas, ed., *Thomas Jones. Whitehall Diary* (OUP, 1969).

E. Monroe, *Philby of Arabia* (1973).

Julia Namier, *Lewis Namier. A Biography* (OUP, 1971).

L. B. Namier, *Germany and Eastern Europe* (1915).

——, *The Structure of Politics at the Accession of George III* (1929, 2nd ed., 1965).

L. B. Namier, *Skyscrapers and Other Essays* (1931).

——, *In the Margin of History* (1939).

——, *Conflicts* (1943).

——, *1848: The Revolution of the Intellectuals* (1946).

——, *Diplomatic Prelude* (1948).

——, *Personalities and Powers* (1955).

——, *Facing East* (New York, 1966).

——, 'Pathological Nationalisms', *Manchester Guardian* (26 Apr. 1933).

——, 'National Character', *Spectator* (28 Feb. 1941).

——, 'Refugee Boats', *Time and Tide* (14 Mar. 1942).

——, 'The Jewish Problem Re-argued. A Palestine State the Only Solution', *Manchester Guardian* (16 Nov. 1943).

——, 'The Jewish Question', *Manchester Guardian* (8 Mar. 1946).

P. Ofer, 'The Role of the High Commissioner in British Policy in Palestine: Sir John Chancellor (unpublished Ph.D. thesis, London, 1972).

J. Owen, 'The Namier Way', *New Statesman and Nation* (26 Jan. 1962).

H. J. Philby, *Arabian Jubliee* (1952).

J. H. Plumb, 'The Atomic Historian', *New Statesman* (1 Aug. 1969).

Norman Rose, *'Baffy'. The Diaries of Blanche Dugdale, 1936–47* (1973).

——, *The Gentile Zionists* (1973).

L. Stein, *The Palestine White Paper of October 1930* (1930).

L. Sutherland, 'Sir Lewis Namier', *Proceedings of the British Academy*, 5, xlviii (1962).

J. L. Talmon, 'The Ordeal of Sir Lewis Namier: The Man, the Historian, the Jew', *Commentary* (March 1963).

A. J. P. Taylor, ed., *Off The Record. Political Interviews 1933–43* (1973).

The Report of the Palestine Royal Committee, Cmd. 5479 (1937).

A. J. Toynbee, *Acquaintances* (OUP, 1967).

——, 'Lewis Namier, Historian', *Encounter* (Jan. 1961).

B. Wasserstein, *Britain and the Jews of Europe, 1939–1945* (Clarendon Press, Oxford, 1979).

J. C. Wedgwood, *The Seventh Dominion* (1928).

C. Weizmann, *Trial and Error* (1950).

——, 'Palestine's Role in the Solution of the Jewish Problem', *Foreign Affairs* (Jan. 1942).

R. Zweig, 'British Policy to Palestine, May 1939 to 1943. The Fate of the White Paper' (unpublished Ph.D. thesis, Cambridge, 1978).

Index

and technical training for Jewish settlers
22–4; as a committed Zionist 24; co-
operates with Weizmann 24–5; returns
to Balliol 26; turns to business and
journalism 26–7; dispossessed of inheritance 27; under Weizmann's spell 28;
arranges meeting between Mrs Dugdale
and Weizmann 28–30; his intellectual
partnership with Mrs Dugdale 30; ex-
pounds his Zionist creed 30–4; offered
job in Zionist Organization 35–6; explains motives for joining Zionist
Organization 36–8; develops
'Namierism' 37n; relationship with
Zionist officials 38–9; dependent upon
Weizmann 39; writes account of 1929
crisis 40–5; incapable of co-operation
44; limitations of as a diplomat 45;
receives Passfield's White Paper 47–8;
his greatest triumph 49–50; appointed
to Chair of Modern History at
Manchester 50; writes account of Anglo-
Zionist negotiations, 1930–31 51–3;
friendship with Weizmann deepens 53–
4; provokes crisis with Zionist Executive
54–5; attacks techniques of Zionist diplomacy 55; confers with Ramsay
MacDonald 56–7; attacks Zionist
Executive 57–9; returns to academic life
59; reflects on Nazi revolution 60–1;
analyses German foreign policy aims
62–3; works on behalf of Jewish refugees
63–5, 72–4; opposes Legislative Council
66–7; refuses Professorship at Hebrew
University 69; excluded from Zionist
Executive 69–70, 79, 83; furious at
Weizmann 70–1; visits Palestine (1935)
71; renews Zionist activity 71–2; attacks
rich Jews 73; believes in 'strong hand'
74; advocates 'real Jewish militarism'
75–6; proposes 'radicalism of deeds' 76–
7; co-operates with Ben Gurion 77–8;
criticizes Weizmann 79; supports partition 79–82; member of Political
Advisory Committee 84; considers
Federalism 85; disappointed at British
policy 86; quarrels with Weizmann 87–
8; opposes participation in St. James's
conference 88–9; reviews Zionist position 90–1; attacks MacDonald 92,
100–1, 105; puts personal affairs in order
93; seconded to JA for war work 94;
involved in Philby plan 94–6; cam-
paigns for creation of JFF 101–13; pra-
ises Lloyd 109; on British imperialism
109n; bitter at British 'pusillanimity'
110–11; as a 'bread-and-butter' diplomatist 111–12; temperamental unpredictability of 113–14; criticized by
Weizmann 114–15; regards Weizmann

in revised light 115–16; renews activity
in Polish question 116–19; fears resurgence of Polish chauvinism 116–17; supports Soviet claims 117–18; puts case for
Jewish State 120–1, 123, 126–8, 129;
attacks Government's immigration policy 131–5; as a controversialist 136–7;
unconcerned by physical dangers of war
138–9; contemplates suicide 139; abhors
terrorism 139–40; leaves Zionist politics
140–1; returns to Manchester 141; analyses post-war Jewish problem 142–3;
attends Executive meetings 144; pays
tribute to Weizmann 145; marries 146;
breach in relations with Weizmann
146–7; reconciles Christianity and
Zionism 147–9; acts unofficially for
Zionism 150; confident in Israel's future
150; hates Germans 151–2; defends unconditional surrender 152–3; attacks
German army 152–3; in twilight of
career 153–4; as an armchair Zionist
154; proposes school for Israeli diplomats 155; proposes British model for
Knesset 155–6; consulted about publication of Weizmann's papers 156–8;
explains tasks of editor 157; visits Israel
157–9; epitaph as a Zionist 159; writes
appraisal of Weizmann 160–4

Newcombe, Col. S. F. 136
Noel-Baker, Philip and Irene 44

Oman, Charles 17

Paderewski, Jan 19
Paget, General 143–4
Palestine 18, 19, 22–4; as a self-governing
Dominion 23, 33, 143; as Jewish
National Home 32; riots in 1929, 41–2;
national consensus on 49; development
of 53; and rise in Jewish immigration 66;
Legislative Council for 66; immigration
restricted in 80, 97, 131–5, 143; Jews
respond to war effort 102; as a supply
base 103; as Southern Syria 119; Jewish
State in 79–87, 120–1, 122–131; Zionist
coup de main in 126; upsurge of terrorism
in 139–40; slips into chaos 143–5; bor-
ders on anarchy 149; termination of
mandate in 150
Pareto, Vilfredo 3
Partition, *see* Jewish State and Palestine
Passfield, Lord, as Colonial Secretary 46–
7; White Paper of 47–8, 49, 163
Patria 132
Peel Report, *see* Report of Royal
Commission for Palestine
Percy, Lord Eustace 12
Philby, H. B., plan of 94–6, 122